MIRROR OF MINDS

The author's aim has been to give some illustrations of the ways in which at various periods English poetry has reflected current views of the human mind, with special reference to such topics as its place in the cosmos, its relations with the body, the connections between sense, passions, and reason, the problem of soul and its possible survival after death. The subject matter is important, for many of the more self-conscious writers have been profoundly affected by their assumptions about the senses and passions, the reason and the imagination.

Poets, of course, have rarely been systematic philosophers or psychologists; they have usually picked out and applied imaginatively only a few notions from contemporary thought. Consequently this study does not attempt to set the history of English poetry squarely against the history of philosophy. Rather, characteristic topics and writers have been selected and the discussion of them will be seen to throw light on some major imaginative preoccupations of each age. The student of English poetry and the history of ideas will find valuable comments on the major writers from Chaucer and Spenser down through Shakespeare and Milton, Dryden, Wordsworth, Shelley, Tennyson, Browning, Hardy and on a variety of modern poets such as Bridges, Eliot, Sitwell, Auden, and Graves.

Alexander Lectures Series.

GEOFFREY BULLOUGH was born in Prestwich, Lancashire, and educated at Manchester University. He taught at Tamworth Grammar School, and did pioneer work in adult education. He has lectured at Manchester, Edinburgh, and Sheffield Universities, and is now Professor of English Language and Literature in King's College in the University of London. He is the co-editor of *The Oxford Book of Seventeenth Century Verse* and *English Studies Today,* author of *The Trend of Modern Poetry,* and editor of a major contribution to scholarship in the volumes of the *Narrative and Dramatic Sources and Analogues of Shakespeare.*

THE ALEXANDER LECTURESHIP

The Alexander Lectureship was founded in honour of Professor W. J. Alexander, who held the Chair of English at University College, University of Toronto, from 1889 to 1926. Each year the Lectureship brings to the University a distinguished scholar or critic to give a course of lectures on a subject related to English Literature.

MIRROR OF MINDS

Changing Psychological Beliefs in English Poetry

GEOFFREY BULLOUGH

University of Toronto Press

COPYRIGHT ©, 1962, BY
GEOFFREY BULLOUGH
TORONTO: UNIVERSITY OF TORONTO PRESS
LONDON: THE ATHLONE PRESS
REPRINTED IN PAPERBACK 2014
ISBN 978-1-4426-5176-0 (PAPER)

THE ALEXANDER LECTURES

(Unless otherwise indicated the lectures have been published by the University of Toronto Press)

1929–30 L. F. CAZAMIAN: "Parallelism in the Recent Development of English and French Literature". Included in the author's *Criticism in the Making* (Macmillan, 1929)
1930–31 H. W. GARROD: *The Study of Poetry* (Clarendon, 1936)
1931–32 IRVING BABBITT: "Wordsworth and Modern Poetry". Included in "The Primitivism of Wordsworth" in the author's *On Being Creation* (Houghton, 1932)
1932–33 W. A. CRAIGIE: *The Northern Element in English Literature* (1933)
1933–34 H. J. C. GRIERSON: "Sir Walter Scott". Included in *Sir Walter Scott, Bart.* (Constable, 1938)
1934–35 G. G. SEDGEWICK: *Of Irony, Especially in Drama* (1934, 1948)
1935–36 E. E. STOLL: *Shakespeare's Young Lovers* (Oxford, 1937)
1936–37 F. B. SNYDER: *Robert Burns, His Personality, His Reputation, and His Art* (1936)
1937–38 D. NICHOL SMITH: *Some Observations on Eighteenth-Century Poetry* (1937, 1960)
1938–39 CARLETON W. STANLEY: *Matthew Arnold* (1938)
1939–40 J. DOUGLAS N. BUSH: *The Renaissance and English Humanism* (1939, 1957)
1940–41 No lectures given
1941–42 H. J. DAVIS: *Stella, a Gentlewoman of the Eighteenth Century* (Macmillan, 1942)
1942–43 H. GRANVILLE-BARKER: "Coriolanus". Included in the author's *Prefaces to Shakespeare*, Vol. II (Princeton, 1947)
1943–44 F. P. WILSON: *Elizabethan and Jacobean* (Clarendon, 1945)
1944–45 F. O. MATTHIESSEN: *Henry James, the Major Phase* (Oxford, 1944)
1945–46 S. C. CHEW: *The Virtues Reconciled, an Iconographical Study* (1947)
1946–47 MARJORIE HOPE NICOLSON: *Voyages to the Moon* (Macmillan, 1948)
1947–48 G. B. HARRISON: "Shakespearean Tragedy". Included in the author's *Shakespeare's Tragedies* (Routledge and Kegan Paul, 1951)

THE ALEXANDER LECTURES

1948–49 E. M. W. TILLYARD: *Shakespeare's Problem Plays* (1949)
1949–50 E. K. BROWN: *Rhythm in the Novel* (1950)
1950–51 MALCOLM W. WALLACE: *English Character and the English Literary Tradition* (1952)
1951–52 R. S. CRANE: *The Languages of Criticism and the Structure of Poetry* (1953)
1952–53 No lectures given
1953–54 F. M. SALTER: *Mediaeval Drama in Chester* (1955)
1954–55 ALFRED HARBAGE: *Theatre for Shakespeare* (1955)
1955–56 LEON EDEL: *Literary Biography* (1957)
1956–57 JAMES SUTHERLAND: *On English Prose* (1957)
1957–58 HARRY LEVIN: *The Question of Hamlet* (Oxford, 1959)
1958–59 BERTRAND H. BRONSON: *In Search of Chaucer* (1960)
1959–60 GEOFFREY BULLOUGH: *Mirror of Minds: Changing Psychological Beliefs in English Poetry* (1962)

TO
ROSEMARY FRANCES JACKSON

PREFACE

This book is a revision and enlargement of five Alexander Lectures delivered in the University of Toronto in October, 1959. They grew out of the Warton Lecture on English Poetry given before the British Academy in 1955 which I was invited to expand. My aim, then and since, has been chiefly to give some illustrations of the ways in which at various periods English poetry has reflected current views of the human mind or soul, with special reference to such topics as its place in the cosmos, its relations with the body, its origin, operation, limitations, and possible survival after death.

The subject has some importance, for though the history of literature cannot be explained as a reflection of changing views about the mind, yet many of the more self-conscious writers have been profoundly affected by their assumptions about the senses and passions, the reason and the imagination. But poets have rarely been systematic philosophers or psychologists. They have usually picked out and applied imaginatively only a few (often subsidiary) notions from contemporary thought. Consequently no attempt is here made to set the history of English poetry squarely against the history of philosophy. A few characteristic topics and writers have been selected to throw light on some major imaginative preoccupations of each age. Apart from some

Morality plays and Shakespeare the drama has been omitted. To discuss this, and the debt of imaginative prose to shifting psychological assumptions, would require another and larger work.

I wish to express my gratitude to the University of Toronto for the honour it bestowed on me, and for the opportunity of visiting Canada, where I received kindnesses from many people, including (at Toronto) Professors A. S. P. Woodhouse, R. S. Knox, K. MacLean and F. E. L. Priestley. I wish also to thank the Librarians of King's College, London, and of the Universities of Edinburgh and Toronto for their services; and the officers of the British Academy for allowing me to include some passages from my Warton Lecture in this volume.

G.B.

CONTENTS

    Preface   ix

I. The Poetry of the Soul's Instruments
    during the Renaissance   1

II. The Development of Shakespeare's Attitude
    to the Mind   48

III. Reason, the Passions, and Associations
    from Dryden to Wordsworth   90

IV. Associations, Intuition, and Immortal
    Longings in the Nineteenth Century   134

V. The Individual and the Racial Image
    in Modern Poetry   188

    Notes   256

    Index   265

ACKNOWLEDGEMENTS

W. H. AUDEN: lines from *Poems*, copyright 1934 by The Modern Library, Inc.; lines from *Another Time*, copyright 1940 by W. H. Auden; lines from *Double Man, Collected Poetry*, copyright 1941 by W. H. Auden; lines from *Collected Poetry*, copyright 1945 by W. H. Auden—all reprinted from *The Collected Poetry of W. H. Auden* by permission of Random House, Inc. for the United States. Permission for Canada granted by Faber and Faber Ltd.

GEORGE BARKER: lines from the *Collected Poems, 1930–1955*. By permission of Criterion Books, Inc. for the United States and Faber and Faber Ltd. for Canada.

ROBERT BRIDGES: lines from *The Testament of Beauty*. By permission of Oxford University Press.

RUPERT BROOKE: lines from *The Collected Poems of Rupert Brooke*, copyright 1915 by Dodd, Mead and Company, Inc., copyright 1943 by Edward Marsh; by permission of Dodd, Mead and Company, Inc. for the United States. Permission for Canada granted by McClelland and Stewart Limited.

W. H. DAVIES: lines from "The Jolly Tramp" and "A Great Time". By permission of Jonathan Cape Limited and Mrs. H. M. Davies.

WALTER DE LA MARE: lines from "Dreams". By permission of the Society of Authors.

T. S. ELIOT: lines from "The Love Song of J. Alfred Prufrock" from *Collected Poems 1909–1935*, copyright 1936 by Harcourt, Brace and World, Inc.; lines from "Burnt Norton", "East Coker", "The Dry Salvages", and "Little Gidding" from *Four Quartets*, copyright 1943 by T. S. Eliot—by permission of Harcourt, Brace and World, Inc. for the United States. Permission for Canada granted by Faber and Faber Ltd.

ACKNOWLEDGEMENTS

Roy Fuller: "Mythological Sonnet" appearing in *Brutus' Orchard* (1957). By permission of the Macmillan Company for the United States and André Deutsch for Canada.

David Gascoyne: lines from "And the Seventh Dream is the Dream of Isis". By permission of David Higham Associates Ltd.

Robert Graves: lines from "Incubus" and "The Marmosite's Miscellany" by permission of Roturman S. A. Lines from "The Haunted House", "Reproach", "Lost Love", from *Collected Poems* published by Doubleday and Co. Inc. and Cassell and Co. Ltd., by permission of Roturman S.A.

D. H. Lawrence: lines from "Fish", "Tortoise", and "She said as well to me". By permission of the Viking Press Inc.

John Masefield: lines from the collected *Poems*. By permission of The Macmillan Company.

Kathleen Raine: lines from *Collected Poems*. By permission of Miss Raine and Hamish Hamilton Ltd.

Herbert Read: lines from the *Collected Poems*. By permission of New Directions and Faber and Faber Ltd.

Edith Sitwell: lines reprinted from *Collected Poems* (from "Gold Coast Customs", copyright 1948, 1954 by Edith Sitwell; "Song of the Cold"‘ copyright 1948, 1954 by Edith Sitwell; "Harvest", copyright 1946, 1954 by Edith Sitwell; "Eurydice", copyright 1948, 1949, 1954 by Edith Sitwell). By permission of the Vanguard Press, Inc. for the United States and the William Morris Agency for Canada.

Arthur Symons: lines from *Collected Works* by permission of Martin Secker and Warburg Limited.

W. J. Turner: lines from *New Poems* (1928). By permission of Messrs. Chatto and Windus.

Dorothy Wellesley: lines from "Genesis" in *Early Light*. By permission of Rupert Hart-Davis Limited.

W. B. Yeats: lines from *Collected Poems*. By permission of The Macmillan Company.

MIRROR OF MINDS

Chapter One ↜ THE POETRY OF THE SOUL'S INSTRUMENTS DURING THE RENAISSANCE

In recent years considerable attention has been paid to the influence of psychology on literature in particular periods of literary history. There have been good books on the Elizabethan world picture in which the theories of mind current in Tudor times have been related to the work of Shakespeare and others; the importance of the idea of the Ruling Passion in Pope has been noted; and much has been made of Freudian influence in the modern novel. Nevertheless, it has not yet been adequately realized how continuously English literature has been affected, both in matter and in form, by changes in men's notions of the human mind and of its relation to the body and the world about it.

Discoveries in medicine, in the sciences of the body, new philosophical or theological beliefs, may bring fresh ideas about the functions of, and relations between, senses, emotions, and thought. At one time the Humours may seem all-important, at another Sensibility or the Memory. Scientific theories about the body-mind relationship may influence ideas about the validity of human knowledge, the hereafter, sex, morality, man's place in the universe. It is not my purpose (nor am I competent) to enter into philosophical questions, though psychology was for so long a handmaid of philosophy that I am bound to draw upon the psychological and ethical ideas of philosophers. My aim is to select some aspects of the body-mind relationship, some ideas about the processes of thought and feeling, about the proper balance of senses, passions, and reason, and about the place of the human mind in the universe, which imaginative writers in several ages have taken over and used. I wish to show, not how accurately imitative poets have been, but how theories or popular assumptions about the mind have been adapted and transformed in the work of some representative poets.

Poets are men of their age even when they rebel against it. Most of them are as aware as most other men of the intellectual currents of the time. A Shakespeare or a Henry James may transcend that knowledge; more conventional writers will be content to portray emotion and character in terms of contemporary theory or popular assumptions. Their imaginations will indeed be conditioned by the ideas about human nature prevalent in their age, and the scope and character of their art will be limited accordingly.

The system of psychology and ethics accepted in the Middle Ages and Renaissance was that inherited from Aristotle and Galen, adapted by St. Augustine and St. Thomas Aquinas, and handed down through schools and Universities. Theological in its basis, and mainly deductive in its method, though not lacking in shrewd observation, this system explained with the help of a few leading ideas such diverse problems as the relation of body and mind, the processes of thought and feeling, the differences between the sexes, races, ages, and temperaments, the nature of diseases, the path of virtue, and the principles of civil government.[1] The following summary of basic beliefs may be helpful though it ignores many details and diversities of opinion:

1. Man is an immortal soul, and his soul operates through all his physical, mental, and spiritual functions. These functions are "motions" of the soul.

2. Man is a microcosm—a little world—and an elaborate series of parallels or correspondences may be drawn between his nature and that of the universe in general.

3. Thus the soul works through three functions which correspond to a threefold division in the universe: the Vegetative Principle, the Sensitive Principle, and the Reasoning Principle.

4. The Vegetative Principle man shares with inanimate nature and plants. It includes unconscious operations like digestion, growth, and generation.

5. The Sensitive Principle links man to the animals; it comprises the powers of apprehension and motion; to it belongs the work of the senses which send messages to the brain. In the brain dwell three faculties: (i) the Common Sense (often thought to be sited in the forehead), which is a kind of clearing-house for sense-impressions; (ii) the Imagination or Fancy (in the middle of the head), which is the power of image-making in the absence of objects; and (iii) the Memory (in the back of the head), which is the storehouse of images.

6. Closely connected to the Sensitive Principle are the Passions. These are of two kinds: the Concupiscible and the Irascible. Both are appetitive, concerned with desires and their fulfilment. Classed as Concupiscible by St. Thomas Aquinas are: Love and its opposite Hatred; Desire and Loathing; Joy and Sadness. Classed as Irascible are Hope and Despair; Courage and Fear; and Anger. Many other passions were admitted, but usually as subdivisions or combinations of these elemental passions.

7. The Reasoning Principle of the soul is superior to all these other faculties. Absent in animals, it links man to the angels. This principle has two powers: Understanding or Judgment; and Will.

8. In a well-balanced soul the Reasoning Principle dominates the others, controls the senses, which are liable to err, moderates the passions, and directs the will only towards those activities which are for the ultimate good of the whole.

9. The operation of the soul through these instruments, however, is affected by the nature of the four elements of which man, like the rest of the cosmos, is composed: fire, air, water, and earth. In the human body these produce the Four Humours: Blood, which like air is hot and moist; Choler, like fire, hot and dry; Phlegm, like water, cold and moist; and Melancholy, like earth, cold and dry. To the combination of the humours in body and mind are ascribed not only differences of individual dispositions, but also differences between ages and races. The Ages of Man were clearly defined in the text-books. Heat and moisture were greatest in youth, whereas old age was cold and dry. The influence of climate on humours and so on national character was also discussed.

10. From the working of the humours in the body comes the natural heat which sustains life. This energy is carried through the body by the Spirits, of which there are three distinct grades. *Natural* spirits come from the liver, make dark blood, and pass through the veins to the heart. There they are transformed into *Vital* spirits, which make light blood and pass through the arteries. In the brain these Vital spirits are further refined into *Animal* spirits, which are the media by which messages are sent to and from the senses and limbs by the mind: they are called *Animal* because they spring from the Soul (*Anima*) and animate the body.

About the details of the all-embracing scheme of the universe there was much disagreement, and only in comparatively few didactic writers do we find a systematic exposition of the relations between body and mind.[2] In the main both lyrical poets and dramatists took what they needed in passing from the system, and a list of their debts to it would often be no more interesting than a heap of potsherds in an archaeological excavation is to an uninformed visitor. Nor was this (mainly Aristotelian) system the only psychology used by mediaeval and Renaissance poets; for under the broad wings of the microcosmic theory sheltered codes of erotic and religious behaviour which developed an almost independent existence. So Chaucer, Spenser, and Shakespeare drew not only on the medical and ethical text-books but also on direct observation and on other sources such as the crude conventions of folk-belief and more purely literary traditions.

From Chaucer's work, indeed, could be compiled a handbook of human nature as the Middle Ages conceived it. He refers frequently to the influence of the planets, to the humours; he cites differing theories about dreams (*Nonne Prestes Tale*), and describes the mental illusions caused by astrological magic (*Franklyn's Tale*).[3] He uses the physiology of his time in describing symptoms of passion—for instance, the grief of the Man in Black (John of Gaunt) at the death of the Duchess Blanche:

> His sorrowful herte gan faste faynte,
> And his spirites wexen dede;
> The blood was fled for pure drede,
> Doun to his hertè, to make hym warme—
> Ful wel it feled the herte hadde harme . . .
> For hit is membre principal
> Of the body; and that made al
> His hewè chaunge and waxè grene
> And pale, for ther no blood was sene
> In no maner lyme of his.
>   (*Boke of the Duchesse*, ll. 488–99)

In *Troilus and Criseyde* Chaucer elaborates Boccaccio's description of the emotions of the two lovers, being more interested than Boccaccio in the analysis of their passion. Here the symptoms are often in accordance with the romantic code of love. When Troilus hears Criseyde approach his heart trembles and he sighs (III. 57): he is paralysed when she speaks (III. 92–8):

> In chaungèd vois right for his verray drede,
> Which vois ek quook, and therto his manere
> Goodly abayst, and now his hewes rede,
> Now pale, unto Criseyde, his lady dere,
> With look down-cast and humble yolden chere,—
> Lo, th'alder firste worde that him asterte
> Was, twyes, "Mercy, mercy, swete herte!"

Almost invariably the courtly lover conforms to a pattern, of wooing on his part and diffidence or retreat on his mistress's, of despair and cruelty, service and reward. For those who had inherited the code developed out of Ovid by Chrétien de Troyes and the *Roman de la Rose*, courtly love was a way of life which conditioned both outward behaviour and inner thoughts by its "gentle craft"; so that Chaucer could write in all sincerity:

> The lyf so short, the craft so long to lerne,
> Thassay so hard, so sharp the conquerynge,
> The dredful joye, alwey that slit so yerne,*
> Al this mene I be love, that my felyng
> A-stonyeth with his wondyrful werkyng,
> So sore y-wis, that whan I on hym thynke,
> Nat wol I wel wher that I flete or synke.
>
> (*Parlement of Foules*, 1–7)

This attitude was passed on to early Tudor love-poets such as Wyatt and Surrey, with help from the Italian sonnet, but it was always complicated by the presence of rival traditions.

Thus what may be called a "folk-psychology" is apparent in the satiric and comic literature which delineates the behaviour and motives of men below the level of court and castle, showing professional, class, amorous, or domestic habits of thought, for example, among priests, lawyers, tradesmen, and plebeian wives. Late mediaeval popular poetry presents many stereotypes of this kind, and many degrees of individuation based on them. In particular one may note the opposed views about the characters of women. An early alliterative antifeminist piece states an attitude which continued into the citizen comedies of Middleton and beyond:

> There were three wily, three wily there were,—
> A fox, a friar, and a woman,
> There were three angry, three angry there were,—
> A wasp, a weasel, and a woman.

* I.e., slideth away so quickly.

> There were three chattering, three chattering there
>   were,—
> A pie, a jay, and a woman.
> There were three would be beaten, three would be
>   beaten there were,—
> A mill, a stockfish, and a woman.[4]

There were many such poems, some of ironical praise ("Of all Creatures women be best: Cuius contrarium verum est"), of impossibilities (anticipating Donne's "Goe and catch a falling starre"), of moral warning, of frightful example ("If I aske our dame bred, Che takyt a staf and brekit myn hed").[5] There were also poems in praise of women, and laments by young girls who had loved not wisely but too well.

Of psychological analysis in poetry the Middle Ages produced little, preferring action, speech, and gnomic generalization to lengthy exploration. In the Complaint, and in character-studies such as Chaucer's Pardoner and Wife of Bath, the representatives of a class reveal their inner selves. The contributions of the Wife of Bath to the gaiety of the Canterbury pilgrims show an unusual combination of the folk-psychology with a more sophisticated idea of sex-relations.

The Wife's Prologue is fabliau-stuff, illustrating the conventional determination of the "weaker sex" to dominate their lords and masters. Her tale of Arviragus and Aurelius begins likewise. She tells of a knight trapped into marrying an old crone after she has let him into the secret of what women love most. What they love most, as we might expect, is (ll. 1038–40) to

> "have sovereynetie
> As wel over hir housbond, as hir love
> And for to been in maistrye hym above."

This makes us expect something in tone like Shakespeare's *Taming of the Shrew*, where Petruchio opposes the curst aggressiveness of Katharine. But the Wife of Bath makes her old woman win mastery over her husband (who has called her loathly, old, and low of birth) by shaming him into courtesy (see ll. 1100–64). She says:

> But for ye speken of swich gentillesse
> As is descended out of old richesse,
> That therfore sholden ye be gentil men,
> Swich arrogance is nat worth an hen.
> Looke who that is moost vertuous alway,
> Pryvee and apert, and moost entendeth ay
> To do the gentil dedes that he kan,
> Taak hym for the grettest gentil man.

This lesson (which Shakespeare later applies in *All's Well* where he contrasts the natural nobility of Helena with the high-born ignominy of Bertram) underlies Chaucer's thinking about the highest quality of the chivalrous mind:

> Crist, wole we clayme of hym oure gentillesse,
> Nat of oure eldres for hire old richesse.

Another psychological influence potent in the Middle Ages and Renaissance appears when Chaucer's Man in Black, grieving for his dead Duchess, declares (ll. 567–72):

> May noght make my sorwes slyde,
> Nought al the remedies of Ovyde . . .
> Ne hele me may no phisicien
> Noght Ypocras, ne Galyen.

The juxtaposition of Ovid's *Remedia Amoris* with Hippocrates and Galen reminds us that there was an Ovidian element in mediaeval love psychology. This tended to replace the Dantesque idea of love as a feudal prince, a "mighty lord", by the more capricious and tyrannical Cupid and a strain of sensual realism. Some effects of this will be touched on later. Enough has perhaps been said to indicate that in mediaeval poetry the general microcosmic psychology was accompanied, and sometimes overlaid, by particular views of the mind derived from other literary and traditional sources, and that it would be wrong to assume that in all mediaeval and Renaissance literature the basic view of man's relation to the universe was everywhere constantly explicit, moulding poetic mood and imagery.

In Renaissance humanism, however, the changing patterns of society, new religious impulses, the rise of secular codes of conduct, and the spread of education through printing popularized the systematic study of human nature by books of medicine, philosophy, and rhetoric. Obviously the professional man, the doctor, or the lawyer must know the workings of the mind. The courtier too must be something of a psychologist, if only, as Castiglione declared, so that he might know

> how to behave himself readily in all occurents to drive into his Prince's head what honour and profit shall ensue to him and to his by justice, liberality, valiantness of courage, meekness, and by the other virtues that belong to a good Prince, and contrariwise, what slander and damage cometh of the vices contrary to them. (*The Courtier*, trans. T. Hoby.)

Sir Thomas Eliot devoted the second and third books of *The Governour* (1531) to a survey and analysis of the attitudes necessary to furnish a statesman "with honourable maners and qualities, whereof very nobilitie is compacte", including such virtues as Affability, Mercifulness, Benevolence, Amity, Justice, Fortitude, Temperance. The study of rhetoric, including poetry, was advocated because it gave knowledge of men's minds. So Eliot thought all young nobles should learn "that part of rhetoric, principally, which concerneth persuasion; for as muche as it is most apt for consultations". He defended comedies, and poetry in general, against their detractors because they represented men's actions and motives, giving incentives to virtue. A long line of writers from Ascham to Bacon took a similar stand. Thomas Wilson in his *Art of Rhetoric* (1553) pointed out that the dramatist, like the rhetorician, must know how to move the spectator through language, whether the situation represented demands "proof and refutation" or just "the arousing of feelings". This could be achieved only through the study of human nature, its good and bad qualities, and Wilson gave considerable space to discussing these under the divisions of oratory. For Bacon, the duty and office of rhetoric was "to apply Reason to Imagination for the better moving of the Will. . . . The end of Rhetoric is to fill the Imagination to second Reason, and not to oppress it" (*Advancement of Learning*, Bk. II). Sir Philip Sidney thought the poet superior to the philosopher because "Whatsoever the Philosopher saith should be done, he gives a perfect picture of it by some one, by whom hee presupposeth it was done, so as hee coupleth the generall notion with the particular example." Like Wilson, he gives illustrations of the portrayal of passions in classical literature:

> See whether wisdome and temperance in *Ulisses* and *Diomedes*, valure in *Achilles*, friendship in *Nisus* and *Eurialus*, even to an ignoraunt man carry not an apparent shining, and contrarily, the remorse of conscience in *Oedipus*, the soone repenting pride in *Agamemnon*, the selfe-devouring crueltie in his father *Atreus*, the violence of ambition in the two *Pheban* brothers, the sower-sweetnesse of revenge in *Medea*, and to fall lower, the *Terentian Gnatho* and our *Chaucers Pander* so expresst that we now use their names to signifie their Trades: And finally, all vertues, vices, and passions, so in their own naturall states laide to the view, that wee seeme not to heare of them, but clearly to see through them. (*Apologie for Poetrie*, 1595 ed.)

Naturally enough an age which saw poetry as a delightful way of teaching the strength and weaknesses of human nature produced a literature in which the working of the microcosm was often explicitly explored, and the faculties and operations of the mind were distinguished in the description of mood and motive and the representation of human character.

In religion "applied" psychology complicated the Aristotelian system with two other elements: first, the Christian moral tradition according to which the Fall of Man had tainted all the instruments of the soul, so that senses, passions, intellect, will, were involved in perpetual conflict, the Seven Deadly Sins were set over against the Cardinal Virtues, and the direct intervention of Satan introduced the concepts of Temptation, Conscience, fear of Damnation, Repentance, and Grace; second, and arising from this, the psychology of piety, which produced systems of mental and spiritual exercises suited to the various stages of the mystic way.

To explore this complex body of imaginative material would require many books; I must confine my attention to only a few ways in which mental relationships entered poetry in the sixteenth and early seventeenth centuries. And first, some examples of allegory, which show how Tudor writers saw the human mind as a battleground of opposing principles.

The microcosmic view of man brought with it a vast and intricate system of analogies or correspondences based on the community in difference of the two worlds. The duplicity of thought by which everything in the little world of man could be paralleled in the macrocosm was favourable to the development of symbolism and allegory in biblical exegesis and homilies, where fourfold meaning was often discovered. It is therefore not surprising to find an allegorical treatment of psychological themes in art.

The Morality play substituted for the narratives from Scripture and saints' lives used in Miracle plays a more sophisticated drama based on the moral conflicts within the soul, in accordance with the Church's teaching about the soul's temptations on its journey from birth to death. Many mediaeval preachers delighted in classifying the elements of the human and divine nature; some of them even ventured into dialogue form, and it was only a short step from this to a drama in which the Will of Man was assailed by the Passions or Senses under Satanic direction, and the proper balance of the mind was shown to be achieved by directing it wholly to the service of God. Not the Aristotelian temperance but scorn of all earthly things was usually the aim.

As W. R. Mackenzie showed long ago,[6] a number of Moralities portrayed a psychological struggle between good and evil, some directly for man's soul, others in the first place for his mind. To the first (Soul) group belong *Perseverance, Mankind, Nature,*

Magnifycence, Lusty Juventus, The Interlude of Youth, The Longer Thou Livest, and *The Conflict of Conscience*; to the second (Mind) group belong *The Four Elements, Wisdom Who is Christ, Wit and Science, The Marriage of Wit and Science,* and *The Marriage of Wit and Wisdom.*

In both groups the relationship between reason and the senses is given a religious direction. One of the best and earliest English Moralities, *The Castle of Perseverance*, shows that the new dramatic form owes something to the *Psychomachia* of Prudentius (c. A.D. 400) where the Christian Virtues were assailed by the pagan Vices and overcame them physically in single combat. Dr. Owst has shown that "the figure of the 'Castle of Mansoul' in English preaching can actually be traced back to a sermon of the so-called *Lambeth Homilies* compiled approximately at the end of the twelfth century".[7]

In *The Castle of Perseverance* Mankind, to the grief of his Good Angel, is misled by the Bad Angel and gives himself up to the World, the Flesh, the Devil, and the Seven Deadly Sins till finally Penance and Shrift lead him back to God. To escape the Seven Deadly Sins, Mankind goes into the Castle of Perseverance where he is counselled by the Seven Cardinal Virtues. The Castle is assailed by the Deadly Sins and their leader, who are repulsed in single combat, each by his opposite. Mankind however is not yet safe, for he falls victim to the wiles of Covetyse, and using his free will he leaves the Castle. When Death comes, Mankind appeals to the World to save him, in vain. He dies; his Soul appears and reproaches the Body; the Good and Bad Angels argue about the possibility of his salvation; Mercy and Peace wish to save him, but Righteousness and Truth declare that Mankind has damned his soul by his free will. The matter is debated at the throne of God, who decides for Mercy and Peace; they bring Mankind to heaven. The mixture here of mental processes and more general moral principles is characteristic of the psychological allegory found in many Morality plays. The Good and Bad Angels persist in Marlowe's *Faustus* and the debate in Heaven recurs as late as Giles Fletcher and Milton.

The typical pattern of many of these plays includes a presentation of opposing forces; a fall from grace; progress in vice; a conversion and repentance.[8] Sometimes, as in *Lusty Juventus* (1547–53), the temptations are subtle, but dramatically dull because the didactic statement prevents characterization; sometimes, as in *The Interlude of Youth* (1553–8), the simple scheme of Youth seduced by Riot is presented with a vivacity which anticipates Falstaff's adventurous gaiety, though the other characters are merely forces within the heart of the hero.

In *Hick Scorner* (c. 1530) we see the rascally adventures of Freewill and Imagination who for a time put Pity in the stocks. When Pity is freed by Contemplation and Perseverance, the three of them work on Freewill and convert him. With his help they convert Imagination, transforming him into Good Remembrance. Hick Scorner, the merry vice, is the scoffer-at-religion, a natural companion of unregenerate Freewill and Imagination. This play is an interesting piece of religious psychology, expounding the doctrine that the will and the imagination corrupt each other when not joined with pity (i.e., goodness). For a good life imagination must be under the control of will. Imagination rightly directed becomes remembrance of God's goodness.

The group of Moralities which describe the temptations affecting the mind is naturally more academic, and the psychological forces involved are set out more clearly, though they still remain generalized. Thus *The Interlude of the Four Elements* (printed 1519) is a tract—probably for schoolboys—on the value of learning. "Natura naturata" first describes the cosmos and the elements which compose it. Humanity listens with delight and discusses with Studious Desire the shape of the earth. When Studious Desire goes out to bring Experience who by "diverse instruments" can prove that it is round, Humanity is tempted by Sensual Appetite, a mild forerunner of Comus.

SEN. I am called Sensual Appetite,
　　　All creatures in me delight;
　　　I comfort the wits five,
　　　The tasting, smelling, and hearing;
　　　I refresh the sight and feeling
　　　To all creatures alive.
　　　For when the body waxeth hungry
　　　For lack of food, or else thirsty,
　　　Then with drinks pleasant
　　　I restore him out of pain,
　　　And oft refresh nature again
　　　With delicate viand.
　　　With pleasant sound of harmony
　　　The hearing alway I satisfy,
　　　I dare this well report;
　　　The smelling with sweet odour.
　　　And the sight with pleasant figure
　　　And colours, I comfort;
　　　The feeling, that is so pleasant,
　　　Of every member, foot, or hand,
　　　What pleasure therein can be
　　　By the touching of soft and hard,
　　　Of hot or cold, nought in regard,
　　　Except it come by me.
HUM. Then I cannot see the contrary,
　　　But ye are for me full necessary,
　　　And right convenient.

The play now turns from questions of learning to problems of good and evil, as Humanity falls under the spell of Sensual Appetite and Ignorance. The latter sings a nonsense song about Robin Hood, and the text breaks off where Nature is reproving the hero for his errors.

In *Wisdom Who is Christ* (1480–95), the central figure Anima (the Soul) is attended by the Five Wits or Senses and Mind, Will, and Understanding ("the three Powers of every Christian Soul") who are treated frankly as faculties of the mind, seduced by Lucifer into leaving the service of God. Mind takes as companions Indignation, Sturdiness, Malice, Hastiness, Wreche (Revenge), and

Discord; Will's group are Recklessness, Idleness, Surfeit, Greediness, Spouse-breach (Adultery), and Fornication. In the end Wisdom first wins over Mind, then Understanding and Will, by showing them the fallen Soul who "appeareth in the most horrible wise, fouler than a fiend" with six devils running out from under her robe. The play closes with a procession, showing the Mind's proper functions—first the Five Wits, then the Soul between Mind and Understanding with Will following them, in accordance with the best moral teaching.

In three closely related plays, *Wit and Science* (by John Redford, c. 1545), *The Marriage of Wit and Science* (a rehandling of the same theme), and *The Marriage of Wit and Wisdom*, the topic is the best means of attaining learning, and the plots discuss the dangers encountered on the road. They are as topical today as in the sixteenth century. In Redford's play Reason wishes his daughter Science (Knowledge) to marry Wit. Wit asks advice of Study and Diligence about his best road. Diligence wants him to go off at once but Study persuades him to ask Instruction, who advises Wit to wait for Science to send the Sword of Comfort; otherwise he may be overcome by the giant Tediousness. Wit goes off impatiently and sure enough he is slain by Tediousness. He is restored to life, however (as studious desires sometimes are even today), by Honest Recreation, attended by Comfort, Quickness, and Strength. He now swings the other way. Dismissing Reason, he tries to abuse the virtue of Honest Recreation and lies down in the lap of Idleness who whistles in Ignorance. In an amusing scene Idleness tries to teach Ignorance to spell his own name and rewards him by putting his coat on Wit and Wit's on him. When Science enters mourning the loss of Wit she does not recognize him now that he is Ignorance. Left alone, Wit looks into the mirror given him by Reason and sees himself disfigured. Full of remorse, he is castigated by Shame and begs Reason's pardon, who bids Study, Diligence, and Instruction back to Wit's service. With their help the reformed and reclothed Wit defeats the giant Tediousness. Science comes down from Mount Parnassus to reward him and she is united to him with the approval of Reason and Experience.

> "If ye use me well in a good sorte [she says]
> Then shall I be your joy and comfort.
> But if ye use me not well then doubt me
> For sure you were better then without me."

The neatness of this allegory will be appreciated by those of my readers who are in danger from the giant Tediousness and are longing for some Honest Recreation. This is a good play, and the mental activities are ingeniously introduced. In reworking the theme *The Marriage of Wit and Science* suggests the passage of years during education and introduces a companion for Wit, namely Will, who seems to represent Wilfulness.

Enough has been said to show the attitude to the mind in the Moralities. The clearcut scheme of scholastic psychology was well adapted for representation in terms of the personified Psychomachia or of the trials and errors of a man's pilgrimage through life. On the whole the style of these plays was simple and down-to-earth. The didactic exposition was given in a plain homiletic manner; the representation of temptation and fall was often made as realistic as possible, the tempter assuming the guise of a man of the world and using suitable speech, a humour rough and familiar. The aim was to link religious principles to the actual life of the audience, using a mixture of simple abstractions with popular idiom, proverbial lore, and everyday imagery of farm and household, all at a level below that of the court.

Though Spenser owed much to the Morality tradition, he transposed the allegory of the mind into a courtly key, as he tried to rival Ariosto but to set in the forefront of his narrative the moral meanings which Ariosto's editors had read into the *Orlando Furioso*. I must limit myself to the first two Books.

Spenser's *Faerie Queene* is a vast portrait gallery of the passions and perturbations of the mind. Here the war in the soul is conceived in terms of the Romantic Quest under influence of the Arthurian legend. The psychological material is still mixed. Spenser includes a Platonic view of the soul's informing power (as in his Hymns to Love and Beauty), which owes much to Marsilio Ficino's treatise on the Immortality of the Soul. In his "Letter to Raleigh" he claims to be using the Aristotelian virtues, but his heroes by no means embody them. In considering Spenser's use of "the twelve moral virtues according to Aristotle and the rest", we must study not so much Aristotle's *Ethics* and *De Anima* as his mediaeval and Renaissance interpreters; and not only these but also the Christian virtues which often depart from them.[9] Thus there is no Aristotelian counterpart for Holiness as sought by the Red Cross Knight in Book I, and the parallel between Arthur's Magnificence (which is Heavenly Grace) and Aristotle's Magnanimity is anything but close, for the habitual mood of the Greek Magnifico would seem to be a Curzonlike effortless superiority (the "Balliol manner") rather than the comprehensive virtue which included humility. St. Thomas Aquinas, however, had tried to include humility in the Aristotelian virtues.

The Red Cross Knight's encounters, his hindrances and errors, are those of Christian, not of Greek, teaching; for example, the reprehension of various kinds of pride. In the House of Pride (Canto IV) we find an attack on the Court of Love idea, and Lucifera is the lighter form of vanity, whereas the Seven Deadly Sins which accompany Pride are darker in their effects. In them Spenser uses a lavishly pictorial method of describing the passions which he inherited from *Piers Plowman*, Gower's *Mirour de l'Omme*, and Sackville's *Induction*. Giant Orgoglio is that other form of pride, arrogance, "Puft up with emptie wynd", whose foster-father is Ignorance. Despair, whom the Knight encounters later, is the defect of which Orgoglio is an excess.

The problem of despair was of course well known centuries before Timothy Bright discussed it in his *Treatise of Melancholy* in 1586. Augustine called it "homicida animae", the murder of the soul. Spenser shows the Knight so tempted by thought of his own sins, hellfire, world-weariness, and desire for rest that he contemplates suicide. The whole incident in Book I, Canto IX, shows how well Spenser can describe the symptoms of passion.

When the Red Cross Knight comes to the House of Holiness the training he receives is a preparation for the mystical vision. The romantic idea may come from Ariosto's account of Ruggiero's visit to the Palace of Logistilla, but this is transformed. Faith, Hope, Charity, Penance, Remorse, Repentance are introduced in accordance with traditional schemes of preparation for the Hill of Contemplation, which is not just a physical viewpoint like the hill from which Huon of Bordeaux saw Oberon's fairy city, but "the way of eying God in heavenly Meditation".

In Book II Sir Guyon seeks Temperance, which might seem to correspond to Aristotle's Temperance or Self-control, and in his journey he faces excesses and deprivations of desirable qualities not unlike those in the *Ethics*. The antitheses agree also with Christian morality and the climax of the book in the House of Alma (Cantos IX, XI, XII) rehandles the Psychomachia theme found in *The Castle of Perseverance*. The irascible passions being overcome with the help of Prince Arthur, Guyon faces concupiscence in the Bower of Bliss and defeats sensual appetite in the person of Acrasia. The scheme may be Aristotelian but the mood is Christian.

The climax of Book II has offended many critics by its allegorical treatment of what is regarded as unsuitable material; but the allegory of body and mind found in the House of Alma was by no means new. St. Bernard's lines "Bonum castrum custodit Qui corpus suum custodit" had been expanded into a description of the Virgin Mary in *The Castle of Love* which Robert Grosseteste translated from French into Anglo-Norman in the thirteenth century. In the *De Planctu Naturae* of Alanus de Insulis the body is described as a city state in which the senses guard the three powers of the soul: Native Strength, Reason, and Memory. Spenser owed something in the physical portion of his description to the Huguenot Du Bartas who in his *Divine Weeks*, Week I, Day 6, worked out parallels between the parts of a body and the parts of a castle. In Spenser the conceit is ingeniously carried through. The hair is like "a wanton ivie", the nose "a faire Portcullis", the tongue is the Porter of the gate. The teeth are twice sixteen warders and (rather oddly)

> By them as Alma passed with her guestes,
> They did obeysaunce, as beseemed right,
> And then againe returned to their restes.
> (Canto IX. 26)

Alma takes Guyon inside the body, where passing Diet and Appetite they reach the Stomach. "The maister Cooke was cald Concoction", the kitchen clerk Digestion; the excreta go out by the Port Esquiline. Alma's court is held in the heart, "a goodly Parlour That was with royall arras richly dight". Mounting thence to the head they find three powers by which the Soul governs well:

> The first of them could things to come foresee:
> The next could of things present best advize;
> The third things past could keepe in memoree.

Phantastes (Fancy) works in the forepart of the brain, Reason or Judgment in the middle, and Memory in the back. The description of Phantastes' chamber (Canto IX. 50-2) is interesting in view of later accounts of Fancy:

> His chamber was dispainted all within,
> With sundry colours, in the which were writ
> Infinite shapes of things dispersed thin;
> Some such as in the world were never yit,
> Ne can devized be of mortall wit;
> Some daily seene, and knowen by their names,
> Such as in idle fantasies doe flit:
> Infernall Hags, *Centaurs*, feendes, *Hippodames*,
> Apes, Lions, Ægles, Owles, fooles, lovers, children,
>   Dames.

> And all the chamber filled was with flyes,
> Which buzzed all about, and made such sound,
> That they encombred all mens eares and eyes,
> Like many swarmes of Bees assembled round,
> After their hives with honny do abound:
> All those were idle thoughts and fantasies,
> Devices, dreames, opinions unsound,
> Shewes, visions, sooth-sayes, and prophesies;
> And all that fained is, as leasings, tales, and lies. . . .

Memory, Eumnestes, the man "of infinite remembrance", has a boy Anamnestes who is the power of particular recollection. (A similar character had appeared in Morality plays.) Spenser uses this to introduce a Canto (X) of historical reminiscence in praise of Queen Elizabeth's ancestors before describing how the enemies of the Soul besieged the castle, assailing the five senses in suitable ways until driven off by Arthur, or Magnificence.

Though the allegory seems trivial and forced today, Spenser's age enjoyed this kind of hard, diagrammatic allegory as much as the richer emblems of the Deadly Sins with their animals and other attributes. Spenser goes still further in this direction in the much-discussed stanza (Canto IX. 22) describing the body in geometrical terms:

> The frame thereof seemd partly circulare,
> And part triangulare, O worke divine;
> Those two the first and last proportions are,
> The one imperfect, mortall, foeminine;
> Th' other immortall, perfect, masculine,
> And twixt them both a quadrate was the base
> Proportioned equally by seven and nine;
> Nine was the circle set in heavens place,
> All which compacted made a goodly diapase.

The body is likened to a circle (the head) set on a rectangle (proportioned 7 by 9), these two supported on a triangle. Spenser's "Cubism" however is far from Picasso's. It is "mystical" in intention, as Sir Kenelm Digby explained in his *Observations* on the stanza, arguing that the head or circle makes the perfect figure, image of eternity; the body is rectangular because of the four humours, and the triangle is "of the lowest rank . . . among figures". More probably the symbolism is of the triple soul of man which the body figures forth, and a passage in Batman's version of Bartolomeus Anglicanus makes the meaning clear:

In diverse bodyes the soule is sayde to be three folde, that is to saye, *Vegetabilis*, that giveth lyfe and no feeling, and that is in plants and rootes, *Sensibilis*, that giveth life and feeling, and not reason, that is in unskilfull beastes, *Racionabilis*, that giveth lyfe, feeling and reason, and this is in men. The Philosopher lykneth the soule that is called *Vegetabilis* to a Triangle. For as a Triangle hath three corners, this manner soule hath three vertues, of begetting, of nourishing, and of growing. And this soule *Vegetabilis* is like to a Triangle in Geometrie. And hee lykneth the soule *Sensibilis* to a quadrangle square, and foure cornered. For in a Quadrangle is a line drawne from one corner to another, before it maketh two Triangles; and the soule sensible maketh two triangles of vertues. For wherever the soule sensible is, there is the soule *Vegetabilis*, but not backwarde [i.e., not *vice versa*]. And hee lykneth the soule *Racionabilis* to a Circle, because of his perfection and conteining.[10]

So much for the shape of the body. The mystic numbers 7 and 9 are invoked, John Upton suggested, because the human mind and body "receive their harmonic proportion, relation, and temperament, from the seven planetary orbs, and from the ninth orb, infolding and containing all the rest". Spenser is "our Pythagorean poet"; to understand his work and that of many other Elizabethan writers one must know not only the Aristotelian view of the mind and body, and the Christian homiletic tradition, but also the hermetic doctrine of shapes and numbers. These ideas fell into disrepute after Descartes and Hobbes, but they were revived in the nineteenth century and affected the imagination of so recent a poet as W. B. Yeats.

Poetry of this kind could be popular only at a time of wide interest in the make-up of the human being. That Spenser's allegory was popular until 1650 is proved by the imitations it evoked, including Phineas Fletcher's didactic *Purple Island* in which the Psychomachia is preceded by a detailed physiological allegory, Strode's play, *The Floating Island*, and passages in Henry More's *Psychozoia*.[11]

In the last quarter of the sixteenth century wonder and joy at the marvellous unity of God's creation were expressed in many writings before Shakespeare penned Hamlet's famous speech on the excellence of man. Even medical treatises such as Timothy Bright's on *Melancholie* (1586) glowed with fervour. Compared with the beasts', man's body is

> made of purer mould as a most precious tabernacle and temple, wherein the image of God should afterward be inshrined, and being formed as it were by God's proper hand, receaved a greater dignitie of beautie, and proportion, and stature erect; thereby to be put in mind whither to direct the religious service of his Creator....
>
> The Spirit (Animal Spirits) is the chief instrument, and immediate, by which the soule bestoweth the exercise of her facultie in her body, that passes to and fro in a moment, nothing in swiftnes and nimblenes being comparable thereunto.[12]

Similarly John Woolton, later Bishop of Exeter, in his *Treatise of the Immortalitie of the Soule* (1576) displays "the marvellous union and conjunction of the body and soule and ... her powers and operations".

> The Reasonable soule is not content with the viewe of Objects externall, and consideration of naturall thinges, but he ascendeth higher, apprehendeth spirituall thinges, and flieth up to the Majestie of God, seeking there his origine and offspring, being the Image of God, not in substance but in similitude....
>
> Consider also [he writes] the manifolde artes and sciences, invented and perceaved by manne, the tilling of the grounde, building of Cyties.

R. Ashley's translation of Le Roy's *Of the Interchangeable Course of Things* (1594) also praises the triumphs of man over his environment, ascribing the invention of arts to economic necessity exercising the human mind, giving an almost Whitmanesque catalogue of achievements which (like Bodin) he sees as affected by geography and history.

Many expositions of man's nature and his place in the Divine Order were associated with the need felt by ethical writers during the Counter-Reformation and the rise of Puritanism to formulate and proclaim their religious position. The Huguenot writers Philippe de Mornay and Pierre de la Primaudaye were well known in England. The former's *The Truenesse of the Christian Religion* was translated in part by Sir Philip Sidney and finished by Arthur Golding (1587). De la Primaudaye's *French Academie* was translated in 1586. Richard Hooker in the next decade introduced into the first Book of his *Ecclesiastical Polity* a superb exposition showing how the several grades of creature keep the law of their being, which is to tend towards the good; and how in man knowledge of goodness grows with command over the appetites by will and reason.[13]

The pleasure taken by the public in such prose writings encouraged poets in the 1590's to break away from the Spenserian method of allegory and to write verse-expositions in which—as if in defiance of the *Faerie Queene*—the plainest of styles was often used and any poetic quality came from the dignity of the subject and the epigrammatic precision of the detail. The didactic strain may be studied in the work of Sir John Davies (*Nosce Teipsum*, 1599), John Davies of Hereford, with his pedestrian *Mirum in Modum* (1602) and *Microcosmos* (1603), and in Fulke Greville's *Treatie of Humane Learning* (1633).[14] These explain how the soul works through the five senses and a sixth, the clearing-house of Common Sense, with Imagination which "doth absent things retaine", and the Fantasie which sorts out the sensuous impressions and

> Compounds in one, things diuers in their kinde;
> Compares the black and white, the great and small, . . .
> And in her ballance doth their values trie.

On this material the Soul exercises its reasoning power, discriminating and relating, and "when by Reason she the truth hath found, And standeth fixt, she Understanding is", which "doth all universall natures know, And all effects unto their causes brings" (Sir J. Davies).

Opinions differed about the reliability of these instruments. On the whole Sir John Davies was inclined to trust the works of the mind. Greville, however, a melancholy Calvinist, saw all our faculties as tainted by the Fall of Adam and drew on Sextus Empiricus and Cornelius Agrippa to decry human knowledge. Thus "Sense, Man's first Instructor, while it showes To free him from deceipt, deceives him most", and Imagination is misinformed by the senses "while our affections cast False shapes and formes on their intelligence". So Memory "can yeeld no Images for man's instruction", and though Understanding retains some "ruinous notions" of general truths, yet they serve only "to convince of ignorance, and sinne, Which where they raigne let no perfection in". Misled by sense and passion, the human mind is incapable of finding truth through sciences and arts. Reason may be of use in practical life and technological inventions, but for ultimate knowledge we must trust faith and revelation.

The *Treatie of Humane Learning* just achieves poetry by its pervading mood of sad disillusionment. Its rejection of reason is repeated in other sceptical verse during the seventeenth century, best of all in Rochester's *Satyr against Mankind*,[15] where man is described as

> that vain *Animal*,
> Who is so proud of being rational.
> The senses are too gross, and he'll contrive
> A Sixth to contradict the other Five;
> And before certain instinct, will prefer
> *Reason*, which Fifty times for one does err.
> *Reason*, an *Ignis fatuus* of the *Mind*,
> Which leaving light of Nature, sense, behind;
> Pathless and dang'rous wandring ways it takes,
> Through error's Fenny *Bogs*, and Thorny *Brakes*;
> Whilst the misguided follower climbs with pain
> *Mountains* of *Whimseys*, heap'd in his own *Brain*—

till at the end of life he realizes

> After a search so painful, and so long,
> That all his Life he has been in the wrong.
> Huddled in dirt, the reas'ning *Engine* lyes,
> Who was so proud, so witty, and so wise.
>
> (ll. 6–30)

While denying the use of reason for metaphysical speculation, Rochester admits its utilitarian value:

> Our *Sphere* of Action is life's happiness,
> And he who thinks Beyond, thinks like an *Ass*.
>
> (96–7)

The "right reason" which he approves

> distinguishes by sense,
> And gives us *Rules* of good and ill from thence:
> That bounds desires with a reforming will,
> To keep 'em more in vigour, not to kill.
>
> (100–3)

He prefers the animal life of simple instinct to the social pretences with which men have surrounded the primordial fear which governs their behaviour. (Rochester had read Hobbes.) In a postscript he praises the "meek, humble man, of modest sense"

> Whose pious life's a proof he does believe
> Mysterious truths, which no *Man* can conceive.
>
> (215–18)

So in the end Rochester reverts to the fideism of Greville and other preachers of *docta ignorantia*.

Most religious writers in the seventeenth century pointed out the imperfections of the human mind even while rejoicing at its potentialities. In its didactic aspect *Paradise Lost* may be regarded as an exposition of this dual attitude as well as a survey of the mediaeval cosmos. While justifying the ways of God to men Milton naturally considers the place of the human mind in the scheme of Creation. The paradisal life of order and harmony is shown in Books IV and V, and Satan praises the "Terrestrial Heav'n" which has all the virtues of the stars:

> in thee,
> Not in themselves, all thir known vertue appears
> Productive in Herb, Plant, and nobler birth
> Of Creatures animate with gradual life
> Of Growth, Sense, Reason, all summ'd up in Man.
> (IX. 109–13)

The innocent use of sense and passion is described, then contrasted with their disorder after the Fall.

The mainspring of the poem is the doctrine of Freewill, which is several times related to man's other faculties. Thus God asserts that Freewill was essential, since He would receive no pleasure from man's obedience

> When Will and Reason (Reason also is choice)
> Useless and vain, of freedom both despoild;
> Made passive both, had servd necessitie,
> Not mee.
> (III. 108–11)

After his fall Adam laments that "my Will Concurr'd not to my being", and sees his future offspring as inheriting the taint,

> But all corrupt, both Mind and Will deprav'd,
> Not to do onely, but to will the same,
> With me.
> (X. 825–7)

The Fall of man, like Lucifer's, comes from freely choosing sense and passion rather than reason, but also from a misuse of reason itself by Eve, whose vanity and curiosity are taught to put on philosophic guise by Satan when he persuades her that if she eats of the fruit

> your Eyes that seem so cleere,
> Yet are but dim, shall perfetly be then
> Op'nd and cleerd, and ye shall be as Gods,
> Knowing both Good and Evil as they know.
> (IX. 706–9)

Man has already been warned that human knowledge must have bounds:

> But Knowledge is as food, and needs no less
> Her Temperance over Appetite, to know
> In measure what the mind may well contain,
> Oppresses else with Surfet, and soon turns
> Wisdom to Folly, as Nourishment to Winde.
>
> (VII. 126–30)

So Eve, the less intellectual of our two parents, falls by intellectual pride. Adam, on the other hand, is misled by her personal charm into uxoriousness.

As he confesses to the Archangel in Book VIII, he was strangely perturbed when he first saw the grace and beauty of Eve: "here passion first I felt, Commotion strange."

> All higher knowledge in her presence falls
> Degraded, Wisdom in discourse with her
> Looses discount'nanc't, and like folly shewes:
> Authoritie and Reason on her waite.
>
> (VIII. 551–4)

He is warned not to subject himself to Eve's beauty but to cherish his self-esteem and balance; and not to surrender himself to the delight of "the sense of touch whereby mankind Is propagated":

> In loving thou dost well, in passion not,
> Wherein true Love consists not; love refines
> The thoughts, and heart enlarges, hath his seat
> In Reason, and is judicious, is the scale
> By which to heav'nly Love thou maist ascend,
> Not sunk in carnal pleasure, for which cause
> Among the Beasts no Mate for thee was found.
>
> (VIII. 588–94)

When Adam falls it is

> Against his better knowledge, not deceav'd,
> But fondly overcome with Femal charm.
>
> (IX. 998–9)

The immediate effect of sin is to excite concupiscence and irascibility. Love turns to lust and then to mutual accusation, until

Adam, who earlier begged God for a companion, cries out against Eve and sex:

> O why did God,
> Creator wise, that peopl'd highest Heav'n
> With Spirits Masculine, create at last
> This noveltie on Earth, this fair defect
> Of Nature, and not fill the World at once
> With Men as Angels without Feminine,
> Or find some other way to generate
> Mankind?
>
> (X. 888–95)

Human sin brings evil passion and discord into subhuman nature. The stars take on malevolent aspects, the climate changes:

> Thus began
> Outrage from liveless things; but Discord first
> Daughter of Sin, among th' irrational,
> Death introduc'd through fierce antipathie;
> Beast now with Beast gan war, and Fowle with Fowle,
> And Fish with Fish. . . .
>
> (X. 706–11)

Self-knowledge, the realization of his sin's effects, adds to Adam's grief. In his vision in Book XI we see the long-term results in human history, the various forms of death, "By Fire, Flood, Famin, by Intemperance more", the diseases caused by "ungovern'd Appetite", the wantonness brought by "Man's effeminate slackness", a pageant of passions. After the Flood the sorry spectacle continues, with the rise of political tyranny and the loss of liberty ("which always with right Reason dwells"):

> Reason in man obscur'd, or not obeyd,
> Immediately inordinate desires
> And upstart Passions catch the Government
> From Reason, and to servitude reduce
> Man till then free.
>
> (XII. 86–90)

The subjection of man "to violent Lords" is an external consequence of the loss of inner freedom.

The lesson concludes when the Angel tells Adam how to live a

Christian life, which is better than to know "All secrets of the deep, all Nature's works". If he learns to add

> Deeds to thy knowledge answerable, add Faith,
> Add Vertue, Patience, Temperance, add Love,
> By name to come call'd Charitie, the soul
> Of all the rest: then wilt thou not be loath
> To leave this Paradise, but shalt possess
> A Paradise within thee, happier farr.
> (XII. 582–87)

The Christian virtues are to direct the passions and senses towards true happiness.

That the pursuit of earthly knowledge and pleasure is a snare is shown again in *Paradise Regained*, where Christ proves his "temperance invincible" by refusing to allay his hunger, his scorn of "Riches and Realms" by explaining that

> he who reigns within himself, and rules
> Passions, Desires, and Fears is more a King
> (II. 466–7),

his contempt of fame when he describes true glory as achieved

> By deeds of peace, by wisdom eminent,
> By patience, temperance.
> (III. 91–2)

Christ further asserts that the classical philosophers, those preachers of the doctrine *Nosce teipsum*, are

> Ignorant of themselves, of God much more,
> And how the world began, and how man fell
> Degraded by himself, on grace depending.
> Much of the Soul they talk, but all awrie,
> And in themselves seek vertue. . . .
> (IV. 310–14)

Some traces in them may appear of "light of Nature not in all quite lost", but

> he who receives
> Light from above, from the fountain of light,
> No other doctrine needs.
> (IV. 288–90)

Thus over against the senses, passions and lower reason of earthbound minds Milton sets the soul's intuition of God, the apprehension of Divine Grace. His major work is indeed moulded to the Christian psychological system; it expounds both epically and didactically God's plan for human nature, and displays both the rightful adjustment of the mind's faculties in a proper relation to God, and also the chaos and self-idolatry into which they fall when diabolical temptation seizes on any weakness or unbalance in the instruments of the soul.

Turning from more formal statements to lyrical poetry, we find frequent reference to the mind and its constituents. If the early Tudor love-poets showed little of the subtlety developed in the mediaeval Italians, they took over the typical situations, emotions, and symptoms of the Petrarchan tradition and used them with considerable appreciation of the psychological relationships involved. The result is a poetry of passionate protest, grief, and longing, celebrating the victory of desire over reason.[16]

> Forget not yet the great assays,
> The cruel wrong, the scornful ways,
> The painful patience in delays,

cries Wyatt, and, comparing his state to a ship in a storm:

> An endless wind doth tear the sail apace
> Of forced sighs, and trusty fearfulness;
> A rain of tears, a cloud of dark disdain
> Hath done the wearied cords great hinderance ...
> Drowned is reason, that should me consort,
> And I remain, despairing of the port.

Usually he tries to stir pity in his cruel mistress's breast, though sometimes he looks to the time when

> Vengeance shall fall on thy disdain,
> That makest but game on earnest pain.

Love is a pain, a wound, a rage, an inevitable but unfortunate perturbation of the mind; the cruel fair one is a "foe", unkind, untrue, a traitress, a passionless thing. In the words of Sandford, who turned away from the Cupid myth to moral teaching,

> Love all the senses doth beguile
> And bleareth all our eyes:
> It cuts off freedom of the mind
> And makes us gape for flies.*
> I think some furious fiend of hell
> The heart doth thus inflame
> And bringeth quite the same a-down
> From lofty reason's frame:
> Ne is this Love a god in deed,
> But lies and bitter bane.

But though many a disappointed lover wrote in similar terms most would not miss the experience:

> Except I love, I cannot have delight,
> It is a care that doth to life belong . . .
> Yet had I rather thus for to remain
> Than laugh, and live, not feeling lover's pain.

The conceits of Elizabethan love-poetry ring the changes on traditional images from classical and mediaeval sources. Some of them derive from psychological relations. Thus the eyes are often praised or blamed as bringers of love to the heart, and debates between eyes and heart (parallel to the religious debates between body and soul) occur in sonnet-sequences by Watson (xx), Constable (Dec. vi, 7), Drayton (xxxiii), and Shakespeare (xlvi):

> Mine eye and heart are at a mortal war,
> How to divide the conquest of thy sight;
> Mine eye my heart thy picture's sight would bar,
> My heart mine eye the freedom of that right. . . .

The impression made by the "bright face" of the mistress in the lover's mind and heart, used in Petrarch's Canzone 13, takes many forms. In Watson (xlv–xlvi) and Shakespeare (xxiv) the image of the beloved is a picture "framed" in the heart. Sometimes the

---

* I.e., blind. "The blind eats many flies" (Churchyard).

lover's heart is a mirror of her beauty or cruelty; or his face may be a mirror of his desires.[17]

Occasionally thoughts or desires become living creatures. "My thoughts are sheep which I both guide and serve", writes Sidney in the *Arcadia*, whereas in Daniel, "My thoughts, like hounds, pursue me to my death" (v). The animal image is also found in Lodge, Griffin, and Shakespeare; but often the poets were content to use mental qualities without dressing them up in concrete form. Spenser, being parted from his mistress, describes how his eyes seek her vainly in the places where he last met her,

> Whose ymage yet I carry fresh in mynd . . .
> And when I hope to see theyr trew object,
> I find my selfe but fed with fancies vayne.
> Ceasse then, myne eyes, to seeke her selfe to see;
> And let my thoughts behold her selfe in mee.
>
> (*Amoretti*, 78)

He frequently treats his thoughts as separable entities. At the beginning of his pursuit, he bids his "unquiet thought" bred "Of th'inward bale of my love-pined hart" to break forth and ask for succour and grace:

> Which if she graunt, then live, and my love cherish;
> If not, die soone; and I with thee will perish. (2)

Later he imagines his thoughts "diving deepe through amorous insight" into the riches of her bosom (76)—

> Sweet thoughts! I envy your so happy rest,
> Which oft I wisht, yet never was so blest;

feasting there like guests at a banquet (77), and visiting her bed only

> to behold her rare perfection,
> And blesse your fortunes faire election.
>
> (83)

Such a habit of abstraction, especially characteristic of poetry from Spenser and Sidney onwards, is associated with ethical and religious interests, but also often with a delight in the figures of rhetoric, which was based on analysis of the passions to be moved. Hence in a "sonnet" which ends "Foole saide my Muse to mee, looke in thy heart and write", Sidney exemplified the invention which he said he lacked in a "Clymax or marching figure" suggesting the mental process he hoped for in his Stella:

> Loving in trueth, and fayne my love in verse to show,
> That the deere *Shee*, might take some pleasure of my paine:
> Pleasure might cause her reade, reading might make her know,
> Knowledge might pittie winne, and pittie grace obtaine,
> I sought fit wordes, to paint the blackest face of woe,
> Studying inventions fine, her wittes to entertaine. . . .
>
> (*Astrophel and Stella*, 1)

Sidney's awareness of mental states and categories is no more varied than Spenser's, but he shows considerable technical agility as he arranges senses, passions, and reason into patterns of compliment.

Sidney plays on the opposition between reason and the senses and with the idea that "naked sense can conquer reason arm'd". "Reason, tell me my mind, if here be reason In this strange violence to make resistance?" he asks when he sees Stella's "sweet graces" coming against him under the banner "Of vertues regiment", and reason must surrender, since "Nought can reason availe in heav'nly matters". Again, love, he says, delights in virtue as well as sense, and

> would not, arm'd with beautie, only raigne
> On those affectes [i.e., passions] which easily yield to sight,
> But vertue sets so high that reason's light
> For all his strife can only bondage gaine. . . .[18]

In the tenth Sonnet to Stella he chides his reason for quarrelling with "sense and love" in him. Reason should turn to poetry and science:

> I rather wish thee climbe the Muses hill
> Or reach the fruit of Natures chiefest tree,
> Or seek heaven's course, or heavens unusde to thee . . .
> But thou wouldst needes fight both with Love and sence,
> With sworde of witte giving woundes of dispraise. . . .

In vain however; one sight of Stella's eyes converts even Reason itself to Love. In the Sixth Sonnet, debating whether Stella's voice or face be more beautiful, he calls in the Common Sense and Reason to decide between the senses of sight and hearing:

> The Common Sense which might
> Be arbiter of this,
> To be forsooth upright,
> To both sides partial is,
> He laies on this chiefe praise,
> Chiefe praise on that he laies.[19]

There is in Sidney a renewal of the consciousness of mental processes found in the poetry of Dante and his circle. Like Dante, Sidney can stand back from his loving, passionate self, and watch what is going on there. He likes to find strange analogies to mental processes. Thus in *The 7 Wonders of England* he likens Stonehenge to his emotions; the Bruertons lake to the power of sensation; and the Barnacle Goose (said to be born from wrack on the seashore) to the sublimation of lust into the higher love.[20] One motive behind the pastoral convention is explained in *The First Eclogues* by Dorus, who prefers the country to the court because

> Then do I thinke indeed, that better it is to be private
> In sorrows torment, than, tied to the pomps of a palace,
> Nurse inward maladies, which have not scope to be breath'd out,
> But perforce disgest all bitter juices of horror
> In silence, from a man's own self with company robbed.
> Better yet do I live, that though by my thoughts I be plunged
> Into my life's bondage, yet may disburden a passion
> (Opprest with ruinous conceits) by the help of an outcry.[21]

Similarly the pastoral lovers of the *Arcadia* and of Lodge's *Rosalynd* reflect freely on love and its effects, and disburden themselves of many a "Passion" or amorous outburst; Shakespeare's characters in *As You Like It* follow suit. Sidney enunciated the long-popular theme of solitary meditation when he cried:

> O sweet woods, the delight of solitariness! . . .
> Where senses do behold the order of heav'nly host,

> And wise thoughts do behold what the Creator is;
> Contemplation here holdeth his only seat,
> Bounded with no limits, borne with a wing of hope
> Climbs even unto the stars: Nature is under it.
> Nought disturbs thy quiet, all to thy service yields,
> Each sight draws on a thought, thought, mother of science.[22]

Renaissance study of the classics brought new interpretations of poets who for centuries had been incompletely known or regarded in the light of mediaeval, not classical, codes of morality and conduct. Ovid, whose pagan eroticism had been transmogrified by Chrétien de Troyes and the Court of Love poets, was seen to have little in common with the chivalric tradition; and in the 1590's his *Amores* (translated by Marlowe), *Ars Amatoria*, and *Remedia Amoris* were enlisted to support the new realism of which Donne in his *Elegies* and earlier *Songs and Sonets* was a major exponent. This Ovidian strain has been wittily expressed by Mr. Robert Graves in his poem "Ovid in Defeat":

> "Let man be ploughshare,
>   Woman his field;
> Flatter, beguile, assault,
>   And she must yield."
>   . . . .
> Ovid instructs you how
>   Neighbours' lands to plough;
> "Love smacks the sweeter
>   For a broken vow."
>
> Follows his conclusion
>   Of which the gist is
> The cold "*post coitum
>   Homo tristis.*"[23]

Donne's *Elegies* involve assumptions about the nature of love, of men's and women's natures and needs, very different from those found in Sidney and Spenser. Thus in Elegy XVII the poet praises Variety, refusing to tie himself to any one woman:

> I love her well, and would, if need were, dye—
> To doe her service. But followes it that I
> Must serve her onely, when I may have choice
> Of other beauties, and in change rejoice?

Change and the love-chase are delightful in themselves,

> And though I fail of my required ends,
> The attempt is glorious, and itself commends.

The techniques of infidelity and secrecy are described without idealization. What might be called the Casanova motif recurs several times. In Elegy XIV the poet comes to an unspoken understanding with a citizen's wife, and in Elegy IV he is betrayed to his mistress's father by the scent he carries. This is a love beset by "spies and rivals", and "father's wrath" or husband's suspicions, by "froward jealousy" and feared or proven inconstancy. Love is a sensual art of deceit to be taught to other men's ingenuous wives and daughters, who learn so readily "the mystique language of the eye or hand", "the Alphabet of flowers", that ere long the dismayed seducer cries,

> I planted knowledge and life's tree in thee,
> Which Oh, shall strangers taste?
>
> *(Elegy VII)*

For the most part the Elegies rate physical enjoyments higher than those of mind or soul (XVIII, XIX) and there is a crudity more like Martial than Ovid in Donne's satire on ugliness and his incitements to copulation. But a warmer feeling endues some of these poems, as when he forbids his mistress to accompany him abroad disguised as a page (XVI), and in his praise of a middle-aged friend (IX),

> No Spring, nor Summer Beauty hath such grace,
> As I have seen in one Autumnall face.

Even in idolizing Variety he concludes by confessing that his allegiance to the "antient liberty" of love is temporary, and that the future will see him

> beauty with true worth securely weighing,
> Which being found assembled in some one,
> Wee'l love her ever, and love her alone.
>   (XVII)

The harsh dissonance of most of the *Elegies* is on the surface related to the style and mood of his *Satires*, but is probably due to a conscious, if often repressed, awareness of the discrepancy between the Ovidian attitude of omnivorous eroticism and a natural desire for spiritual unity and truth in love as well as in religion. So the realistic, cynical thoughts and imagery are crossed by ideas drawn from the scholastic philosophy in which Donne had been reared. That these are particularly frequent and significant in the Elegies of less purely physical import witnesses to Donne's growth out of cynical gallantry into a search for a complete harmony of the soul's instruments.

In his mature work Donne is fascinated by the way the soul works in the body and by their connection in and after this life. Psycho-physical relationships are drawn on for analogies to the simplest relationships in everyday life; hence the accusation made later, in an age which had rejected such doctrines, that he used far-fetched and puzzling conceits. When he tells the Countess of Bedford that both zeal and discretion are needed in religion he draws on the doctrine that man has three souls, the Vegetative, Sensitive, and Rational:

> But as our Soules of growth and Soules of Sense
> Have birthright [i.e., precedence] of our Reason's soule,
>   yet hence
> They flie not from that, nor seeke precedence:—
> Nature's first lesson, so discretion
> Must not grudge zeale a place. . . .

In the same letter he points out that the four elements "Produce all things with which wee are joy'd or fed". The soul, he declares in "Aire and Angels", "takes limbs of flesh, and else could nothing do", and even angels have forms and speak to men in a voice or shapeless flame. We must accept our earthly condition; hence the poem "The Extasie" is more than an exercise in seduction. In it Donne describes the day-long rêverie of two lovers whose souls are fused until they emanate a third soul which overhangs them and is conscious of them both at once. Sex is an instrument of spiritual unity:

> This Extasie doth unperplex
> (We said) and tell us what we love,
> We see by this it was not sex,
> We see we saw not what did move.

Yet the sexual instruments are there to be used:

> They are ours, though they are not we. We are
> The intelligences, they the sphere

(like the angels controlling the planets). On earth souls must normally communicate through the body;

> So must pure lovers souls descend
> T'affections [emotions] and to faculties
> Which sense may reach and comprehend,
> Else a great Prince in prison lies.[24]

In poems as in his *Sermons* later Donne speaks of the bodily spirits in their three kinds: the "natural" spirits born in the liver, the "vital" in the heart, and the "animal" (or soul-like) in the brain. The "animal" spirits from the head govern the body through the hollow tubes of the nerves; hence the celebrated description in "The Funerall" of the immortalizing power of his mistress's hair—that "bracelet of bright hair about the bone" (cf. "The Relic"), here compared with the nerves:

> For if the sinewie thread my brain lets fall
>   Through every part
> Can tie those parts and make me one of all,
>   Those haires which upward grew, and strength and art
>   Have from a better braine,
> Can better do't. . . .

The poetic power of such apparently disparate images consists in

Donne's sense of the unity in the Divine Order of all things material and spiritual. Where all is one nothing is far-fetched.

Donne occasionally deploys the conventional Petrarchan symptoms: tears, sighs, groans, and protests. But he prefers other effects, such as the power of passion to alter one's normal sense of time and place. When with his mistress,

> She is all states, and all princes I,
> Nothing else is
> ("The Sun Rising")

he can transcend absence; or, on the contrary, cry

> For the first twenty years, since yesterday,
> I scarce believ'd thou could'st be gone away,
> For forty more I fed on favours past. . . .
> ("The Computation")

He can treat fruition as an eternal union of souls, or on the contrary sadly describe, Ovid-like, the aftermath of love, which reduces all senses to one,

> And that so lamely, as it leaves behind
> A kind of sorrowing dulnesse to the mind.
> ("Farewell to Love")

Being something of an invalid he is morbid about illness and death and their physical concomitants. He dramatizes himself as dying and being anatomized for a post-mortem. Thinking of his mistress as dead, he mixes his grief with witty fancies on the idea that "all which die To their first Elements resolve" ("The Dissolution").

He plays many variants on this theme. When in *The First Anniversarie* he hyperbolically imagines Elizabeth Drury as the Soul of the World, to her death he ascribes all the chaos and degeneracy used by religious pessimists to prophesy the speedy end of an epoch. "There is no health, Physicians say that we At best enjoy but a neutrality." Men do not live as long as they used to; they are smaller in size. Modern times have brought new diseases. "And with new Physic a worse Engin far." Our minds too are dwarfed. "The new Philosophy calls all in doubt", that is, makes us doubt all the efforts of human reason to discover the truth about the universe; and

>   nothing
> Is worth our travail, grief or perishing
> But those rich joys which did possess her heart,
> Of which she's now partaker, and a part.

In *The Second Anniversarie* he again shows man's ignorance about his origin, his physiology, his humours, and the operations of his senses. The only remedy is to cease "being taught by Sense and Phantasie",

> And see all things despoiled of fallacies:
> Thou shalt not peep through lattices of eyes,
> Nor heare through labyrinths of eares, nor learne
> By circuit, or collections to discerne.
> In heav'n thou straight know'st all. . . .

A conclusion with which the Davieses and Greville would have agreed.

 In the main Donne's interest in the body and mind springs from their participation in a theological system. He does not often anatomize the passions themselves, and the complex force of his poetry comes not so much from the intensity of the emotions excited by immediate circumstances as from their involvement with ideas and sentiments about the laws of the cosmos and the operations of the intellect in science and philosophy. Being movements of the soul, they imply the whole system of the universe. If he wants to tell his mistress that she was a phantom of delight when first she gleamed upon his sight, and that every one of her beauties is too great for him to bear, he writes "Aire and Angels", in which erotic feeling is distracted with angelology. Always there is argument, and the argument tends to supplant its original impulse. His passion is self-consciously aware of its place in the great chain of being; and Donne is often at least as interested in the interrelations of other mental activities as he is in the amorous chase. "The delight of the intellect is to feel itself alive", wrote Pater. For Donne poetry became an exercise of all the faculties as he saw love or religion in terms of a scholastic universe which he could enjoy not only for its ordered totality but also for its astonishing and at times bizarre details, its refined discriminations which fostered his subtle casuistry.

Too much has been made of the "fusion" of thought and feeling in Donne. His work depends rather on an interplay, conflict, and tension between them arising from his sense of the postlapsarian dissonances in man's body and mind. Even when he overrides these conflicts with argument or hyperbole the differences between heavenly and earthly, spiritual and sensual, truth and man's illusive knowledge, remain in his consciousness. His poetry is based in the paradox of human existence, the "wearisome condition of humanity", the limitations of the soul's instruments, and the dramatic quality of his work springs from the effort to resolve dissonance into harmony.

In the early seventeenth century the practice of piety and the revival of mysticism fostered a systematization of religious experience, the division of the work of grace into stages, each with its own emotional and intellectual activities. There was much hair-splitting and confusion of terminology, which led the Cambridge Platonist Benjamin Whichcote, in one of his sermons, to take ten words in common religious use and comment on them. These were Regeneration, Conversion, Adoption, Vocation, Sanctification, Justification, Reconciliation, Redemption, Salvation, Glorification. Whichcote believed that "It is the proper employment of our intellectual faculties to be conversant about God, to conceive aright of him; and then to resemble and imitate him." "A man cannot open his eye, nor lend his ear, but everything will declare more or less of God." But these ten words, he declared, were evidence of "a troublesome multiplicity in religion". They "differ but notionally or gradually, or as to our apprehension only". He briefly describes their import and concludes that "whensoever one of these is, all are, ... they speak the same thing in different states" (*Sermons*, II, 80–2).

To more pedantic or curious seekers the fact that they meant "different states" was important, and, as Louis Martz comments, "both Catholic and Puritan, while accusing each other bitterly of neglecting the inner life, were pursuing the art of self-knowledge by methods equally intense and effective" with "a subtlety of self-awareness that went far beyond the popular achievements of the Middle Ages".[25] St. Augustine's *Confessions*, the mediaeval mystics, *Theologia Germanica*, the *Dark Night of the Soul* of St. John of the Cross, the *Interior Castle* of St. Teresa—all were closely studied. The *Meditations* of St. Bernard were several times reprinted after Wynkyn de Worde published them in 1496. They were re-translated in 1611 and remained popular. The *Divine Considerations* of Juan de Valdes, translated by Nicholas Ferrar, appeared in 1638 with a prefatory epistle by George Herbert, and in 1646 they were adapted to Puritan use. The exercise of meditation and contemplation was popularized by such works as Bishop Joseph Hall's *Art of Divine Meditation* (1606), and his *Meditations and Vows* (1605, etc.). Later Thomas Fuller's *Good Thoughts in Bad Times* (1645) proved immensely popular. Richard Baxter in *The Saints Everlasting Rest* (1650) cited pre-Reformation and Jesuit writers in advocating to Puritans the art of meditation. Hall's exposition of the "Deliberate Meditation"—which he distinguishes from the "Extempore Meditation"—might be profitably examined: "It begins in the understanding, endeth in the affection; It begins in the braine, descends to the heart; Begins on earth, ascends to Heaven, not suddenly, but by certaine staires and degrees till we come to the highest." He gives, from "the Scale of Meditation of an Author, ancient but namelesse", the "degrees of proceeding in the understanding, viz. *Commemoration, Consideration, Attention, Explanation, Tractation, Dijudication, Causation, Rumination*".[26] "From hence to the degrees of Affection", which are equally refined.

Hall himself, Manchester ("Al Mondo"), and many others including the "Sceptical Chymist" Robert Boyle composed prose Meditations on simple schemes. The religious poetry of the first half of the seventeenth century owes much to this practice, and some of the differences between the religious lyrics of Donne, Herbert, Crashaw, and Vaughan are due to the different psychological procedures they had learned in such spiritual exercises. Many of their poems are indeed Meditations, either extempore or deliberate, and the imagery they use is stamped by the particular nature of their reading or their aim. So Herbert, the country parson, will take a simple theme, part of the church building ("The Church-floore", "The Windows") and write a short meditation on it, drawing spiritual lessons from physical objects; or he will meditate on Aaron the priest and his Hebrew vestments, and draw a parallel with his own self-preparation for service; or think about the festivals of the Anglican church, using the simplest of language as befitted one for whom the Bible was a main source of contemplation:

> Oh Book! Infinite sweetnesse! Let my heart
> Suck ev'ry letter, and a honey gain,
> Precious for any grief, in any part;
> To cleare the breast, to mollifie all pain.
> ("The Holy Scriptures")

Crashaw will meditate on the Blessed Sacrament, or the life of St. Teresa, rising to a rapture imitative of hers. Vaughan, on the other hand, a medical doctor and hermetic student of nature, is more concerned with the relationship between the mind of man and other creatures in the cosmic scheme. So, meditating on a verse in the Epistle to the Romans which declares that inanimate objects await the revelation of the sons of God, he realizes that this transcends the Aristotelian categories.

> And do they so? have they a Sense
> Of aught but Influence?
> Can they their heads lift, and expect,

> And grone too? Why th'Elect
> Can do no more: my volumes said
> They were all dull, and dead, . . .
> Go, go; Seal up thy looks,
> And burn thy books.

He goes on here and in other poems to envy the "stedfastness and state" of the mean things which are more innocent than man, who is "ever restless and irregular":

> He knows he hath a home, but scarce knows where,
> He sayes it is so far
> That he hath quite forgot how to go there.
>
> ("Man")

The longing for innocence makes him yearn for the pastoral days of the Hebrew patriarchs, when Angels still came down to talk with men:

> The valley, or the Mountain
> Afforded visits, and still Paradise lay
> In some green shade, or fountain.
>
> ("Corruption")

The remembrance of his infant days brings him to the doctrine of the soul's pre-existence before birth into this world ("The Retreat"). Restlessness of mind and soul spring from our loss of antenatal union and our attempts to regain it.

The practice of self-analysis fostered the tendency, already noted, to treat thought as a special power separable from and superior to the other faculties. Thus Marvell's Resolved Soul answers Created Pleasure who bids him "On these downy Pillows lye" with the rebuke: "My gentler Rest is on a Thought, Conscious of doing what I ought." And Traherne who pushed introspection to the edge of solipsism celebrated thought as the only reality. "Thoughts are things"; "To walk abroad is not with Eys, But Thoughts, the Fields to see and prize." "A delicate and tender thought The Quintessence is of all He wrought." Allied to this was a centrifugal delight in the manifold activity of consciousness. One is reminded of Hamlet's fancy that he might "be bounded in a nutshell and count myself a king of infinite space". The philosophical Sir John Davies, in proving the spirituality of the soul, had asserted the immediacy of its intuitions:

> But she is nighe, and farre, beneath, above,
> In point of time, which thought cannot devide;
>
> She is sent as soone to China as to Spaine,
> And thence returnes, as soone as shee is sent,
> She measures with one time, and with one paine,
> An ell of silke, and heav'ns wide spreading tent.
> (*Nosce Teipsum*)

It was an easy step from this to regard Fancy as the active power of the soul

> Who in a Minute can the Earth surround
> And sinke into her center, then ascend.
> (John Davies of Hereford, *Microcosmos*)

Traherne frequently expressed his joy in the speed and range of imaginative thought. In "Insatiableness" he sought new worlds to conquer:

> 'Tis mean Ambition to desire
>   A single World:
>   To many I aspire,
> Tho one upon another hurl'd:
> Nor will they all, if they be all confin'd,
>   Delight my Mind.
>
> This busy, vast, enquiring Soul
>   Brooks no Controul:
>   'Tis hugely curious too.
> Each one of all those Worlds must be
> Enricht with infinit Variety
>   And Worth; or 'twill not do.

In this aspiration he went little further than other poets of the mid-seventeenth century who praised the treasure-flights of Wit and Fancy, their ability to give to airy nothing a local habitation and a name. Addressing his muse, Cowley celebrated Fancy which goes

> Where never foot of man, or hoof of beast,
>   The passage press'd;
> Where never fish did fly,
> And with short silver wings cut the low liquid sky; . . .
>
> Thou fathom'st the deep gulf of ages past,
>   And canst pluck up with ease
>   The years which thou dost please;
> Like shipwreck'd treasures, by rude tempests cast
>   Long since into the sea,
> Brought up again to light and public use by thee.

But Cowley had read Hobbes, who, in his "Answer to Davenant", pointed out the internal organization of the mind and the stabilizing influence of Memory and Judgment on Fancy,

> So that when she seemeth to fly from one Indies to the other, and from Heaven to Earth, and to penetrate into the hardest matter and obscurest places, into the future and into her self, and all this in a point of time, the voyage is not very great, her self being all she seeks; and her wonderful celerity consists not so much in motion as in copious Imagery discreetly ordered and perfectly registered in the Memory.

Unlike most of his contemporaries, who regarded Fancy or Imagination as a curio-hunter, an Autolycus, a "picker up of unconsidered trifles", Cowley perceived something of its unifying power. And in his ode "Of Wit" he insisted on the *concordia concors*, the harmony of the total effect:

> In a true piece of Wit all things must be,
>   Yet all things there agree;
> As in the ark, join'd without force or strife,
> All creatures dwelt; all creatures that had life:
>   Or, as the primitive forms of all
>   (If we compare great things with small)
> Which, without discord or confusion, lie
> In that strange mirror of the Deity.

So at the end of the period the image of the microcosm recurs in this analogy between the working of the human mind and the Divine. But the prevalence of the ability to hold separate the various functions of the mind in the consciousness of the percipient and to explore their manifold activities helps to explain the climate in which Descartes's *Discours de la méthode* and Locke's *Essay concerning Human Understanding* became popular. With some literary implications of these works we shall be concerned in the third essay.

Chapter Two ↬ THE DEVELOPMENT OF
SHAKESPEARE'S ATTITUDE TO
THE MIND

Should future generations take any interest in the British and American drama of the twentieth century, their scholars will undoubtedly have to consider the views of the mind current in our time and the degree to which these permeated the work of Eugene O'Neill, Tennessee Williams, Bernard Shaw, J. B. Priestley, and T. S. Eliot. For the drama of any age, representing the motives and traits which writers and audiences assume to lie beneath the behaviour of theatrical characters, holds a mirror up to human nature but sees it in the light of contemporary preoccupations and beliefs. Without some knowledge of these assumptions, many nuances of dramatic personality will be ignored, the prevalence of certain kinds of theme and character will be inexplicable, and some turns of plot and mood may seem improbable.

Major Elizabethan drama, beginning in the 1580's, coincided with the popularity of the ethical writings already noted, and the growing interest in mental operations apparent in lyrical and didactic verse. Properly to discuss the influence of Tudor psychology on the dramatists would involve a long series of individual studies. For our purpose the generalizations worked out by

Professor Hardin Craig will suffice.[1] He has pointed out that psychological terms are used more or less extensively, but casually, by the early dramatists, Lyly, Peele, and Greene.

Then came a group of writers who show a knowledge of the details of the science and employ it in an obvious and often penetrating way in their work—Marlowe, Shakespeare, Marston, Chapman, and Jonson. They are at home with the terminology of the subject; it is integral and poetized.

After these came Jacobean dramatists such as Beaumont and Fletcher, Tourneur, Webster, Middleton, and Ford, who were "absorbed in the spectacle of man in the grasp of unruly spirits and driven to insanity, crime, misery, blindness, etc." These later writers were fascinated by abnormal aberrations of passion, by incest, cruelty, lechery, and stories involving violent twists of motive which it tasked all their resources to reconcile with any underlying pattern of character. What has been called a "decadent" morbidity in these writers was often the result of a poetic inquiry into the springs of abnormal behaviour, activated by a desire to explain the extreme situations and dénouements of some Italian *novelle*, to portray a social order in disruption, a moral world tottering on the brink of chaos, even to philosophize on the frailty of the human will and the justice of a universe which demands too much of man's divided nature.

A history of Elizabethan drama might be written in terms of the writers' choice and treatment of themes in relation to psychological and ethical considerations, but that is not my purpose. Nor shall I try to contrast Shakespeare's pervasive but undoctrinaire use of psychology with Jonson's narrow but fruitful insistence on the Humour theory for comic and satiric purposes, or with Chapman's expert conflation in his tragedies of the Stoic theory of the passions with more general theories. That Shakespeare may be regarded as a link between the first and the third group of psychologizing dramatists, a sketch of the development of his use of elements of the current psychology proves.

The earlier English Histories show only a limited interest in contemporary psychological science. In them the exploration of character is less sought than an epic treatment of foreign affairs (*1 Henry VI*), a Senecan orgy of contrasting passions (*2 and 3 Henry VI*), and a combination of this with Marlowesque tragic villainy (*Richard III*). *1 Henry VI* uses the white and red roses as symbolizing anger or fear (II. 4); the disproportion between Talbot's small body and his great mind surprises the Countess of Auvergne (II. 3. 23-4);* symptoms of old age are mentioned by the dying Mortimer (II. 5) and by Talbot (IV. 6) whose "leaden age" is "Quicken'd with youthful spleen and warlike rage". But the piece displays little psychological knowledge—and this is not surprising, since the tone is largely heroic, the portrayal of its figures external.

In *2 Henry VI*, which describes warring animosities in the domestic life of the nation in an age when, as Gloucester exclaims (III. 1. 143-6):

> Virtue is chok'd with foul ambition
> And charity chas'd hence by rancour's hand;
> Foul subornation is predominant,
> And equity exil'd your highness' land,

the irascible passions come to the fore, and, indeed, men are chiefly known by them. Typical words are choler, ambition, envy, treachery, revenge, spite, malice. Suffolk calls Warwick "headstrong Warwick" and Warwick calls Suffolk "Image of pride" (I. 3). Duke Humphrey characterizes the rivals when prophesying that his death will be the prologue to a long tragedy (III. 1. 154-60):

> Beaufort's red sparkling eyes blab his heart's malice,
> And Suffolk's cloudy brow his stormy hate,
> Sharp Buckingham unburdens with his tongue
> The envious load that lies upon his heart;
> And dogged York that reaches at the moon, . . .
> By false accuse doth level at my life.

* Line references are to the three-volume Oxford edition of Shakespeare, by W. J. Craig (1912).

ATTITUDE TO THE MIND

Senecan influence is seen not only in the inflated emotional language, but in the formulation of scenes to reveal conflicting passions at work, for example, Eleanor Cobham's ambition in her colloquy with her meek husband (I. 2), her "invincible spirit" in the conjuration scene (I. 4), her shame and anger at her public humiliation (II. 4), the Queen's fury at Eleanor's arrogance, her impatience with the mild weakness of the King.

Usually the symptoms of passion are described in conventional, general terms: King Henry's "heart is drown'd with grief, Whose flood begins to flow within myne eyes". A sudden accession of animal imagery denotes the inhuman, unnatural qualities represented. York calls himself a "starved snake", his brain is like a "labouring spider"; Gloucester's enemies wrongly call him "a mournful crocodile", a "hungry kite", a "fox" to be slain "by gins, by snares, by subtilty" (III. 1).

We see a reference to physiology when Warwick realizes that Gloucester was murdered because, whereas most corpses are pale through the spirits' descending "to the labouring heart", his face "black and full of blood" is that of a strangled man (III. 2. 160–71). But the banished Suffolk's description of cursing to kill (III. 2. 309–21) is entirely external, with its "bitter-searching terms" delivered through clenched teeth, with a stumbling tongue. Equally external are the symptoms of Beaufort's conscience-struck sickness.

In *3 Henry VI* the passionate words recur: savage, bloody, quenchless fury; the animal images: "O tiger's heart wrapped in a woman's hide!" But there is a movement inwards, from Clifford's assertion that revenge "could not slake mine ire, nor ease my heart" (I. 3. 29) to the Queen's cry to York

> What! hath thy fiery heart so parch'd thy entrails
> That not a tear can fall for Rutland's death?
> Why art thou patient, man? thou shouldst be mad;
> (I. 4. 87–9)

and from York's accusation that Margaret cannot blush, her face

> is visor-like, unchanging
> Made impudent with use of evil deeds
> (I. 4. 116–17)

to his declaration, as he weeps, that "when the rage allays, the rain begins"; and Northumberland is deeply moved "To see how inly sorrow gripes his soul". When Richard, on learning of his father's death, refuses the alleviation of tears, he combines physiological and elemental images:

> I cannot weep, for all my body's moisture
> Scarce serves to quench my furnace-burning heart....
> (II. 1. 79–86)

This play marks an important change in the revelation of the mind, when Richard in Act III, scene 2, ceases to be the gallant son, the faithful brother, the Senecan avenger, and becomes the coldly self-conscious intriguer for a throne. In this soliloquy (ll. 134–95: "Why then, I do but dream on sovereignty...") Shakespeare for the first time catches a mind in the act of deliberating a course of action, swayed hither and thither by difficult considerations. In following out the train of thought it is aware of itself, its own limitations and resources. After describing the physical disadvantages that barred him from the love of women, Richard explains his compensatory love of power, but he is still "like one lost in a thorny wood" until he realizes that a way may be opened by cunning and hypocrisy:

> Why I can smile, and murder while I smile,
> And cry "Content", to that which grieves my heart.

It is a fine speech, but how little psychological terminology it uses! Apart from the initial reference to Edward IV's sexual excesses wasting his marrow, it is all observation, without scientific jargon. In Act V, scene 6, the picture of Richard becomes lurid with King Henry's story of the omens at his birth and Richard's elaboration of the monstrous portent, "Teeth hadst thou in thy head to bite the world". This prepares for his refusal of love:

> And this word "love" which greyheads call divine,
> Be resident in men like one another,
> And not in me: I am myself alone. . . .

Here the psychology, like the portents, is cosmic, religious rather than medical. The overweening worship of the Self was the root of all evil: "For the Self, the I, the Me and the like all belong to the Evil Spirit, and therefore it is that he is an Evil Spirit" (*Theologia Germanica*).

Physical abnormality is thus accompanied by a spiritual monstrosity which disturbs the harmony of the interdependent universe by a self-sufficient, all-exclusive egoism. The sickness of self-love was to afflict other of Shakespeare's characters, Malvolio, Phoebe, Edmund, but never with better grounds than in this self-portrait of ugly lovelessness turning to hypocrisy and domination.

The first soliloquy of *Richard III* is crude in comparison with these two of the previous play, but rightly so since it serves mainly for recapitulation, exposition, and promise of plentiful action—a promise faithfully carried out in one of the busiest plays Shakespeare ever wrote. Here the Senecan "passions" recur, in scenes where Queen Margaret, Queen Elizabeth, and the Duchess of York rival each other in woeful reminiscence, foreboding, and recrimination (e.g., IV. 4). There is a self-consciousness about some of these speeches which shows the author reflecting on the rhetoric as he writes it. Increasing fluency is apparent in describing emotional symptoms, and in one place (III. 5. 5–10) the author's awareness of "theatrical psychology", the actor's craft of simulating emotions, appears when Buckingham, asked by Gloucester if he can pretend fear, answers

> Tut! I can counterfeit the deep tragedian,
> Speak and look back, and pry on every side,
> Tremble and start at wagging of a straw,
> Intending deep suspicion: ghastly looks
> Are at my service, like enforced smiles;
> And both are ready in their offices.

An awareness of psychological topics is frequently shown. Thus the value of letting grief express itself is discussed by the Duchess of York and Queen Elizabeth (IV. 4). "Why should calamity be full of words?" asks the Duchess; and the Queen replies:

> Windy attorneys to their client woes,
> Airy succeeders of intestate joys,
> Poor breathing orators of miseries!
> Let them have scope: though what they do impart
> Help nothing else, yet do they ease the heart.

Later in the same scene the Duchess describes the four ages of Richard III, his infancy "Tetchy and wayward", his schooldays "frightful, desperate, wild and furious", his "prime of manhood daring, bold and venturous", his age "confirm'd, proud, subtle, sly, and bloody". On the night before Bosworth, in his soliloquy after the vision of the Ghosts, the religious psychology of *2 Henry VI* returns when Richard's conscience confronts his egoism in an antithesis of self-love and self-hate, and he comes near desperation at the collapse of his central self-esteem:

> I shall despair. There is no creature loves me;
> And if I die, no soul will pity me:
> Nay, wherefore should they, since that I myself
> Find in myself no pity to myself?
> 				(V. 3. 201-4)

But he recovers, and accepts his damnation,

> Let not our babbling dreams affright our souls;
> Conscience is but a word that cowards use. . . .
> Our strong arms be our conscience, swords our law.
> March on, join bravely, let us to't pell-mell;
> If not to heaven, then hand in hand to hell.
> 				(V. 3. 309-14)

Again no use is made of psychological terms; the moral issues are made clear enough without describing their mechanism. Shakespeare has clearly added, to emulation of Italian Senecan tragedy, with its catalogues and display of passions, the new technique of mental analysis adumbrated by Marlowe in the final scene of *Doctor Faustus*.

The dreams and visions in the early Histories show Senecan influence modified by moral symbolism. Shakespeare inherited the theory of sleep and dreams about which Chaucer had written and which most Elizabethans accepted. There is no need to suppose that he was deeply learned in all the nice distinctions made by Macrobius, Augustine, Vincent de Beauvais, Pietro de Alano, and others. But the use he makes of the portents and dreams beloved of Italian Senecans is by no means stereotyped. The vision of our Lady described so finely by Joan of Arc in *1 Henry VI*, Act I, scene 2, must be regarded as an "Illusion" cast by the demons which appear and abandon her in Act V, scene 3. The ill-boding dream of Gloucester in *2 Henry VI*, Act I, scene 2, is what Macrobius would call "*Somnium proprium*", since it needs interpretation, and the Duchess interprets it differently from her husband. Her own dream of success is either an "Insomnium", a vain wish-fulfilment, or an "Illusion", a false *visio spirituale*. The appearance of the spirit in Act I, scene 4 is not an illusion but the sayings are oracular in kind. The dying Winchester in his delirium sees a phantasm of the murdered Gloucester (III. 3). In *3 Henry VI* dreams have less place. The three suns seen in Act II, scene 1 are not a vision but a real occurrence noted by chroniclers. More is made of dreams in *Richard III*, perhaps because they were referred to in Hall and Holinshed. Clarence's dream in Act I, scene 4 that he is struck overboard by Gloucester, is a "*somnium proprium*" developed at great length with a wealth of fancy new to the dramatist. Stanley's warning *somnium*, which Hastings disregards (III. 2) is adapted from the Chronicles. We learn through Queen Anne that Richard's sleep is troubled by "timorous dreams" (*insomnia*). When before Bosworth the two rivals are asleep in their tents on the stage, the ghosts of those whom Richard has killed come to them in dreams with opposite messages, promising catastrophe to Richard and success to Richmond. These are oracular visions; and Richard, who previously ascribed his bad nights to fear of the Princes in the Tower (IV. 2. 71–2), realizes that the visitation is the effect of conscience ("O coward conscience, how dost thou afflict me!") and that he is loved by none. The depth of his damnation is shown by his refusal to accept the warning.

Imagery drawn from dreams is not infrequent in other plays; for example, when Marcus in *Titus Andronicus* sees his niece Lavinia after her ravishment

> If I do dream, would all my wealth awake me?
> If I do wake, some planet strike me down
> That I may slumber in eternal sleep.
> (II. 4. 13–15)

In the early Comedies the dream idea is often coupled with enchantment. Shakespeare's idea of comedy seems to have started with laughter at ludicrous mistakes of identity and meaning, and the ludicrous situations caused by misapprehensions. If these are improbable, so much the better; they may be caused by dream or enchantment.

In *The Comedy of Errors* the dream gives place to the idea of sorcery and witchcraft, for

> They say this town is full of cozenage:
> As nimble jugglers that deceive the eyes,
> Dark working sorcerers that change the mind,
> Soul-killing witches that deform the body.
> (I. 2. 97–100)

Antipholus of Syracuse and his servant Dromio frequently ascribe their bewilderment to witchcraft. When the visitor to Ephesus is claimed as her husband by Adriana and accused of infidelity, he exclaims (II. 2. 191–3):

> What! was I married to her in my dream?
> Or sleep I now and think I dream all this?
> What error drives our eyes and ears amiss?

and his Dromio, when ordered by Luciana to see the table set:

> O for my beads! I cross me for a sinner.
> This is the fairy land: O! spite of spites,
> We talk with goblins, owls, and elvish sprites...
> I am transformed, master, am not I?
> (II. 2. 197-204)

Obviously dreams and magic spells resemble each other. Both produce an atmosphere of fantasy, freedom from ordinary logic, and mention of them, by lifting the mind out of the workaday world, prepares the audience for improbable events, surprising turns, gossamer fancy, a mad world of apparent delusions. Madness is indeed relevant. Shakespeare, adapting Plautus, has the unfortunate Antipholus of Ephesus accused of madness, examined by a quack and bound in a dark room.

The notion of lunatic farce, whimsical caprice, is carried on in *The Taming of the Shrew* where Sly's adventure (called in another version *The Waking Man's Dreame*) is described by the Lord who invents it as likely to seem in retrospect "Even as a flattering dream or worthless fancy" (*Ind* I. 44). When Sly, transported into the mansion, wakes in luxury, the servants are to

> Persuade him that he hath been lunatic;
> And when he says he is—say that he dreams,
> For he is nothing but a mighty lord.
> (ll. 63-5)

Scene 2 is largely occupied with making the tinker believe that he has been mad for many years:

> Heaven cease this idle humour in your honour!
> O, that a mighty man of such descent,
> Of such possessions, and so high esteem,
> Should be infused with so foul a spirit!
> (ll. 13-16)

It takes only a little time for Sly to "banish hence these abject lowly dreams" and imagine himself a lord; and at the end of the inset comedy of Katharine and Bianca, it is doubtless intended (as in *The Taming of a Shrew*) that he should be carried out asleep to the alehouse where he was found, and that we should see him wake again, imagining that

> I know now how to tame a shrew.
> I dreamt upon it all this night till now
> And thou hast wak't me out of the best dreame
> That ever I had in my life, but Ile to my
> Wife presently, and tame her too
> And if she anger me. . . .²

In *The Shrew* the "dream" is set in a realistic frame, invented and imposed on the comic butt, and the main play, the comedy performed before Sly, is part of the dream. In *A Midsummer Night's Dream* the dream is also inset, this time into a romantic-classical setting. Part of the fun of the comedy consists in doubt whether there is a dream in it or not. It is true that Titania and Lysander and Hermia fall asleep in Act II, scene 2, but the spells cast on them and others are not to be thought of as only dreams. We have seen them prepared for by the quarrels of Oberon and Titania and Puck's service to his master which leads him into error. But when the four courtly lovers awake (IV. 1. 143), Lysander is bemused "Half sleep, half waking"; Demetrius, realizing that some power has switched his love from Hermia to Helena, adds, "It seems to me That yet we sleep, we dream"; and the two women "see these things with parted eye, When everything seems double". The lovers are willing to accept their misadventures as dreams. Theseus dismisses their stories as fabrications of the waking imagination:

> The lunatic, the lover and the poet,
> Are of imagination all compact. . . .

But Hippolyta thinks that their stories are consistent,

> And all their minds transfigur'd so together,
> More witnesseth than fancy's images. . . .
> (V. 1. 24-5)

We know that the dreamlike quality of events has been caused by these very "antic [anticke F_1] fables and these fairy toys" which the Duke cannot believe. So this is a play in which enchantment does the work of dream, in the twelve hours before "the first cockcrow" during which, on Midsummer Night, the fairies take command. This is the impression left, though Puck in his final address excuses the entire play as like a series of visions

> And this weak and idle theme
> No more yielding than a dream. . . .

The implication running through it all is that young love (as distinct from the stable mature union of Theseus and Hippolyta) is itself an enchantment of the mind; and what Theseus says of poetry and love is true: they are indeed like madness in their emotional manipulation of the fancy and judgment.

If to relate comedy to dreams and the vagaries of magic was an early impulse in Shakespeare, he did not altogether ignore the ethical implications of contemporary psychology even in his first two comedies of incident. Twice in *The Comedy of Errors* do we get below the surface of the action. The Abbess accuses Adriana of driving her husband mad by her nagging jealousy:

> The venomous clamours of a jealous woman
> Poison more deadly than a mad dog's tooth; . . .
> Sweet recreation barred, what doth ensue
> But moody and dull melancholy,
> Kinsman to grim and comfortless despair;
> And at her heels a huge infectious troop
> Of pale distemperatures and foes to life?
> (V. 1. 69–86)

This is a piece of comic irony, for Antipholus of Ephesus is quite sane; but it is a shrewd lesson for a bad wife. The other instance also occurs in a discussion of marriage: Luciana says to Adriana, who disagrees,

> The beasts, the fishes, and the winged fowls
> Are their males' subjects and at their controls;
> Men more divine, the masters of all these,
> Lords of the wide world and wild watery seas,

> Indued with intellectual sense and souls,
> Of more pre-eminence than fish and fowls,
> Are masters to their females and their lords:
> Then, let your will attend on their accords.
> (II. 1. 18–25)

Here we have a common contemporary notion which was expressed by Pierre Charron as follows:

> The distinction of superiority and inferiority consisteth in this, that the husband hath power over the wife, and the wife is subject to the husband.... In all things the wife, though she be far more noble, and more rich, yet is subject to the husband. This superiority and inferiority is natural, founded on the strength of one, the weakness and insufficiency of the other. The Divines ground it upon other reasons drawn from the Bible. [I.e., the woman was born after man, and sinned before him.] The woman then, the last in good and in generation and, by occasion, the first in evill and the occasion thereof, is justly subject unto man, the first in good, and last in evill.[3]

In *The Comedy of Errors* the reflections on the relations of husband and wife are mainly confined to two scenes. In *The Taming of the Shrew* the idea forms the basis of the whole play: for Petruchio's aim is to reduce Katharine not to equality but to a humble subordination, which she accepts in the last scene (when the more romantically wooed Bianca refuses): "Thy husband is thy lord, thy life and keeper."

The theme of *The Shrew* is the subordination of women, though it cannot be said that Katharine is inferior in anything but endurance and a sense of humour. Petruchio's are not the methods of the text-books of ethics, which agree with Charron that a husband's duties are: "(i) to instruct his wife with mildness in all things that belong to her duty, her honour, and good whereof she is capable; (ii) to clothe her whether she brought dowry with her or not; (iii) to nourish her; (iv) to lie with her; (v) to love and defend her."[4] Petruchio does none of these things; in fact he conquers her by his refusal to do them. He would come under the reproof of la Primaudaye, who declares "the best way to bring an unruly wife into good order is to make her more honest", and attacks them who "studie to pull them downe, perswading themselves that they will come to better order when they have abased and brought them low".[5] Shakespeare is not writing an ethical treatise but a "fabliau play" with the morality of "the biter bit". It is rough justice. Yet an attempt is made to give Katharine's behaviour and Petruchio's treatment of her a psychological foundation. As a shrew, she suffers from an excess of choler, which according to la Primaudaye "is bred of a custome to be angry for small things, and afterward becometh easily a fire of sudden wrath, a revenging bitternesse, and an untractable sharpnesse, working a man forward and furious disliking everything".[6] That is why Petruchio refuses to let her eat meat on the ground that it is over-roasted:

> And I expressly am forbid to touch it,
> For it engenders choler, planteth anger,
> And better 'twere that both of us did fast,
> Since, of ourselves, ourselves are choleric.
> (IV. 1. 168–71)

Note that he includes himself as suffering from the same humour. This is a clue to much of his behaviour: his actions are the result of *assumed* choler.

All this is general and elementary. Shakespeare's view of the sexes here is socially orthodox enough, and applied with a zest for the humours of fabliau and jest-book anecdote which does not mean that he would have approved of Petruchio in real life, or that he thought women could easily be mastered in this way; indeed the last line of the play suggests a doubt:

LUCENTIO. 'Tis a wonder, by your leave, she will be tam'd so.

In *The Two Gentlemen of Verona* Shakespeare turns from this crude, if classical, conception of love and marriage to write in terms of the psychology of romances such as the *Diana* of Montemayor and the story of *Titus and Gisippus*, in which the aspirations and yearnings of courtly love and friendship are displayed.[7]

In *The Shrew* a marriage of convenience proves to be as successful (from the dominant sex's point of view) as one of romantic wooing. Now the emphasis shifts to the emotional opportunities afforded by romantic wooing. Marriage is not a state to be analysed in itself but just the goal to be won through many interesting vicissitudes. The psychology of amorous passion and its conflict with romantic friendship is explored to show "how wayward is this foolish love", how various its moods, how inevitably it overmasters men and women so that gentle ladies will follow their lovers to the world's end, and a hitherto faithful friend will suddenly turn traitor at its behest. Proteus, who in Act II, scene 2 swears eternal fidelity to Julia, declares in scene 4 that

> Even as one heat another heat expels,
> Or as one nail by strength drives out another,
> So the remembrance of my former love
> Is by a newer object quite forgotten.
> (II. 4. 193–6)

All the characters might confess with Valentine

> Love's a mighty lord,
> And hath so humbled me as I confess,
> There is no woe to his correction,
> Nor to his service no such joy on earth.
> (II. 4. 137–40)

The psychology of this play is that of the Petrarchan love sonnets, of Wyatt and Surrey and Sidney. It is all very serious and overwrought and *A Midsummer Night's Dream* may well be a witty revulsion against its excessive sentiment. Puck's "Lord, what fools these mortals be" is certainly a comment on lovers and their ways.

That Shakespeare by now had become very interested in the mind especially in so far as current theory gave an account of the relations between senses and passions is shown by *Love's Labour's Lost*. Here there is a remarkable increase in psychological terms. The triple soul is behind Nathaniel's description of Dull:

His intellect is not replenished; he is only an animal, only sensible in the duller parts: And such barren plants are set before us, that we thankful should be—which we of taste and feeling are—for those parts that do fructify in us more than he (IV. 2).

But Nathaniel is one of the pedants, and it is noticeable that an exaggerated use of psychological terms is part of the satire against him and Holofernes, who, for instance, speaks of his poetry as

a gift that I have ... a foolish extravagant spirit, full of forms, figures, shapes, objects, ideas, apprehensions, motions, revolutions: these are begot in the ventricle of memory, nourished in the womb of *pia mater* and deliver'd upon the mellowing of occasion (IV. 2).

There is also, however, an appreciable increase in the more serious use of such language among the courtly characters in this play. Their conversation is much concerned with the relationship between wit or understanding and the senses, and between the passions and the senses, particularly the sense of sight (which many writers thought the noblest of the outer instruments). Boyet, describing Navarre in love (II. 1), calls on the doctrine that the vital forces were concentrated in whichever sense was operative under any passion:

> Why all his behaviours did make their retire
> To the court of his eye, peeping through desire:
> His heart, like an agate, with your print impress'd,
> Proud with his form, in his eye pride express'd:
> His tongue, all impatient to speak and not see,
> Did stumble with haste in his eyesight to be;
> All senses to that sense did make their repair,
> To feel only looking on fairest of fair. . . .

There is more in such examples than scraps of learning turned to the use of conceit. The theme of the play is the conflict between bookish and actual experience, and the supremacy of love over learning. On several occasions the diverse effects of love and learning are compared, with special reference to the use of the eyes, through which experience is gained in either case. Bookishness, says Berowne (IV. 3. 302-10), dims the eyes without giving the primary experience for which the eyes exist:

> Why, universal plodding poisons up
> The nimble spirits in the arteries . . .
> Now, for not looking on a woman's face,
> You have in that forsworn the use of eyes,
> And study too, the causer of your vow.
> For where is any author in the world
> Teaches such beauty as a woman's eye?

No study is so enlivening to body and mind as love, he continues, and describes its quickening power in language approved by the old psychology:

> But love, first learned in a lady's eyes,
> Lives not alone immured in the brain,
> But, with the motion of all elements,
> Courses as swift as thought in every power,
> And gives to every power a double power,
> Above their functions and their offices.
>
> (324-9)

Thus the science of the time is used to prove the superiority, the ethical necessity, of the power which inspires and fructifies mankind. In all this there is a touch of fantasy, an ingenuity, a playful zest which suggests that behind Berowne stands the poet, who has just realized the immense value, for image-making and for the generalized description of passion, of the popular psychology with its dynamic vitalism.

Here, as in *A Midsummer Night's Dream* (probably written in the same year), Shakespeare seems more interested than before in the relations between the several faculties of the human organism. He knew how the mind was thought to work, and had mastered the difficult art of assimilating a technical vocabulary into his romantic poetry; but so far his psychology was mainly theoretic and general; he had still to take the arduous step of applying his scientific knowledge to the analysis of characters more subtle than Katharine's or Navarre's. That step he took in *The Merchant of Venice* where for the first time in comedy he shows not only his supreme mastery of human nature in diversity of characterization, but also an interest in ethical problems akin to that found in the Tudor books of conduct.

The change in technique and stress appears at the beginning of *The Merchant of Venice*, for the first 120 lines, which tell us little of the plot, are devoted to analysis of mood and temperament. Shakespeare uses the newly fashionable idea of melancholy in the first scene, where Antonio's unaccountable sadness is discussed (incidentally with some excellent illustrations of the working of imagination under fear) not, as Quiller-Couch thought, to contrast him with the prevailing shallowness of Venetian life, but to set the tone of his almost tragic part in the play. Also, because Shakespeare has become interested in diversity of personalities, his gravity is contrasted with Gratiano's

> Let me play the fool!
> With mirth and laughter let old wrinkles come....
> (I. I. 79–102)

For the wildness of the long speech expressive of his sanguine temperament Gratiano is later rebuked by the well-balanced Bassanio:

> Pray thee, take pain
> To allay with some cold drops of modesty
> Thy skipping spirit, lest, through thy wild behaviour,
> I be misconstru'd in the place I go to,
> And lose my hopes.
> (II. 2. 184–8)

Obviously there is a new ethical element in Shakespeare's observation of even his minor characters, and the play contains many other evidences of his pleasure in the variety of human manners and follies. Thus when we first see Portia (I. 2) she runs through the list of her suitors with an unerring eye for characteristic national differences. Take for instance the Frenchman, Monsieur le Bon, and the Englishman, Falconbridge. The Frenchman "is every man in no man; if a throstle sing, he falls a-capering; he will fence with his own shadow: if I should marry him I should marry twenty husbands...."

NERISSA. What say you then to Falconbridge, the young baron of England?
PORTIA. You know I say nothing of him, for he understands not me, nor I him; he hath neither Latin, French, nor Italian: and you will come into the court and swear that I have a poor pennyworth in the English. He is a proper man's picture, but alas! who can converse with a dumb show? How oddly he is suited? I think he bought his doublet in Italy, his round hose in France, his bonnet in Germany and his behaviour everywhere.

Such diversions are not merely padding. They reveal Portia's comic poise and gaiety and remind us that the play is not only about bonds, wooing, generosity, but also about national differences. Shylock is a racial type as well as an individual; he is "a very Jew", the Jew of evil legend, and if Shakespeare overstepped the mark (and this I doubt) by making him more sympathetic than for comedy's sake he should, it was because in order to make the Jew of legend plausible, he had to give him affections and passions which a Christian might understand. But we are not meant to sympathize deeply with him in his great cry:

> Hath not a Jew eyes? Hath not a Jew hands, organs, dimensions, senses, affections, passions?... If you prick us, do we not bleed? If you tickle us do we not laugh? If you poison us do we not die? And if you wrong us, shall we not revenge? (III. 1. 56-65)

Shylock is a man of passion, driven by hate, cruelty, meanness, avarice, revenge. Reason and judgment are not in him save as a mask for hypocrisy; and so when he explains himself to Salarino (and the audience) he looks no higher than "affections and passions" for his guide. When, sure of his legal position, he comes to court and is asked to be reasonable and merciful, he defiantly takes his stand upon the letter of the law—and his own humour:

> affection,
> Mistress of passion, sways it to the mood
> Of what it likes, or loathes ...
> So can I give no reason, nor I will not

> More than a lodg'd hate, and a certain loathing
> I bear Antonio.
> (IV. 1. 50-61)

Over against this passion-driven wretch stands Portia, the spirit of reason and mercy, and Bassanio, who in his wooing as well as in his rebuke to Gratiano proves himself a man of judgment. Morocco fails before the Caskets, being ridden by passion—pride of mind; Aragon by pride of place. But the song sung while Bassanio reflects upon the Caskets (III. 2. 63-4),

> Tell me where is Fancy bred,
> Or in the heart or in the head?
> How begot, how nourished?

is a hint that he should not be misled by the eyes or the heart's passions as the others had been, but that he should use his judgment, which he does when he says "So may the outward shows be least themselves...." When he chooses right, Portia's delight is expressed in terms of the theory of passions: doubt, despair, fear, jealousy—all flee before love; and, struggling for poise, she begs (ll. 111-14) that this may restrain itself:

> O love, be moderate; allay thy ecstasy;
> In measure rain thy joy; scant this excess;
> I fear too much thy blessing; make it less,
> For fear I surfeit!

Similarly, Bassanio, when she offers herself to him so completely and so beautifully, describes his confusion in quasi-scientific terms (ll. 176-84):

> Madam, you have bereft me of all words,
> Only my blood speaks to you in my veins;
> And there is such confusion in my powers,
> As, after some oration fairly spoke
> By a beloved prince, there doth appear
> Among the buzzing pleased multitude;
> Where every something, being blent together,
> Turns to a wild of nothing, save of joy,
> Express'd and not express'd.

The remarkable thing is that this sort of talk does not strike us as strange; but by 1595 Shakespeare had developed such a power of ideal lyrical expression that it does not shock us when his characters show themselves, in moments of passion, conscious of the internal workings of their bodies and minds, and define their own states with an accuracy which would be the despair of a psychiatrist. What is often done with satire, even pedantry, by Ben Jonson becomes in Shakespeare a revelation of souls refined by emotion or intelligence until they seem conscious in all their instruments as well as in the informing spirits. Part of the secret receipt which makes his romantic heroes and heroines incomparable is that their love does, as Berowne says, "give every power a double power Above their functions and their offices".

The interest in particular temperaments and national types expands in the History plays of the next few years. Thus *1 Henry IV* opens with another study in melancholy. "So shaken as we are, so wan with care" are the King's first words, and the scene shows his hopes of peace and a crusade shortly dashed. Soon we hear Hotspur's description of the King's popinjay messenger (I. 3. 36–45).

> He was perfumed like a milliner,
> And 'twixt his finger and his thumb he held
> A pouncet-box, which ever and anon
> He gave his nose, and took't away again; ...
> And as the soldiers bore dead bodies by,
> He call'd them untaught knaves, unmannerly,
> To bring a slovenly unhandsome corpse
> Betwixt the wind and his nobility. ...

Shakespeare became fond of these incidental thumbnail sketches. They are instances of the social comment which grew popular with the flourishing of the Latinate epigram and the Theophrastan character-sketch (itself a psychological study). Compare the interview of Hamlet (V. 2. 107–93) with the "water

ATTITUDE TO THE MIND

fly" Osric, the foppish courtier who invites him to the fencing-match, refuses to wear his hat in the Prince's presence, and praises Laertes in an elaborate servile manner:

> Sir, here is newly come to court Laertes; believe me, an absolute gentleman, full of most excellent differences, of very soft society and great showing; indeed, to speak feelingly of him, he is the card or calendar of gentry, for you shall find in him the continent of what part a gentleman would see.

Hamlet mocks at Osric and comments when he leaves:

> He did comply with his dug before he sucked it. Thus has he—and many more of the same bevy, that I know the drossy age dotes on—only got the tune of the time and outward habit of encounter, a kind of yesty collection which carries them through and through the most fond and winnowed opinions; and do but blow them to their trial, the bubbles are out.

The passage from *1 Henry IV* gives a particular portrait of manners. In this later sketch the speaker reveals more of himself as he describes the waterfly, teases him, and parodies his style while relating him to his general class of folly. Neither sketch makes much use of the psychology books. The insistence is on the manners which make the man rather than on his mental activities or "humours".

After *The Merchant of Venice* Shakespeare used the jargon of contemporary psychology less than in the plays written just previously. Except during a short phase of excited discovery, he was not primarily interested in the mechanism of the mind as a separate phenomenon or as part of the cosmic scheme. He preferred to suggest character through outward behaviour, in the clash of dialogue and action, and not in technical jargon so much as in the language of the court, the camp, and the tavern, and especially through imagery. Yet he did not ignore the ethical psychology. An example of this, showing that Shakespeare was aware (through his characters) of his technique, occurs in *1 Henry IV* (I. 3. 190 ff.) where, after Hotspur has ranted lengthily against the King, Worcester interrupts him with promise of

> matter deep and dangerous
> As full of peril and adventurous spirit
> As to o'erwalk a current roaring loud,
> On the unsteadfast footing of a spear.

Kindled by this, Hotspur's perfervid mind continues the image and adds new ones:

> If he fall in, good night! or sink or swim:
> Send danger from the east unto the west,
> So honour cross it from the north to south,
> And let them grapple; O! the blood more stirs
> To rouse a lion than to start a hare.

Northumberland's comment on all this:

> Imagination of some great exploit
> Drives him beyond the bounds of patience,

gives the psychological explanation of Hotspur's rhetoric. Similarly, after Hotspur has plunged on into his great panegyric on honour ("By heaven methinks it were an easy leap . . ."), Worcester interprets the symptoms and recalls Hotspur to the business in hand:

> He apprehends a world of figures here,
> But not the form of what he should attend.
> Good cousin, give me audience for a while.

Shakespeare was interested in individuals and the individual poetic expression of their passions. He took cognizance of the psychological system which "explained" their mental processes, but (at the time when Jonson was all-too-rigidly embodying his "Humour" theory of behaviour) he would not confine his characters within an intellectual strait-jacket. The system was secondary, an occasional aid in interpretation. It would have been easy, when there was a fashion for putting comic foreigners on the stage, to have represented his Welshmen, Scots, Irish, and French as conventional figures. But Shakespeare did not: Glendower, Sir Hugh Evans, Fluellen, are all Welsh and all different. The fecundity of Shakespeare's invention makes him avoid the stereotype; he shows the variety within the species. This love of the diversity within the unity makes him devote much of *1 Henry IV* to presenting in the King, Hal, Hotspur, and Falstaff several attitudes to the desire for Honour—that passion of Aristotle's "high-minded man" which for the Renaissance Christian too was "the last infirmity of a noble mind".

Shakespeare had never accepted the ideas of dramatic decorum and propriety which Sidney and other classicists handed on from Horace and the Italians and which included the psychology of theatrical stock-characters. In *The Duty of a Player* at the end of the seventeenth century, the writer (said to be Thomas Betterton) declares that an actor

> must perfectly express the Quality and Manners of the Man whose Person he assumes, that is, he must know how his Manners are compounded, and from thence know the several Features ... of his Passions. A Patriot, a Prince, a Beggar, a Clown etc. must each have their Propriety, and Distinction in Action as well as Words and Language.[8]

This is orthodox neoclassic doctrine. Miss L. B. Campbell asserts that Betterton gave here "not only the ideal method for the actor but also the actual method used to present men in the plays of Shakespeare". This is dubious. No doubt at times Shakespeare worked to a formula, especially in the early plays, where the influence of classical and earlier Tudor drama is strong. So we have the twin servants in *The Comedy of Errors*, the scarcely distinguishable lovers Lysander and Demetrius in *A Midsummer Night's Dream*, Proteus in *Two Gentlemen of Verona*, the conventional faithless friend of the romances, and Valentine the conventional faithful friend who will even give up his mistress to the man who betrayed him. But the success of Shakespeare's characterization mainly depends on his additions to the Propriety or Distinction, and the variety he gave to the Features of Passion. He used both the ethical psychology of the age and the theatrical psychology of types as a jumping-off ground for a complex portrayal not to be explained in terms of the books. So Orlando and

Rosalind may frequently behave in accordance with the love code and as Shakespeare found them in Lodge's novel, but they have a range of interests, a vivacity and tenderness all their own.

Falstaff is the supreme example of a figure who transcends his theatrical and ethical sources and purpose. He has been called a Vice, a descendant of Riot in *The Interlude of Youth*, but the source play *The Famous Victories of Henry V* where Shakespeare found him a merry rake and boon companion should not be overlooked.[9] For Shakespeare combines the two ideas, the immoral misleader and the gay dog, in a personality who transcends both. Falstaff is a Coward, the *miles gloriosus*, he is Riot, Insolence, a Tempter of Youth, the antithesis of the chivalric hero, of the patriotic military officer. He is all these, but in addition has all the qualities which make him the most exciting of humorous characters—wit, versatility, readiness and resource, mastery of words, a coarse lovableness, a frank self-indulgence expressed in an infinite variety of moods.

In using the cult of melancholy prevalent in the 1590's, Shakespeare was in no danger of finding its psychology restrictive, for melancholy (as Robert Burton showed later), the "hot dry humour", had many often apparently incompatible effects: hypochondria, amorousness, alternate surliness and "sodeyn incontinence of the tongue". It made men fearful, torpid, introspective, given to delusions, or fitfully witty, prophetic, satiric. One special social type was the Malcontent, the clever underling at odds with his environment, lacking advancement.[10] Shakespeare's melancholy men range from Antonio and the young gentlemen seen by Prince Arthur in France, who "would be sad as night Only for wantonness", to Prince Hamlet; his Malcontents from Jaques to Iago.

The melancholy of Jaques in *As You Like It* is very different from the premonitory sadness of Antonio and the conscience-struck sickness of Henry IV. He is a libertine traveller at odds with "th'infected world" who seeks liberty "To blow on whom I please". The Duke loves his "sullen fits For then he is full of matter". The mildest of malcontents, in his sensibility he curiously anticipates an eighteenth-century mood, weeping over a dying deer and moralizing "into a thousand similes" the spectacle of the animal abandoned by his kind (II. 1. 55–7):

> Sweep on, you fat and greasy citizens;
> 'Tis just the fashion; wherefore do you look
> Upon that poor and broken bankrupt there?

Don John in *Much Ado* is darker in cast, bitter, malicious, ready for any plot against the successful whom he envies: "I cannot hide what I am", he boasts, "I must be sad when I have cause, and smile at no man's jests". Having been forgiven for opposing his brother he says (I. 3. 28–34):

I'd rather be a canker in a hedge than a rose in his grace; and it better fits my blood to be disdained of all than to fashion a carriage to rob love from any: in this, though I cannot be said to be a flattering honest man, it must not be denied but I am a plain-dealing villain.

He adds little to the type, and is so weak and fumbling a villain that we are surprised when his plot against Claudio and Hero proves temporarily successful. Compare him with Thersites in *Troilus and Cressida*, the Malcontent whose malice finds expression in a stupid grotesque railing, who says "Ile learn to conjure and rouse devils; but Ile see some issue of my spiteful execrations", yet is ineffective except as a parody of Elizabethan Juvenalian satire, for he is "lost in the labyrinth of his fury". Different from both of these is Iago, whose natural malignity invents motives as it goes along in its extemporary but subtle schemes to trap Othello, all under cover of friendship and service. One concludes that although Shakespeare knew that men, like dogs, could be put into categories, when his plot needed a man of any type he usually created him as a unique person. The principle of individuality, of variety is all-important.

The growth of ethical concern in Shakespeare's handling of the melancholy man corresponds to a gradual change apparent in his dramatic attitude to life. Moral considerations, dominant in the early Histories, are lightly but increasingly touched in the comedies before 1600. They occur strongly in *Henry IV*, where they cause the decline and banishment of Falstaff; and they deepen the seriousness of tragicomedy in *All's Well* and *Measure for Measure*. It is unnecessary to postulate a "dark period" of grief, unrest, and illness in Shakespeare's life when he wrote the so-called dark comedies and the major tragedies.[11] They can be accounted for by the natural deepening of ethical interests in a mind which was always growing. This coincided with changes in theatrical fashion and the pleasure taken by the public in themes involving paradoxes of situation and motive, satire on manners and morals, tragedies of revenge and intrigue. Nevertheless, *Troilus and Cressida* presents a problem, for here is a play more violent and savage than anything else he ever wrote. It is indeed Shakespeare's only completely anti-romantic comedy. It includes a complete reversal of the heroics found in most classical and mediaeval versions of the Troy tale. If you care to believe (without much evidence) that Chapman was the Rival Poet of the Sonnets, this might supply a motive for Shakespeare's deliberate reversal of the epic loftiness of Chapman's *Iliad* translation. But recently Shakespeare, I suspect, had been reading ancient history with some disillusionment, and he had written in *Julius Caesar* about two groups of celebrated leaders who when examined closely were no better than modern politicians struggling for mastery; so that play became the tragedy of the idealist Brutus whose very nobility and stoic virtue turned him into a murderer and let loose on the state all the evils he wished to avoid. Similarly *Troilus and Cressida* is a realistic re-interpretation of the "Homeric" story in terms of the baser side of human nature. It attributes to the personages characteristics which accord with their known behaviour in some previous accounts, smoothing out inconsistencies in the original tale by altering facts to suit character. Thus Achilles is made to murder Hector with the help of his gang of ruffians; and this is what might be expected of the man who even in Homer sulked in his tent and showed such brutality to the body of his foe. In its satire, in its comparative lack of lyricism, in its use of set discussion, above all in the character portrayal, *Troilus and Cressida* is an anatomy of politics and love. The mask of romance is torn from war, government, and youthful desires, and the epic tale becomes a pageant of souls at odds with themselves, driven by passions, their wills separated from their judgments. Since this is the aim of the dramatist, we are not surprised that he makes great use, in dissecting motive, of the mental analysis with which we are now familiar.

It is in keeping with the chaos of human nature revealed in *Troilus and Cressida* that the clown is Thersites, obscene railer, braggart, and coward, who yet "tells no little of shameful truth" (Dowden); and that so large a part is played by Ajax, a man without a dominant passion, a confusion of humours:

This man, lady, hath robbed many beasts of their particular additions; he is as valiant as the lion, churlish as the bear, slow as the elephant: a man into whom nature hath so crowded humours, that his valour is crushed into folly, his folly sauced with discretion (I. 2. 18–23).

The political discussions which occupy so much time in the play turn on ethical questions related to man's inmost nature. Thus Agamemnon's praise of constancy in difficulties is a commonplace of the text-books, while Nestor's praise of courage in difficulties draws its force from the fact that courage is one of the irascible passions, which according to Aquinas exist to help man in difficulties:

> the thing of courage
> As rous'd with rage, with rage doth sympathise,
> And with an accent tuned in selfsame key
> Retorts to chiding fortune.
> (I. 3. 51–4)

When Ulysses asserts the need for order and degree in the camp, he talks good contemporary political theory and relates it to man's nature: if degree be abolished,

> Then everything includes itself in power,
> Power into will, will into appetite,
> And appetite, a universal wolf,
> So doubly seconded with will and power,
> Must make perforce a universal prey,
> And last eat up himself.
>   (I. 3. 119–24)

Ulysses has a special function in the stripping bare of motives; he knows the secret workings of the mind, and through him we are enabled to see the self-interest of the Greeks and the baseness of Achilles, on whose conceit he plays like a musical instrument. On the Trojan side Hector bears a similar part in the scene where the Trojan leaders discuss the surrender of Helen.

Hector, almost alone, is a man of understanding. He sees that to give up Helen is the reasonable course to end a bloody war. He recognizes the laws of states, which agree in supporting Menelaus's right to her (II. 2. 173–93):

> Nature craves
> All dues be render'd to their owners: now,
> What nearer debt in all humanity
> Than wife is to the husband? if this law
> Of nature be corrupted through affection,
> And that great minds, of partial indulgence
> To their benumbed wills, resist the same;
> There is a law in each well-order'd nation
> To curb those raging appetites that are
> Most disobedient and refractory.
> If Helen then be wife to Sparta's king,
> As it is known she is, these moral laws
> Of nature, and of nations, speak aloud
> To have her back return'd: thus to persist
> In doing wrong extenuates not wrong,
> But makes it much more heavy.

Troilus on the other hand is an opponent of "crammed reason":

> reason and respect
> Make livers pale and lustihood deject.

He backs up his plea for retaining Helen with a piece of weak argument (II. 2. 61–8):

> I take today a wife, and my election
> Is led on in the conduct of my will;
> My will enkindled by mine eyes and ears,
> Two traded pilots 'twixt the dangerous shores
> Of will and judgment. How may I avoid,
> Although my will distaste what it elected,
> The wife I chose? there can be no evasion
> To blench from this and to stand firm by honour.

He forgets that for love to be ethically sound it must not be the result of a will enkindled merely by the eyes and ears, but should be considered by the understanding, namely the very reason which he is rejecting. He takes his stand upon honour, and Hector in the last resort weakly agrees that their dignity is at stake and they must fight on in an unrighteous cause. There is thus no glory on either side in the war. Self-interest and passion are paramount. And so in love. Helen is a silly vain doll, Paris an uxorious fop. Cressida's changeable nature is ruthlessly exposed, from her early statement: "Things won are done; joy's soul lies in the doing", to her badinage with the Greek generals and her surrender to Diomed.

Troilus here again proves himself a man of passion and excessive sentiment. His love for Cressida is as unreasoning as his political counsel. What Paris says of Pandarus is true of him also (III. 1. 131–7): "He eats nothing but doves, love; and that breeds hot blood, and hot blood begets hot thoughts, and hot thoughts beget hot deeds, and hot deeds is love." And there is truth behind Pandarus's reply: "Is this the generation of love? hot blood? hot thoughts, and hot deeds? Why, they are vipers: is love a generation of vipers?"

When Troilus waits for Cressida in Pandarus's orchard, he describes his feelings (III. 2. 17–28):

> I am giddy, expectation whirls me round.
> The imaginary relish is so sweet
> That it enchants my sense. What will it be
> When that the watery palate tastes indeed
> Love's thrice-repured nectar? death, I fear me,
> Swounding destruction, or some joy too fine,
> Too subtle-potent, tun'd too sharp in sweetness
> For the capacity of my ruder powers:
> I fear it much; and I do fear besides
> That I shall lose distinction in my joys;
> As doth a battle, when they charge on heaps
> The enemy flying.

Both feeling and manner of expression anticipate Shelley's swooning raptures. No wonder that, when betrayed, the young idealist cuts a sorry figure as, lurking with Ulysses, he watches her coquetting with his rival, and that he feels his reason divided against itself as it tries to distinguish "Diomed's Cressida" from the true mistress of his fancy. His reasoning power was never very strong, so we are not surprised when his jealousy combines with his martial passion and he pursues Diomed up and down the battle. He is cured of his amorous illusions, but his rage is merely transferred to another object:

> For the love of all the gods,
> Let's leave the hermit pity with our mothers,
> And when we have our armours buckled on,
> The venom'd vengeance ride upon our swords,
> Spur them to ruthful work, rein them from ruth!
>
> (V. 3. 44–8)

To which the more sober Hector's answer is, I think, Shakespeare's too: "Fie, savage, fie!" The pursuit of martial glory is perhaps better than the pursuit of a light woman, but it is not the highest activity of the reasonable soul.

If *Troilus and Cressida* is a savage comedy of shattered illusions about heroism and love in which both the better and the baser passions ally themselves against nobility and happiness, what of the four great tragedies? Here I must be brief.

Miss L. B. Campbell has argued in detail that they are tragedies of passion, and indeed nobody with the evidence about Tudor thought which she provides could doubt it. According to the best classical and Christian teaching the function of reason, morality, and religion was to control the passions to good ends; failure to do so brought confusion of mind, perturbations, errors of judgment and will, sins, and crimes. As Plutarch wrote (in Holland's translation),

moral vertue being a motion and facultie about the unreasonable part of the soule, tempereth the remission and intention; and in one word taketh away the excesse and defect of the passions, reducing each of them to a certaine Mediocritie and moderation that falleth not on any side.

And Thomas Wright in his *Passions of the Mind* (ch. IV):

the Passions well used, may consist with wisdom against the Stoicks; and if they be moderated, to be very serviceable to vertue; if they be abused, and overruled by sinne, to be the nurserie of vices, and pathway to all wickednesse.[12]

All tragedies tend to be tragedies of passion, either passion in the hero or passions in the persons who cause his downfall.

In his early Histories Shakespeare had presented a great pageant of the passions revolving round ambition and family feuds, as he extracted from Hall and Holinshed the motives which had brought kings and nobles in the fifteenth century to civil strife. But the characters in these plays were not just embodiments of one passion only, for Shakespeare knew—and would read in the Chronicles—that men are governed by mixed motives. The ruthless Queen Margaret loves Suffolk; Richard III might seem nothing but a hater of humanity, but already in *3 Henry VI* he was depicted as a wild jester, and in *Richard III* his Machiavellian intrigues are alleviated by his sense of humour, his virtuosity in playing on the sympathy and goodwill and ambition of others—as when he woos Anne, his enemy's widow, by the bier of the King he has murdered.

Romeo and Juliet is a simple tragedy of passion in another sense, in that the innocent love of the unfortunate pair dashes them to destruction against the hatred between their families. Romeo and Juliet are "star-crost" lovers, and this helps to cover up a lack of inevitability, a dependence on coincidence in the catastrophe, but in the main the tragedy occurs because an overmastering but virtuous passion (and we sympathize throughout with the rash young couple, though we may fear that "these violent delights have violent ends") is its own undoing when aroused in unfavourable circumstances and crossed by the evil passions of feud and vendetta. This idea that virtuous passion might cause its own overthrow struck deep into Shakespeare's mind, to be elaborated some years later in *Hamlet*.

Miss L. B. Campbell has argued that *Hamlet* is a tragedy of grief, which produces in a naturally sanguine man a state of "melancholy adust". Undoubtedly Hamlet's melancholy is what Timothy Bright called an "unnatural melancholie" which preys on his other humours. The term "melancholy adust" was used when any humour was affected by "excessive distemper of heate":

This sort raiseth the greatest tempest of perturbations and most of all destroyeth the braine with all his faculties and disposition of action, and maketh both it, and the harte cheere more uncomfortably; and if it rise of the naturall melancholy, beyond all likelihood of truth, frame monstrous terrors of feare and heavinesse without cause. If it rise of choler, then rage playeth her part, and fury joyned with madnesse, putteth all out of frame. If bloud minister to this fire, every serious thing for a time is turned into a jest, and tragedies into comedies, and lamentation into jigges and dances.[13]

Certainly Hamlet's behaviour agrees with these symptoms: he frames an unjustified and "monstrous terror" of the Ghost (after accepting it as his father); he falls into heaviness (though scarcely without a cause); he indulges in extravagant rage and fury (but again justified); he is hysterical (but surely never mad); and he turns serious things into a jest. Hamlet is not melancholy by nature. The picture we are given of him before the play opens is of a man well balanced as Brutus was, with all the elements well mixed in him. The shock of his father's death and his mother's o'er-hasty marriage, his mistrust of his uncle, the Ghost's visit, the revelation of Claudius's crime and his mother's adultery, set not one but all his humours in commotion. Melancholy is involved in the grief and disillusionment which spread out from his father's loss and his mother's treachery to include the state of Denmark and the realization of his difficult mission. His self-dedicated parting from Ophelia is followed by suspicion that she has betrayed him. Choler is involved in his bursts of anger against uncle, mother, Polonius, Ophelia, and in the thought of a revenge which he assumes must be achieved by devious means. Phlegm we see less of, since Hamlet is essentially an active person, but dull moods are mentioned, his loss of joy in the powers of man's mind, and his self-accusations of inactivity. The sanguine humour, which shows itself now and again in lively conversations with Horatio, the Players, Rosencrantz and Guildenstern, produces also his wild jests against Ophelia and his mockery of Polonius.

Not grief alone but the self-frustration of manifold conflicting passions evoked by his peculiar situation seems to be the inner cause of Hamlet's tragedy. He is given to "wild and whirling words"; he envies the player who "in a fiction, in a dream of passion Could force his soul so to his own conceit". Having imitated him, Hamlet berates himself (II. 2. 591–5):

> That I, the son of a dear father murder'd,
> Prompted to my revenge by heaven and hell,
> Must, like a whore, unpack my heart with words,
> And fall a-cursing, like a very drab,
> A scullion! ...

When the Ghost returns to rebuke him for flagging in his mission, Hamlet recognizes his fault (III. 4. 106–10):

HAM. Do you not come your tardy son to chide,
     That, laps'd in time and passion, let's go by
     The important acting of your dread command?
     O say!
GHOST. Do not forget: this visitation
     Is but to whet thy almost blunted purpose.

Hamlet has delayed; he has "laps'd in time and passion"; that is he has wasted time and wasted his passion, let it wane, or exercised it unprofitably for his purpose. He has failed because he has let himself be shifted from his revenge by all kinds of diversions: the antic disposition and its opportunities for a game of "hide and seek" with the murderer and for satire on Polonius, etc.; the parting from Ophelia and his subsequent suspicion of her; his doubts about the Ghost, made specious though not justified by the doubts shared by many religious people about the existence and nature of ghosts; the visit of the Players; the King at prayer; anger at his mother. All these side-issues have improperly occupied his emotions and led his will astray because his nature is in confusion and all his humours are upset by the "unnatural melancholie". This, though excited by grief and rage in co-operation, is not just a matter of grief and rage but extends to the whole man; so that now he unpacks his heart with words, now he darts into action with amazing agility, now

> the native hue of resolution
> Is sicklied o'er with the pale cast of thought,
> And enterprises of great pith and moment
> With this regard their currents turn awry,
> (III. 1. 84-8)

Hamlet, then, is a whole play built round the idea expressed by Brutus in *Julius Caesar* (II. 1. 63-9):

> Between the acting of a dreadful thing
> And the first motion, all the interim is
> Like a phantasma, or a hideous dream:
> The genius and the mortal instruments
> Are then in council; and the state of man,
> Like to a little kingdom, suffers then
> The nature of an insurrection.

In *Hamlet* the period of chaos between intent and performance is extended over four acts owing to the upheaval caused by the hero's peculiar situation in a nature essentially courtly, civilized, and nicely poised. The play is a study in distraction—meaning by that not madness but the effects of the several passions which, being excited by temporary occasions relating to a central issue, divert the hero's will from the main issue itself.

In *Othello* we again see the limitations of any narrow psychological scheme. *Othello* is a tragedy of jealousy, and the hero, once his suspicions are aroused, betrays jealous symptoms catalogued in the books of ethics. But there is more in him than that. He is also a Moor, an African, and the play has been called a tragedy of colour. There are many references to Othello's race, but they are uttered either by himself in self-depreciation or by his enemies. Brabantio, excited by Iago and Roderigo, does not want his daughter to marry Othello, but comes to accept the union. Iago, himself a slave of envy and jealousy, makes the most of the difference in race. But we know that his insinuations are wrong. The nobility of the individual makes a mockery of all colour-prejudices. Shakespeare, indeed, seems to be flying in the face of English insularity and suggesting that a mixed marriage may be a beautiful union. It takes a diabolical villain to break the bond between Othello and his wife. Yet the fact that Othello is a Moor has some significance. According to the text-books a Moor, an African, born under a hot sun, was by nature sensual, soft, gentle, and amiable, but savage and ruthless if his anger were aroused. Maybe this affected Shakespeare's treatment of his hero, so easy, gracious, and trusting till mistrust is excited, when his mind falls into chaos. But how far Othello is from that other Moor, Aaron, in *Titus Andronicus*! Othello's quality resembles that of the Prince of Morocco in *The Merchant of Venice*, whose characteristic is pride of mind. *Othello* is rather a tragedy of personal honour than of race. And whereas in the source story by Cinthio the murder of the wife is carried out with vile brutality, Othello goes to his murderous deed like a priest to the sacrifice. This is not so much the operation of jealousy as of a diseased sense of honour and justice, almost Spanish in its inevitability.[14] To this sense of honour race and jealousy are subordinate.

Similarly, *Macbeth* is not a tragedy of ambition simply, but of conscience suppressed in a tainted mind which welcomes suggestions of evil from supernatural sources but deliberately shuts itself against suggestions of the good. And *King Lear* is not so much a tragedy of Wrath in Old Age (as Miss Campbell suggests) as one of unnatural relationships ("unkindness") between parents and children wherein the errors in passion and judgment, the misplaced trust and mistrust of the parents Lear and Gloucester, excite the ingratitude of the evil children and bring suffering and catastrophe on innocent and guilty alike. To reduce so great a tragedy to such simple terms may seem trivial; but for Shakespeare the rightful affections between parents and children were as much part of the universal order as the political "degree" celebrated by Ulysses in *Troilus and Cressida*. Remove the love and kindness due to ties of blood, and the state of things will be like that described by Ulysses and already cited (*T.C.*, I. 3. 114–24):

> Strength should be lord of imbecility,
> And the rude son should strike his father dead;
> Force should be right . . .
> Then everything includes itself in power,
> Power into will, will into appetite,
> And appetite, a universal wolf,
> Must make perforce a universal prey,
> And last eat up himself.

That is precisely the theme of *King Lear*, where human nature turned "unnatural" is accompanied by chaos in the state and chaos in the firmament. Gloucester, indeed, blames the prevalent disorder upon the stars ("These late eclipses in the sun and moon portend no good to us") and later cries

> As flies to wanton boys are we to th' gods;
> They kill us for their sport.

King Lear is not an anti-religious play; neither is it a play of Christian reconciliation, although it contains much pious imagery. It is a tragedy of Christian ethics without Christian faith. It discusses the problems set by passions turned evil in the mind and their effects in *this* world, in which nature proves as unkind as men, and a great king enwrapped in a self-induced confusion of anger, pride, and humiliation stumbles through the storm to become naked, essential man, the victim of his daughters' passions and the insane prey of his own. This is human life bereft of reason, without human kindness, and it culminates in the dire scene where Lear comes in with the dead Cordelia in his arms and dies trying to persuade himself that she is still alive.

The moral assumption throughout the play is that men should respect and love one another and that when the bonds of natural piety are broken, as Albany says (IV. 2. 46–50),

> If that the heavens do not their visible spirits
> Send quickly down to tame these vile offences,
> It will come,
> Humanity must perforce prey on itself,
> Like monsters of the deep.

In *Hamlet* a "visible spirit" comes in the Ghost; even so, doubt and delay bring despair and slaughter before the evil is purged. In *Lear* there is no "visible spirit", and the triumph of goodness is so narrow as to seem almost an empty victory. Almost, but not quite. For goodness as revealed to us in the personality of Cordelia ("a Queen over her passion"), the loyalty of Kent, the filial piety of Edgar, and the rise of Lear to self-knowledge and gentleness is not merely "its own reward" but a justification of existence. No flights of angels sing Lear to his rest, and we are not invited to look beyond death. Yet even in life at its most horrible there is a soul of goodness which by suffering transcends an evil that inevitably consumes itself.

> Men must endure
> Their going hence, even as their coming hither.
> Ripeness is all.
> (V. 2. 9–11)

And ripeness is achieved by persevering in the good, by controlling the selfish appetites, by learning the endurance which makes possible the patient acceptance of the worst that fate can bring.

Shakespeare has come a long way since his pageant of warring ambitions in the first Histories, the conventional marriage lore of the first comedies, and the light sketches of a variety of young people under the ineluctable spell of love in the romantic comedies. His ethical preoccupations have grown until in the major works he embodies a view of tragedy as the exploration of a deep moral disturbance in the mind and environment of noble characters. This is caused by some overgrowth or misapplication of passion bringing errors of judgment and misdirection of the will. One effect of excessive passion in a sensitive mixture of humours is to infect all functions of the mind, including the imagination; hence the gross imagery caught by Othello from Iago, the phantasms seen by Macbeth, Hamlet's hysteria, and the true madness of Lear. Shakespeare's mature tragedy makes us contemplate a mind breaking down through internal disharmonies caused or increased by pressure from without. It involves public as well as private relationships, and these former are particularly important in the Roman plays. Brutus's tragedy is that a good man in private life is led by his public zeal and ignorance of the baser passions of his colleagues to make disastrous errors of judgment about the need to kill Caesar and the results of his assassination. Antony's tragedy consists more simply in a sexual dotage which overrides his sense of public duty. Coriolanus, the extreme aristocrat, lets his pride fester until he is willing to destroy Rome.

In the three last plays Shakespeare turns to comic use the experience he has gained in writing the great tragedies and especially *King Lear*. The moods of repentance and reconciliation after passionate excess, which in *Lear* were impotent (in a worldly sense) against the accumulated though self-destructive energy of evil, are now allowed to work their way towards happiness, and an initial state of moral and mental perturbation is transformed to one of rational balance. Something of the sort had happened in *As You Like It* and *Measure for Measure*, but now the contrast between the evil sway of passion and the geniality of a peaceful order is emphasized, especially in *A Winter's Tale*, where the first two and a half acts make a study in violent passion and the last two are mainly idyllic. In *Cymbeline* the court with its envy and intrigue is contrasted with the wild pastoral life of freedom and generosity. In *The Tempest* courtly passions invade the magic-guarded island. In all three plays there is a preoccupation with the ties between the generations, ideas of birth and breeding, and the power of young love to counteract the sins of the older generation.

Psychological terminology is not very frequent in *A Winter's Tale* and *Cymbeline*. It occurs more in *The Tempest* because the theme of this play is explicitly an ethical transformation; and some characters are conceived as intermixtures of the elements. Ariel is air and fire (I. 2. 189–206, etc.); Caliban is water and earth ("Thou earth thou!" "Legged like a man; and his fins like arms . . . no fish, but an islander"); Miranda is all primal innocence; and the intruders into Prospero's realm are variously governed by base passions which Prospero uses his arts to subdue and purge. So Antonio, having usurped Prospero's dukedom of Milan with the help of the King of Naples, persuades Sebastian to murder the latter; Stephano and Trinculo, drunken sailors, are tempted to kill Prospero and take Miranda.

The highborn "men of sin", "'mongst men Being most unfit to live", are brought to the island where as Ariel tells them, the powers of destiny

> do pronounce by me,
> Ling'ring perdition . . . shall step by step attend
> You and your ways; whose wraths to guard you from
> . . . is nothing but heart-sorrow
> And a clear life ensuing.
> (III. 3. 76–82)

By Prospero's charms his enemies "are all knit up In their destructions",

> their great guilt,
> Like poison given to work a great time after,
> Now 'gins to bite the spirits.

The lowborn sinners are dazzled with false shows and "glistering apparel", hunted by "divers Spirits, in shape of hounds", and physically anguished. But Prospero is touched by Ariel's appeal for them (V. 1. 21–4):

> Hast thou, which art but air, a touch, a feeling
> Of their afflictions, and shall not myself,
> One of their kind, that relish all as sharply,
> Passion as they, be kindlier mov'd than thou art?

he declares, and so,

> they being penitent,
> The sole drift of my purpose doth extend
> Not a frown further.

By the end they have all come to know themselves, as Gonzalo puts it; "and all of us [found] ourselves, When no man was his own".

In this play (unlike *King Lear*) the heavens send their "visible spirits" to amend the unruly passions of men; and this is Shakespeare's greatest achievement in ethical comedy. Prospero, the Providence of the island, is a wiser Oberon, as Ariel is a more subtle Puck, and there is no irony in the fact that the good man triumphs only by using magic. For just as in *A Midsummer Night's Dream* and other early plays love itself was a sort of magic, so here the wisdom born of goodness and suffering is revealed in secret powers over nature and over the human mind. But a note of seriousness in Prospero's Epilogue perhaps reflects back on the play:

> Now I want
> Spirits to enforce, art to enchant;
> And my ending is despair
> Unless I be reliev'd by prayer,
> Which pierces so that it assaults
> Mercy itself and frees all faults.

As the whole of *The Tempest* has implied, the last word is not with stoic patience, or magic, but with religion.

Chapter Three ∽ REASON, THE PASSIONS, AND ASSOCIATIONS FROM DRYDEN TO WORDSWORTH

A few years ago one of the accepted commonplaces of criticism was the phrase "dissociation of sensibility" invented by Mr. T. S. Eliot in an essay on "The Metaphysical Poets" in which he contrasted the omnivorous mechanism of sensibility in Donne and Marvell with the less unified imaginations of poets such as Collins, Gray, Johnson, Tennyson, and Browning, whose language may have been more refined but whose feeling was more crude, for they "thought and felt by fits, unbalanced; they reflected".[1] Mr. Eliot implied that between Dante and Donne a fusion of thought and feeling was general in poetry and drama. This is far from true; fusion of thought and feeling of the kind found in Donne is rare in any age. To take Donne as typical of mediaeval and Tudor poetry is quite unhistorical.

Nevertheless there are differences in content and manner between Jacobean and Augustan verse, and these arise in part from a change in the content and direction of the poetic imagination, from a shift in ideas about the relationship between God, man, and the universe, and about the functions of the mind and their place in art.

The microcosmic view of the world discussed in the opening

essay was shattered in the latter half of the seventeenth century by new movements in philosophy. Gassendi's study of Epicurus (1647) heralded a new physics based on the assumption that "the atoms, endowed with weight, size and order, are the primary elements of things".[2] Their motions might be bestowed by God, but once men came to believe, like Walter Charleton in his *Physiologie* (1654), that the forms of all things living and inanimate were "only a certain contexture of the most subtle and moveable atoms", they lost their certainty that the entire world order was a suffusion of spirit emanating from God and aspiring back to Him. And when Boyle, seeking to establish "a good intelligence betwixt the corpuscularian philosophers and the chemists", attacked the adequacy of the classical four elements to explain the nature of things, the new philosophy indeed called all in doubt and, though religion speedily adapted itself to the new ideas (indeed Boyle was a very pious man), it lost some of its imaginative force as a unifying principle.

A second factor was the growth of inductive science, the insistence on natural causes and effects associated with Bacon and the Royal Society, which brought all things to the test of observation and experiment. The practical achievements of the Royal Society had perhaps less significance for literature than their spirit of independent sceptical enquiry and humanist ideals. More important for us were the mathematical and mechanistic speculations of Galileo and Descartes. In the 1650's their doctrines were excitedly discussed in Cambridge, and in the first edition of *The Vanity of Dogmatizing* (1661) Joseph Glanvill declared that "the grand Secretary of Nature, the miraculous Descartes, had infinitely outdone all the Philosophers who went before him, in giving a particular and analytical account of the Universall Fabric".[3] From Galileo came the new idea that in true philosophy the mind should use "mathematics, and its symbols are mathematical figures". The objectively measurable qualities of things are alone significant, whereas "Tastes, odours, colours, on the side of the object in which they seem to exist are nothing but mere names, and reside solely in the sensitive body."[4] The importance given to mathematics fostered a kind of abstraction very different from that which lay behind the Morality plays or Spenser's *Faerie Queene*; but although scientists might suspect the secondary, subjective qualities, defenders of the artistic imagination did not, and Addison, who learned of "that great modern discovery" from Locke's *Essay concerning Human Understanding* (Bk. II. ch. viii) wrote:

> Things would make but a poor appearance to the eye, if we saw them only in their proper figures and motions: and what reason can we assign for their exciting in us many of those ideas which are different from anything that exists in the objects themselves, (for such are light and colours,) were not it to add supernumary ornaments to the universe, and make it more agreeable to the imagination? (*Spectator*, No. 413).

The relations of body and soul were much debated in this period, and poets re-worked the problems of Sir John Davies. For Descartes the body of man must be separable from the soul. The body is a machine, and the heat and motions in us "in so far as they do not anywise depend on thought, appertain exclusively to the body". "The body of a living man differs from that of a dead man just as any machine that moves of itself (e.g. a watch or other automaton when it is wound up . . .) differs from itself when it is broken and the principle of its movement ceases to act." (*Passions of the Soul*, Art. 6.) The soul operates temporarily in the body but its works must be distinguished from those of the body itself. This dualism was responsible for the change in attitude to Descartes observable in writers like Joseph Glanvill and Henry More, who at first hailed his definitions of matter and spirit as useful aids against Hobbes's materialism. The vigorous Christian-Platonist movement radiating from Cambridge owed something both positively and negatively to the Cartesian philosophy; and the mystical poetry of John Norris of Bemerton and the treatise in which that enthusiastic man attempted to answer John Locke,[5] were the last offshoot in the seventeenth century of the great Platonic tradition.

Attempts were made to bridge the gulf between soul and matter. Locke suggested that possibly the power of thought might be "superadded" to matter. But this solution raised more questions than it answered. Was the mind mortal like the body? Dr. William Coward developed Locke's speculation in his *Second Thoughts Concerning the Human Soul* (1702) demonstrating "the notion of human soul as believed to be a spiritual, immortal substance united to a human body to be a plain heathenish invention". The soul he held not to be separate from the body which would, however, be raised to immortality at the Last Day. Coward also ridiculed Descartes's theory that the soul was immaterial and had its seat in the pineal gland. The *Second Thoughts* caused scandal so great that Coward was summoned before a committee of the House of Commons and his book condemned to be burned by the common hangman (1704). But the author was not put down; he published a second edition of the work in 1705.

Coward is satirized in the *Bibliotheca* of Archbishop William King (1712) as a wandering doctor who

> needs would have mankind control
> The universe without a soul;
> That matter nicely wrought and spun
> Might all those mighty feats have done
> Which ancient dotards were inclin'd
> To attribute to Thought and Mind . . .
> A proof within himself he feels
> That all mankind is mov'd by wheels;
> That chains, and pendulums, and springs,
> With twenty other curious things,
> Were first by artful Nature made
> Ere clocks and watches form'd a trade.
>
> (ll. 886–907)

Matthew Prior's Hudibrastic poem *Alma: or The Progress of the*

Mind (1718) plays amusingly on warring theories about the soul's seat in the body.[6] In a debate between the poet and his friend Dick Shelton the chief current notions are humorously presented. First, the Aristotelian theory as adapted by St. Thomas Aquinas (Canto I, 13-21):

> Alma in verse, in prose the mind,
> By Aristotle's pen defined,
> Throughout the body squat or tall,
> Is bona fide all in all.
> And yet, slap-dash, is all again
> In every sinew, nerve and vein;
> Runs here and there, like Hamlet's ghost;
> While everywhere she rules the roast.

Against this view, held by "the men of Oxford", Prior sets that of "the Cambridge wits" influenced by Descartes (I. 30-4):

> Alma, they strenuously maintain,
> Sits cock-horse on her throne the brain;
> And from that seat of thought dispenses
> Her sovereign pleasure to the senses.

The contemporary scientific doctrine that the nerves are messengers between the outer points of sensation and the brain is parodied, and Coward's objection to regarding the pineal gland or conarion as seat of an immaterial entity is given to the Aristotelians (I. 94-101):

> The Mind, say they, while you sustain
> To hold her station in the brain;
> You grant, at least, she is extended:
> *Ergo*, the whole Dispute is ended . . .
> The mind as visibly is seen
> Extended through the whole Machine.

On the other hand, the Epicurean notion of Lucretius that the bodily organs were formed by chance and not for any functional purpose—that "heedless Nature did produce The members first and then the use"—is mocked at and rejected.

Prior now proposes a theory of his own (I. 252 ff.), to reconcile "Old Aristotle with Gassendus". This theory he took from Montaigne, who suggested that "natural heat" dwelt in a different part of the body at each different stage of life.

> My simple system shall suppose
> That Alma enters at the toes;
> That then she mounts by just degrees
> Up to the ankles, legs and knees....

And so on until

> From thence compelled by craft and age
> She makes the head her latest stage.

The theory is applied with a wealth of comic illustration, all tending to show that

> where Fancy or Desire
> Collects the beams of vital fire;
> Into that limb fair Alma slides,
> And there, *pro tempore*, resides.
>
> (II. 773-6)

The method is burlesque, but a serious idea lies behind it, for Prior is a sceptical Pyrrhonist who refuses to accept either the degradation of the body into a machine or the separation from it of the rational soul. The dispute is ridiculous, but Prior implies a preference for the Aristotelian doctrine that soul and body are one and inseparable,[7] while insisting on the relativity of opinion, the dependence of the mind on the body's humours, and the functional nature of the body.

A view at once more traditional and more forward-looking was presented by Edward Young in his *Night Thoughts* (1741-5). In *Night I* Young expressed his wonder at the central position of man "in being's endless chain, Midway from nothing to the deity", and used the fancy's speedy wanderings in dream to prove the soul's essential difference from the material body:

> What though my soul fantastic measures trod
> O'er fairy fields; or mourn'd along the gloom
> Of pathless woods; ...

> ... or danced on hollow winds,
> With antic shapes, wild natives of the brain?
> Her ceaseless flight, though devious, speaks her nature
> Of subtler essence than the trodden clod;
> Active, aerial, tow'ring, unconfined,
> Unfetter'd with her gross companion's fall.
> Ev'n silent night proclaims my soul immortal. ...

The soul being immortal,

> Embryos we must be, till we burst the shell,
> Yon ambient azure shell, and spring to life,
> The life of gods, O transport! and of man.

In *Night IV* he discusses the relation between reason and faith. "Man know thyself; all wisdom centres there", he exclaims, but this implies the recognition of God's immanence:

> he tunes
> My voice (if tuned); the nerve that writes sustains:
> Wrapp'd in his being, I resound his praise.

When Young praises reason in men he means not just the work of logic but rather that higher power of intellection called by the Cambridge Platonists "Divine Sagacity".

> He, the great Father, kindled at one flame
> The world of rationals; one spirit pour'd
> From spirit's awful fountain; pour'd himself
> Through all their souls; but not in equal stream;
> Profuse, or frugal, of th'inspiring God
> As his wise plan demanded; and when past
> Their various trials, in their various spheres,
> If they continue rational, as made,
> Resorbs them all into himself again;
> His throne their centre, and his smile their crown.

Hence in an age which disliked Enthusiasm he attacked the lower rationalism which clung to sense and earth.

> Think you my song too turbulent? too warm?
> Are passions then the pagans of the soul?
> Reason alone baptis'd? alone ordain'd
> To touch things sacred?

He tells "cold-hearted, frozen, formalists" that

> On such a theme, 'tis impious to be calm;
> Passion is reason, transport temper, here;

and answers the disbeliever who declares

> "On argument alone my faith is built."
> Reason pursued is faith; and, unpursued
> Where proof invites, 'tis reason then no more.
> And such our proof, that, or our faith is right
> Or reason lies, and Heav'n design'd it wrong.

In thus asserting that faith should transcend the ordinary work of reason Young is a link between the ages of Donne and Newman. That he was not just carried away by religious zeal but wished to vindicate the power of the mind to go far beyond the suggestions of ratiocination or authority is proved by his prose *Conjectures on Original Composition* (1759) in which he wrote:

who hath fathom'd the mind of man? Its bounds are as unknown as those of the Creation. . . . Forming our judgments, altogether by what *has* been done, without knowing, or at all inquiring, what possibly *might* have been done, we naturally enough fall into too mean an opinion of the human mind. . . . Nor are we only ignorant of the dimensions of the human mind in general, but even of our own.

He urges the young writer to "know himself", "to prefer the native growth of thy own mind to the richest import from abroad", and whereas Pope based his *Essay on Criticism* on the assumption that the human mind is so much the same in all ages that all great thoughts have already been discovered by the Ancients, so that "To follow Nature is to follow them", Young asserts the possibility of "new thought", "rare imagination and singular design", and contrasts "the divinely-inspired enthusiast" in literature with "the well-accomplished scholar", who "up to the knees in antiquity, is treading the sacred footsteps of great examples, with the blind veneration of a bigot saluting the papal toe." "It is prudence to read, genius to relish, glory to surpass, antient authors."[8] In his anticipation of the Romantic view of genius and private inspiration, in his advocacy of the singular and idiosyncratic, in his revolt against authority, he is a rare figure in eighteenth-century thought about the potentialities of the mind.

Young wrote in the forties and fifties when the first impact of Cartesianism had long spent its force. Yet the influence on literary style of Descartes's ideas about the human mind was great and lasting. The celebrated dictum, "Cogito, ergo sum", which based the whole structure of knowledge upon the fact of the thinking self, fostered a revulsion against emotionalism and towards ratiocination. Moreover, his initial introspection gave new point to Horace's demand that the writer examine his available mental resources before embarking on any project. Hence Pope, at the beginning of his *Essay on Criticism* (ll. 46–9):

> But you who seek to give and merit fame
> And justly bear a Critic's noble name,
> Be sure yourself and your own reach to know,
> How far your genius, taste and learning go.

The insistence on the value of general ideas influenced literature in many ways, not least in the idea that "nothing can please many, and please long, but just representations of general nature", whether in painting the tulip without its streaks[9] or in depicting human characters as quintessential types rather than as individuals. The Ruling Passion fits in here, as we shall observe later. Undoubtedly Descartes's absolute distinction between soul and matter, the frank relegation of the natural world to a subordinate place as a setting and a convenience for man's use, the insistence on moral philosophy and on the examination of human nature, led in imaginative literature to a corresponding preoccupation with man.

Descartes's approach might to a modern reader seem likely to have produced a spate of egocentric writings. But Descartes was not interested in the kind of introspection which later inspired Rousseau's *Confessions*. What mattered to him was mathematical logic, and he handed on to Locke his interest in abstract relations, and the search for clear ideas like those which the science of geometry best affords.

Denying the existence of innate ideas, which Descartes accepted, and on which so much Renaissance poetry had depended, Locke asserted that all our knowledge is founded on experience:

> Let us then suppose the mind to be, as we say, white paper, void of all characters, without any ideas; How comes it to be furnished? Whence comes it by that vast store, which the busy and boundless fancy of man has painted on it with an almost endless variety? Whence has it all the materials of reason and knowledge? To this I answer, in one word, From experience (Bk. II, ch. 1, § 2.)

The consequence is plain: "Since the mind, in all its thoughts and reasonings, has no other immediate object but its own ideas, which it alone does or can contemplate, it is evident that our knowledge is only conversant about them".

The ideas are of two kinds, sensation and reflection (which "might properly be called internal sense"); they may be simple and unanalysable, or complex and resolvable into the simple ideas from which they are compounded. Reflection interprets and clarifies the often confused messages of sensation. To obtain and to organize clear ideas is the primary aim of thought, and Locke in the Third Book of his *Essay concerning Human Understanding* (1690) wrote much of value about the imperfections of language and the common use of "words without clear and distinct ideas" of what they stand for, and without any consistency in their use:

> Men take the words they find in use amongst their neighbours, and that they may not seem ignorant of what they stand for, use them confidently, without much troubling their heads about a certain fixed meaning. . . .

> Words being intended for signs of my ideas, to make them known to others, not by any natural signification, but by a voluntary imposition, it is plain cheat and abuse when I make them stand sometimes for one thing, and sometimes for another: the wilful doing whereof can be imputed to nothing but great folly or greater dishonesty (Bk. III, ch. x, § 4-5).

Though "Knowledge and reasoning require precise determinate

ideas", men too rarely "desire the explication of words whose sense seems dubious", and "this abuse of taking words upon trust has nowhere spread so far, nor with so ill effects, as amongst men of letters". Like Sprat in the *History of the Royal Society*, Locke considers "figurative speech also an abuse of language".

If we would speak of things as they are we must allow that all the art of rhetoric besides order and clearness, all the artificial and figurative application of words eloquence hath invented, are for nothing else but to insinuate wrong ideas, move the passions, and thereby mislead the judgment; and so indeed are perfect cheats; and therefore however laudable or allowable oratory may render them in harangues and popular addresses, they are certainly, in all discourses that pretend to inform or instruct, wholly to be avoided (Bk. III, ch. x, § 31-4).

Against these abuses of language Locke urges that no word should be used without a corresponding idea: if a simple idea, "clear and distinct"; if a complex idea, with "the precise collection of simple ideas settled in the mind, with that sound annexed to it as the sign of that precise, determined collection, and no other". Where a simple idea (which cannot be defined) is not likely to be understood, a synonym or similitude may be given; mixed ideas, "especially those belonging to morality", should be defined with reference to the relevant aspects.[10]

The scientific and philosophic desire for clarity, plainness, precision, and consistency in thought and the expression of thought affected literature at the same time as the movement towards an urbane easy elegance due partly to direct French influence and partly to the new cultural ideal which Dryden and Addison wished to spread. Locke was not interested in poetry, and his remarks were meant for philosophic and didactic prose writers; but that they would extend further was already shown in Descartes's letters to his friend Balzac and his comments on Balzac's style.

The desire for clarity was combined in Descartes with a passion for order and unity. Just as life is present in all parts of the human body, so in good style:

Grace and politeness shine there like the beauty of a perfectly beautiful woman, which does not consist in the striking effect of any one part in particular but in a harmony and tempering of all the parts which are so well arranged that not one of them dominates over the others, lest, proportion not being kept with the rest, the whole composition be less perfect.[11]

We find the same idea in Pope, who owed much to Descartes through Boileau:

> In wit, as nature, what affects our hearts,
> Is not th'exactness of peculiar parts;
> 'Tis not a lip, or eye, we beauty call,
> But the joint force and full result of all.
> (*Essay on Criticism*, ll. 243–6)

The Cartesian pursuit of clarity and order led to a dislike of all discordancy and contraries, of mingling opposites. Applied to style it involved the unity of matter and expression. Descartes indicates four undesirable types of inequality and unfitness: (1) where the style pleases the ear but the matter is low and unworthy of it (compare Pope's attack (l. 320) on False Eloquence, the "vile conceit in pompous words express'd"); (2) where richness and sublimity of thought are spoiled by faulty expression, as in a too concise or obscure style; (3) the rough style of the writers who, indifferent to the pomp and abundance of words, use them rudely and baldly in an attempt at direct expression; (4) lastly the "bon mots", word-play, ridiculous ambiguities, sophisticated arguments, and puerile subtleties used by the Précieux and writers of burlesque. With all this Pope agreed, when he declared (ll. 318–19; 315–16)

> Expression is the dress of thought, and still
> Appears more decent as more suitable,

and

> true expression, like th'unchanging Sun
> Clears and improves whate'er it shines upon.

Locke would not have admired Pope's variable use of words like "Wit" and "Nature" in the *Essay on Criticism*, but the general elegance and perspicuity of Pope's writings (and Prior's and Gay's) is associated with a comparative simplicity of vocabulary and syntax. The trend towards a gentlemanly and philosophic ease of style was crossed by a desire to distinguish verse from prose, and by the classical tradition of epic, pastoral, and georgic which affected other forms of poetry in diction, figures, and word-order. Hence the practice of a heavily stylized poetic diction which had started in the sixteenth century was augmented.[12] Yet it has been well argued that many neo-classical periphrases arose from an attempt to define the ideas intended in terms of the scientific tendency to generic classification.[13] The circumlocution is an analytic description, bringing together two or more aspects of the object while avoiding the use of its proper name. The essential thing is that the qualities or functions thus selected should be relevant. When in his *Autumn* Thomson calls eggs "ovarious food" he is not telling us much; when he writes, a few lines before, of swallows and other birds: "O'er the calm sky in convolution swift The feather'd eddy floats", there is more to be said for the phrase; and there is real observation again as well as definition when he writes of herrings as "the glittering finny swarms That heave our friths and crowd upon our shores". In the main, it must be confessed that periphrases were *not* used by English poets with any philosophic end, but as a refined trick which soon degenerated into *cliché*.

In his reply to Davenant, Hobbes described the main factors in poetry thus: "Time and Education begets experience; Experience begets Memory; Memory begets Judgement and Fancy: Judgement begets the strength and structure, and Fancy begets the ornaments of a Poem."[14] Fancy gathers the materials of a poem from the "copious Imagery discreetly ordered and perfectly registred in the Memory"; she invents new conceptions for the Judgment to organize, but her work is subordinate to his.

The intimate relation in literature between Fancy and Judgment became a main theme of criticism. Thus the Earl of Mulgrave's *Essay upon Poetry* (1682), starting from the assertion that

> Of things in which Mankind does most excell,
> Nature's chief Masterpiece is writing well,

goes on to argue that this is not done by the occasional "Flash of Fancy" but by the infusion of

> A Spirit which inspires the work throughout,
> As that of Nature moves this World about.

The controlling influence of genius is Judgment, which is the work of Reason:

> As all is dullness, when the Fancy's bad,
> So without Judgment, Fancy is but mad . . .
> Fancy is but the Feather of the Pen;
> Reason is that substantial, useful part,
> Which gains the Head, while t'other wins the Heart.

In the several kinds of poetry this principle is seen working. So a Song without a fault must have

> Exact propriety of words and thought,
> Th'expression easy, and the fancy high . . .
> No words transpos'd, but in such just cadence,
> As, though hard wrought, may seem the effect of chance.

Similarly an Elegy fails

> If yet a just coherence be not made
> Between each thought, and the whole model layed
> So right that every step may higher rise,
> As in a Ladder, till it reach the Skies.

Moderation and order must govern even the Ode; the best Satire has "sharpest thoughts in smoothest words convey'd"; in drama a rare grace is given by the Unities, while figures of speech which Mulgrave calls

> Art's needless Varnish to make Nature shine,
> Are all but Paint upon a beauteous Face,
> And in Descriptions only claim a place.

The image of the vital spirits omnipresent in the body was used by the Earl of Roscommon in his *Essay on Translated Verse* two years later, where he insists that in a translation (as in an original composition) the fabric must rise by

> strict *harmonious Symmetry* of *Parts*
> Which through the *Whole* insensibly must pass,
> With vital Heat to animate the Mass.

This involves a complete understanding of the original and an ability to "*Fall*, when *He falls*; and when *He Rises, Rise*".

A third noble author, George Granville, Lord Lansdowne, in a short verse-essay on *Unnatural Flights in Poetry* (1701) followed the Frenchman Bouhours very closely in allowing the use of fables, metaphors, and hyperboles provided that they were kept under control.

> Mistake me not: No Figures I exclude,
> And but forbid Intemperance, not Food....
>   As Veils transparent cover, but not hide,
> Such metaphors appear, when right apply'd;
> When thro' the phrase we plainly see the sense,
> Truth, when the meaning's obvious, will dispense.
> The Reader, what in Reason's due, believes,
> Nor can we call that false which not deceives.

Pope's discussion of Wit in the *Essay on Criticism* should be viewed in the light of such opinions. Pope was in a difficulty, for the word "Wit" had been used diversely by psychologists and literary critics. On the one hand, Wit was almost identified with Fancy as the sprightly power of ranging over the storehouse of memory to find vivid resemblances and novel turns of thought and expression. On the other, it was the poets' power "to invigorate their conceptions and strike life into a whole Piece" (Dryden); it was the informing creative "spirit which inspires the work throughout" described by Mulgrave.

In the first sense Wit became suspect in the age which idolized Judgment, and Locke contrasted the two, seeing Wit as

lying most in the assemblage of ideas, and putting these together with quickness and variety wherein can be found any resemblance or congruity, whereby to make up pleasant pictures and agreeable visions in the fancy: judgment on the contrary, lies quite on the other side, in separating carefully one from the other ideas wherein can be found the least difference, thereby to avoid being misled by similitude and by affinity to take one thing for another (*Essay concerning Human Understanding*, Bk. II, ch. XI, § 2).

Locke's further remarks show that while admitting the "agreeableness of the picture and the gaiety of the fancy" he disapproved of Wit because it was not perfectly conformable to "the severe rules of truth and good reason".

As the late E. N. Hooker showed, Pope's *Essay* attempted to reconcile the conflicting views.[15] Rejecting Dennis's notion that "careless, irregular and boldest Strokes are most admirable", he attacked works which present "One glaring Chaos and wild heap of Wit", and presented a view of Wit as moving hand in hand with Judgment, so that it becomes an easy, sparkling way of communicating truth, of expressing general principles of human nature in a lively, new, but decorous manner. When Pope declared (ll. 297-8) that

> True Wit is Nature to advantage dress'd,
> What oft was thought but ne'er so well express'd,

he was restating Dryden's definition, "thought and words elegantly adapted to the subject". Wit was an attitude of mind as well as a form of expression. It kept a balance between the tendency of Fancy to wild extravagance and the Understanding's tendency to reject all but universal, general truths.

Enough has been said to show that the Cartesian school, in rejecting the microcosmic view of the universe, did not reject the idea of order; quite the contrary. Attention was diverted from the extravagant potentialities of the Fancy and the mind's power of perceiving mystical correspondences, towards the internal order of the mind as a thing in itself and the order which it could find in, or impose on, the external world by using the instruments of thought. Pope's version of "Nosce teipsum" (*Essay on Man*, II. 1-2),

> Know then thyself, presume not God to scan,
> The proper study of Mankind is Man,

marked an important change in the direction of enquiry, and for more than a century philosophers were mainly concerned with the investigation of man as a rational animal, or thinking machine with a soul, living in a world designed largely for his convenience.

The new science was both theoretical and utilitarian, and it is not surprising that the "age of enlightenment" produced a large crop of didactic poems, not only in the field of poetic criticism, but on manifold topics of contemporary interest, showing the powers of the mind at work either in reasoning, as in Dryden's *Religio Laici*, or ingeniously controlling nature to man's use, as in the description of the wool industry in Dyer's *The Fleece*.

No doubt some scholar has made a study of the diverse ways in which these poets made their didacticism interesting, no easy feat where the material was so often argumentative, practical, and prosaic. Often the form was that of a verse-essay in which the poet could avoid rigorous argument but utter his thoughts loosely in witty epigram and aphorism. This was Pope's method in the *Essay on Man* in which he sketched the optimistic philosophy of Leibnitz and Bolingbroke. James Bramston's *The Art of Politicks* (1729) was a satiric imitation of Horace's epistolary *Art of Poetry*. William King imitated the same poem genially in his *Art of Cookery* and adapted Ovid's *Ars Amatoria* in a more respectable *Art of Love*. Dryden's argument for Christianity against Deism in *Religio Laici* was more closely knit as he tried to bolster the fallibility of human reason with appeals to tradition and authority. In *The Hind and the Panther*, where as a Catholic convert he attacked the Anglican position, he combined debate with animal fable.

If it was more usual to treat solemn or utilitarian themes seriously, as in John Philips's georgic *Cider* (1708), at times a comic tone alleviated the tedium of instruction, as in the same author's earlier *Cerealia* (1706) in praise of beer. Two poems of a medical nature, one by a doctor, the other by a layman, are not only relevant to our subject, but also excellent examples of contrasted techniques. These are Dr. John Armstrong's *The Art of Preserving Health* (1744) and Matthew Green's *The Spleen* (pubd. 1737). Armstrong's poem is a solemn treatise in which the mind is referred to chiefly as it affects the body. In Book I he gives advice on choosing a place to live in, with regard to soil, air, and weather. In Book II, turning to diet, he describes the way food builds up the body, points out the allergies to which some men are subject, and says that man is the only animal who often eats unsuitably.

> Learn a juster taste;
> And know that temperance is true luxury,

he urges, telling us not to eat too often,

> nor protract the feast
> To dull satiety; till soft and slow
> A drowsy death creeps in, th'expansive soul
> Oppressed, and smothered the celestial fire.

He praises the water drinkers of the Golden Age, but

> We curse not wine; the vile excess we blame.

It is even wise to learn to drink alcohol, if only in order to keep up with one's business rivals or take part in elections:

> Ah! when ambition, meagre love of gold,
> Or sacred country calls, with mellowing wine
> To moisten well the thirsty suffrages,
> Say how, unseasoned to the midnight frays
> Of Comus and his rout, wilt thou contend
> With Centaurs long to doughty deeds inured?
> Then learn to revel; but by slow degrees:
> By slow degrees the liberal arts are won,
> And Hercules grew strong. . . .

If one must get tipsy, let it be

> only with your friends.
> There are sweet follies; frailties to be seen
> By friends alone, and men of generous minds.

He treats in Book III of Exercise, and again preaches moderation and gradualness. Men of different natures need different amounts of exercise:

> Th'athletic fool, to whom what Heaven denied
> Of soul is well compensated in limbs,
> Oft from his rage, or brainless frolic, feels
> His vegetation and brute force decay.
> The men of better clay and finer mould
> Know nature, feel the human dignity,
> And scorn to vie with oxen or with apes.

He tells us when men of different physical complexions should work or stop work, and how to ensure sweet dreams instead of nightmares.

Book IV turns from external influences to describe "What good, what evil from ourselves proceeds", and how the passions affect the body, likening the "Subtle fluids poured through subtle tubes" by which thought works, to the "viewless atoms" by which "Nature moves The mighty wheels of this stupendous world". Not thought in general but "painful thought" harms the mind; the passions influence the body, which "betrays each fretful motion of the mind". Love and grief should not be indulged in solitude: "Go, seek the cheerful haunts of men, and mingle with the bustling crowd"; seek distractions in business, travel or war—with such platitudes Armstrong counsels men. He describes the effects of fear, of rage—both on the mind and on one's friendships—and continues "whatever cheerful and serene Supports the mind, supports the body too", and ends by praising music as "a power, that sways the breast, Bids every passion revel or be still".

Apart from a few moments of dry humour, Armstrong's blank verse poem has little to recommend it save as an instance of current medical opinion.

Matthew Green on *The Spleen* is more interesting. In Hudibrastic couplets he declares,

> First know, my friend, I do not mean
> To write a treatise on the Spleen;

he is merely going to describe how he avoids the morbid melancholy then known abroad as "the English disease". His manner is now burlesque, now serious:

> I always choose the plainest food
> To mend viscidity of blood.
> Hail, water-gruel, healing power,
> Of easy access to the poor;
> Thy help love's confessors implore,
> And doctors secretly adore;
> To thee I fly. By thee dilute,
> Through veins my blood doth quicker shoot,
> And by swift current throws off clean
> Prolific particles of spleen.

He finds hunting and other exercise beneficial, also laughter at ridiculous people (he gives examples), music, books (on rainy days), gossip and cards in the coffee-house. He avoids marriage, and has ceased attending Quaker meetings (he had been a Friend). He shuns political strife and all attempts to improve other people, and finally he gives a recipe to cure the Spleen for ever:

> Two hundred pounds half-yearly paid,
> Annuity securely made,
> A farm some twenty miles from town,
> Small, tight, salubrious, and my own;
> Two maids, that never saw the town,
> A serving-man not quite a clown,
> A boy to help to tread the mow,
> And drive, while t'other holds the plough; . . .
> May heaven (it's all I wish for) send
> One genial room to treat a friend,
> Where decent cupboard, little plate,
> Display benevolence, not state.
> And may my humble dwelling stand
> Upon some chosen spot of land:
> A pond before full to the brim

> Where cows may cool, and geese may swim;
> Behind a green like velvet neat,
> Soft to the eye, and to the feet;
> Where odorous plants in evening fair
> Breathe all around ambrosial air; . . .
> With trips to town life to amuse,
> To purchase books, and hear the news,
> To see old friends, brush off the clown,
> And quicken taste at coming down,
> Unhurt by sickness' blasting rage,
> And slowly mellowing in age,
> When Fate extends its gathering gripe,
> Fall off like fruit grown fully ripe,
> Quit a worn being without pain,
> Perhaps to blossom soon again.

This is the typical Englishman's wish for a moderate competence so often expressed in the seventeenth and eighteenth centuries, and inherited from Martial and Horace. Green concludes that he has lost the superstitious fear of his youth by using his reason; he has become a freethinker.

> The enthusiast's hope, and raptures wild,
> Have never yet my reason foiled. . . .
> Such thoughts as love the gloom of night,
> I close examine by the light;
> For who, though bribed by gain to lie,
> Dare sunbeam-written truths deny,
> And execute plain common sense
> On faith's mere hearsay evidence? . . .
> Thus in opinions I commence
> Freeholder in the proper sense,
> And neither suit nor service do,
> Nor homage to pretenders show,
> Who boast themselves by spurious roll
> Lords of the manor of the soul;
> Preferring sense, from chin that's bare,
> To nonsense throned in whiskered hair.

Dr. Johnson thought there was no poetry in this piece, perhaps because he suffered from the spleen himself and did not like to see it treated lightly; perhaps he disapproved of Green's final and contented scepticism. But it is as good a piece of serio-comic writing as the century produced.

In his treatise on the *Passions of the Soul* (1650), Descartes rejected the Aristotelian classification of the passions as either concupiscible or irascible, and while preserving the basic distinction between the soul and the body, he treated the passions, along with the volitions, as direct functions of the soul, to be distinguished from feelings "such as odours, sounds, colours, referred to external objects, others, such as hunger, thirst, pain, referring to our body". Descartes deduced all the passions from six primary ones: wonder, love, hatred, joy, sadness, and desire. Their seat is not in the heart, as many have thought; they are caused by some movement of the animal spirits, and they are affected in and work in the body by the "inclinations" of the pineal gland. The passions cannot be directly controlled by the will, but only "indirectly through representation of the things which are conjoined with the passions we wish to have, and contrary to those we wish to suppress". But the powers of men to use their wills in this way differ widely. A strong character is a man whose will is fortified by "firm and determinate judgements bearing on good and evil".

Broadly speaking the new philosophers accepted the traditional view that the mind of man was an arena in which reason or judgment and the passions fought for supremacy, and although the seventeenth century brought the mediaeval mechanism of humours and the several "souls" into disrepute, moral philosophy still preached rational self-control and temperance. In the century and a half after Descartes English philosophy was marked by tentative explorations of the machinery of the mind, including the functions of the passions. The preponderantly social direction of Augustan ethics did not diminish the stress laid on the passions, rather the reverse. The so-called Age of Reason was in fact an age in which the passions, moods, and sensibility were at least equally important for literature.

The old theory of Humours did not die without a long struggle, and in Restoration drama it cropped up again and again, notably among the imitators of Ben Jonson's comedy. Thus Shadwell in his Preface to *The Sullen Lovers* (1668) declared:

> I have endeavoured to represent variety of humours (most of the persons of the Play differing in their characters from one another) which was the practice of Ben Jonson ... who never wrote comedy without seven or eight excellent humours. I never saw one, except that of Falstaff, that was in my judgement comparable to any of Jonson's considerable humours.

A more subtle and flexible attitude is found in Dryden, who made the first considerable attempt in England to analyse and illustrate the various aspects of dramatic effect including the representation of passions. In his essay on "The Grounds of Criticism in Tragedy" (1679) Dryden considered tragedy under such headings as aim ("to rectify or purge our passions, fear or pity"), plot, and manners. He defines manners as

> those inclinations, whether natural or acquired, which move and carry us to actions, good, bad, or indifferent, in a play; or which incline the persons to such or such actions.

They are

> distinguished by complexion or by the differences of age or sex, of climates, or quality [rank] of the persons, or their present condition. They are likewise to be gathered from the several virtues, vices, or passions, and many other commonplaces, which a poet must be supposed to have learned from Natural Philosophy, Ethics, and History; of all which whosoever is ignorant does not deserve the name of poet.

Dryden insists that a man's character does not "consist of one particular virtue, or vice or passion only; but 'tis a composition of qualities which are not contrary to one another in the same person". So "Falstaff is a liar, and a coward, a glutton, and a buffoon, because all these qualities may agree in the same man".

"Yet", he continues, "one virtue, vice and passion ought to be shown in every man as predominant over the rest: as covetousness in Crassus, love of his country in Brutus; and the same in characters which are feigned".

Dryden is typical of the Augustan age in this treatment of particular passions. The ability to describe and make the audience share them he regards as a notable quality, born in the poet, yet fostered by acquired knowledge of "what they are in their own nature, and by what springs they are to be moved". But Dryden differs from some of his contemporaries in seeing the need for differences of tension in dramatic emotion. The poet whose judgment is not increased by skill "in the principles of moral philosophy" will not know how to trace "the crises and turns" of passions "in their cooling and decay". Constant vehemence, "the roar of passion", soon palls; the dramatist must not stay (as Longinus accused Aeschylus of doing) "always at high flood of passion, even in the dead ebb and lowest water-mark of the scene".

No doubt most contemporary writers agreed with Dryden—in theory at least—but John Dennis did not, when, attacking the use of the chorus in modern tragedy in *The Impartial Critic* (1693), he argued that the choruses between episodes must destroy tragic tension:

the Chorus in some measure must calm an Audience which the Episode disturb'd by its Sublimity and by its Pathetick; and therefore he who makes use of a Chorus in Tragedy seems to do like a Physitian, who, prescribing a Dose for the evacuation of Peccant Humors, should afterwards order Restringents to be taken in the midst of its kind Operation.[16]

Dryden opposes this doctrine when he asserts that the passions "suffer violence when they are perpetually maintained at the same height". In his own plays he did not sufficiently provide gradations of feeling and shifts of tension; but we can see his awareness of the problem in *The Conquest of Granada* (Pt. I, Act II, scene 1) where Prince Abdalla, after Lyndaraxa has left him, says:

> Howe'er imperious in her words she were,
> Her parting looks had nothing of severe;
> A glancing smile allured me to command,
> And her soft fingers gently pressed my hand:
> I felt the pleasure glide through every part;
> Her hand went through me to my very heart.
> For such another pleasure, did he live,
> I could my father of a crown deprive.—
> Why did I say?—
> Father!—That impious thought has shocked my mind:
> How bold our passions are, and yet how blind—
> She's gone; and now,
> Methinks, there is less glory in a crown:
> My boiling passions settle, and go down.
> Like amber chafed, when she is near, she acts;
> When further off, inclines, but not attracts.

The great scene in *Aureng-Zebe* (Act IV, scene 1), where the condemned prince is tempted by his stepmother Nourmahal, is a good illustration of Dryden's skill in suggesting the rise and fall of passions. In this play, as in *The Conquest of Granada*, he tries to draw characters "which are the nearest to those of an heroic poem", and to show contrast of passions issuing from contrast of "inclinations" (or manners and situations), and every scene contains at least one study in a passion, good or bad.

Dryden's advocacy of the dominant inclination is one proof that Pope's pet idea of the Ruling Passion was not new. Pope's *Essay on Man* has often been called unoriginal. Its significance lies partly in the daring and steadfastness with which Pope combined ideas taken over from the moderns—Shaftesbury, Hobbes, Mandeville, Bolingbroke—with scholastic and Platonic ideas which he may have imbibed in his Roman Catholic youth. As Mr. Maynard Mack has shown,[17] the theodicy of Epistle I looks back to the Renaissance and beyond:

> All are but parts of one stupendous whole
> Whose body Nature is, and God the Soul.
> (I. 267-8)

The image of transfusion by the animal spirits found in the *Essay on Criticism* has become one of Divine Immanence in a universe so perfectly poised that

> The least confusion but in one, not all
> That system only, but the whole must fall.
> (I. 249-50)

In Epistle II Man's internal nature and the implications of his "middle state" are discussed. He is a creature of paradox,

> Plac'd on this isthmus of a middle state,
> A Being darkly wise and rudely great: . . .
> In doubt to deem himself a God, or Beast; . . .
> Chaos of Thought and Passion, all confus'd; . . .
> Sole judge of Truth, in endless Error hurl'd:
> The glory, jest, and riddle of the world!
> (II. 3-18)

The marvels of human reason and science go together with ignorance and impotence. Even Newton could not "Describe or fix one movement of his Mind" (l. 36); "What Reason weaves, by Passion is undone" (l. 42). The two principles act like clockwork, Self-love (the impulse to self-fulfilment) being "the spring of motion" and Reason the balance which controls it by thoughts of consequences. Their common aim is to seek pleasure and avoid pain, but there are good and bad pleasures. The passions arising from Self-love become good when ruled by Reason, so the Stoics were wrong who advocated apathy. The contrary qualities

> Love, Hope and Joy, fair pleasure's smiling train,
> Hate, Fear and Grief, the family of pain,
> These mix'd with art, and to due bounds confin'd,
> Make and maintain the balance of the mind.
> (II. 117-20)

The multiplicity of pleasures possible to body and mind excite the passions in different ways and degrees; but each man has his Ruling Passion, for, as Montaigne wrote, "though the Soul have in it divers motions to give it Agitation, yet must there of necessity be one to overrule the rest". Under the dangerous sway of this predominant inclination fall all the other powers of the mind, imagination, habit, wit, the spirits; and "Reason itself but gives it edge and pow'r" unless it be given arms, those "strong determinate judgments of good and evil" which, Descartes explained, enable Reason to temper a passion by representations of its opposite:

> 'Tis hers to rectify, not overthrow,
> And treat this passion more as friend than foe.
> (II. 163–4)

Reason thus grafts fruitful scions on "savage stocks" and "Surest Virtues thus from Passions shoot".

One of the finest aspects of Pope's brilliant exposition is his perception of the antitheses of the mind, the delicate balance of moral qualities, the devious means by which "Reason the bias turns to good from ill" so that we may attain "the Virtue nearest to our vice ally'd". At best "virtuous and vicious ev'ry Man must be" as our several passions send us towards our individual goals. But the passions have a valuable function to perform in human life:

> Here then the truth: 'Tis Heav'n each Passion sends,
> And diff'rent men directs to diff'rent ends.
> Extremes in Nature equal good produce,
> Extremes in Man concur to general use.
> (*Moral Essays*, III. 159–62)

Human society enables us to live securely and to temper each other's Self-love away from mean selfishness towards benevolence and the common interest. Thus Pope effects a transition to Epistle III where he discusses man's place in the great chain of being and the individual's place in society where God "bade Self-love and Social be the same".

The *Essay on Man* has been regarded as merely a cento of commonplaces from Christian theology and the moral tradition. This is sadly to underrate the poem. In the consistency of its general picture, in the energy of its movement, and the combination of epigrammatic point with an all-pervading sense of the Divine

Order working through the conflicts of the parts of creation, it has no equal.

Pope's *Moral Essays* apply the doctrine of the Ruling Passion to social observation and satire. The theory often led to excessive simplification in such sweeping antitheses as Hogarth's *Idle and Industrious Apprentice* and Mrs. Inchbald's moral novel *Nature and Art*. But to Pope the variety was as important as the unity, and he was fascinated by the bewildering inconsistencies apparent in any man's behaviour:

> See the same man, in vigour, in the gout;
> Alone, in company; in place, or out;
> Early at Bus'ness, and at Hazard late;
> Mad at a Fox-chase, wise at a Debate;
> Drunk at a Borough, civil at a Ball;
> Friendly at Hackney, faithless at Whitehall.
> (Essay I. 71–6)

Much of Pope's pleasure in watching his fellow-men came from tracing the manifold forms taken by the Ruling Passion, and though in his second Essay he reduced the ruling passions of women to two, "The Love of Pleasure, and the Love of Sway", the diversity of his female portraits makes nonsense of this limitation.

Edward Young in *The Universal Passion* (1725–8) reduced the ruling passions of men to one, Love of Fame, which he traced in seven "Characteristical Satires", often very distantly—and dully. His theory of satire merits notice when he declares:

Laughter at the misconduct of the world will, in a great measure ease us of any more disagreeable passion about it. One passion is more effectually driven out by another than by reason, whatever some may teach (Preface).

The idea that satire should be passionate was an old one. Cinthio had seen it as a combination of comedy and tragedy, of laughter, pity, and terror, and Sir Philip Sidney declared that while making us laugh, it "giveth us to feele howe many head-aches a passionate life bringeth us to". To drive out passion by passion had been the aim of Juvenal and Marston. Young, however, favours Horace because of his "delicacy" and because "he appears in good humour while he censures; and therefore his censure has more weight as supposed to proceed from judgement, not from passion". Young's satire is more negative than positive, and there is little sign in the eighteenth century of any deliberate attempt to follow out Descartes's idea that the only way to drive out erring passions is to excite pleasing representations of their opposites. Perhaps Goldsmith's *Deserted Village* came as near as any to using this technique.

Apart from satire the delight in individual forms or strange types of eccentricity was potent in an age which was taught that all men were imperfect and so "out of centre". The "humourists" of the de Coverley Papers, the Quixotic figures of the novel, the lovable oddities such as Parson Adams, Uncle Toby, and Dr. Primrose were tributes to the diversity of human nature and its more amiable weaknesses.

The passions themselves multiplied and were explored by poets who believed with Dryden that to describe the rise and fall of emotions, their cause and cure, was a major aspect of their art. The Ode in particular (called by Mulgrave "the Muse's most unruly Horse", for "Judgment yields and Fancy governs there") became the safety-valve of passionate writers, and the union of music and poetry in such commissioned pieces as the odes composed annually (from 1683 onwards) for St. Cecilia's Day produced a long series of pieces in which the effect of music in exciting or allaying passion was shown with copious imitation of musical effects in verse. One of the first, by John Oldham (set by Dr. Blow, 1684), initiated a custom by mentioning the orchestral instruments and praising music as:

> The gentle spell that charms our care to rest,
> And calms the ruffled passions of the mind,
> Music does all our joy refine,
> It gives the relish to our wine,
> 'Tis that gives rapture to our love,
> And wings devotion to a pitch divine. . . .

Dryden's *Song for St. Cecilia's Day* (1687) and his *Alexander's Feast* (1697) displayed more virtuosity. In the first, after exclaiming, "What passion cannot Music raise and quell?" he shows the passionate effects of various instruments:

> The trumpet's loud clangor
> Excites us to arms . . .
> Sharp violins proclaim
> Their jealous pangs and desperation
> Fury, frantic indignation. . . .

And the organ produces "Notes inspiring holy love". No doubt the Italian musician Draghi who set the poem tried to make the instruments do what the poet claimed. In *Alexander's Feast* Dryden approached the theme historically, giving an instance of the power of music from the life of Alexander the Great. At a banquet Timotheus chants to the lyre a series of songs. When he sings of Jove, the king

> Assumes the god,
> Affects to nod,
> And seems to shake the spheres.

At a song of Bacchus with its reminder that "Drinking is the soldier's pleasure", Alexander "Fought all his battles o'er again". That mood was soon transformed to one of pity for the fallen Darius. From this it was an easy transition to emotions of love, and finally Timotheus, by a song of revenge, excited the king to such an ecstasy that he set fire to the city.

If music was regarded as most magically potent, poetry too was praised for its effects. Dodsley in his ode, *Melpomene, or the Regions of Terror and Pity*, sees a vision of tragedies in which

> Revenge stands threatning o'er
> A pale delinquent . . .

and

> This slave of passion rends his scatter'd hair,
> Beats his sad breast, and execrates his birth . . .
> And sees, or fancies, all the fiends below
> Beckoning his frighted soul to realms of endless woe. . . .

The poet sees the jealous man (Othello), the man growing mad (Lear), Macbeth, Romeo and Juliet, and "A thousand tender scenes of soft distress", "The types of every theme that suits the tragic strain", and he is given banal hints on how to move the passions in this way.

The passions became as real to the eighteenth century as were the classical deities and the Seven Deadly Sins to the Renaissance. Indeed they constituted a new mythology which had behind it the moral and psychological authority of philosophy and religion. So Parnell in his *Essay on the Different Styles of Poetry* (1713) describes how each passion has its own proper poetic mode:

> Brisk Joy with transport fills the rising strain . . .
> By frightful accents Fear produces fears;
> By sad expression Sorrow melts to tears. . . .

He discusses the psychological significance of the figures of rhetoric, and then goes on to welcome

> the new creations of the Muse,
> Poetic Persons, whom the Writers use
> Whene'er a course magnificently great
> Would fix attention with peculiar weight . . .
> 'Tis hence the Virtues are no more confin'd
> To be but rules of reason in the mind;
> The heav'nly Forms start forth, appear to breathe,
> And in bright shapes converse with men beneath;
> And, as a God in combat Valour leads,
> In Council Prudence as a Goddess aids.

Dr. Johnson defended the use of such figures when in his "Life of Milton" he wrote: "To exalt causes into agents, to invest abstract ideas with form, and animate them with activity, has always been the right of poetry", though he disliked their extended use as mythological agents.[18] The fatal facility of personifications made concrete merely by a capital letter, and the disrepute into which they fell with changes in the literary and philosophical fashion, should not make us forget that to Gray's readers (much more than to the Victorian Etty who painted them), his "Youth at the prow and Pleasure at the helm" was a pictorial allegory with considerable ethical significance. Gray's attitude to the passions was indeed moral. On the whole he belonged to that phase of poetry which regarded them as disturbers of the rational mind; as when, considering the Eton schoolboys as little victims of life, he prophesied:

> These shall the fury Passions tear,
> The vultures of the mind,
> Disdainful Anger, pallid Fear,
> And Shame that skulks behind. . . .

The cult of Sensibility, however, whether derived from French romances or the humanitarian optimism preached by Samuel Clarke and Shaftesbury, gave warrant for an unashamed emotional self-display which early affected Pope's "Eloisa to Abelard" and his "Elegy on an Unfortunate Lady", and soon sapped the foundations of rationalist and neo-classical restraint. By the midcentury, Fancy, the poetic ally of libertine wit, was hailed by Joseph Warton as "Parent of each lovely Muse". The "Nymph with loosely-flowing hair" and "all-commanding magic wand" conducted the poet through emotions and imaginary scenes by turns joyous, melancholy, martial, and amorous, and was invoked to bring back poetry to England:

> Animate some chosen swain,
> Who, filled with unexhausted fire . . .
> May rise above the rhyming throng,
> O'er all our listn'ing passions reign,
> O'erwhelm our souls with joy and pain;
> With terror shake, with pity move,
> Rouse with revenge, or melt with love . . .
> [And] bid Britannia rival Greece!
>
> ("Ode to Fancy")

Poetry came to be regarded as the liberator of the mind from the shackles of reason, and the return to popularity of Spenser, the early Milton, and Shakespeare's romantic comedies was partly due to their vindication of the free-ranging imagination.

> What are the lays of artful Addison,
> Coldly correct, to Shakespear's warblings wild?

exclaimed Warton in *The Enthusiast*. There were few moral or descriptive pieces in which some flight of fancy or dream-excursion was not admitted. The matter-of-fact William King, following Petronius, had dismissed dreams as

> Not by Heav'n for prophecies design'd
> Nor by ethereal beings sent us down.
> But each man is creator of his own;
> For when their weary limbs are sunk in ease
> The souls essay to wander where they please,
> The scatter'd images have space to play,
> And night repeats the labours of the day.
> ("Of Dreams")

For many writers dreams were still either prophetic or a delightful realm of fantasy, and poetry itself an activity in which "the scatter'd images have space to play".

Interest in the supernatural, in ghosts, witches, fairies, had never vanished. The Royal Society remained sceptical despite the efforts of Glanvill and Henry More to prove the existence of spirits. Hobbes declared that the worship of "Satyres, Fawnes, Nymphs and the like" and the modern belief "that rude people have of Fayries, Ghosts, and Goblins; and of the power of Witches" arose from inability "how to distinguish Dreams, and other strong Fancies, from Vision and Sense" (*Leviathan*, Pt. I, ch. II). Mulgrave praised Hobbes because he "by plain Reason's light Put such fantastic Forms to shameful Flight". But few poets were able wholeheartedly to agree with Sprat in his *History* that "The course of things goes quietly along, in its own true channel of *Natural Causes and Effects*." For Dryden as for many others: " 'Tis enough that, in all ages and religions, the greatest part of mankind have believed the power of magic, and that there are spirits and spectres which have appeared." In poetry references to the supernatural abounded, and, especially as the influence of Shakespeare, the ballads, and romances grew, accompanied by acquaintance with Celtic and Norse literature, allusions to fairies, witches, visionary Bards, and ghosts made up a minor tributary of mid-eighteenth-century poetry. In cruder form the supernatural fashion produced the Terror-Novel, the demoniac oriental tale, and the Germanized ballads of the century's end, whose shock-tactics were invariably less effective than the poetry which linked itself more modestly to folk-lore (as in Collins's *Ode on the Superstitions of the Western Highlands*) or to the tradition of *A Midsummer Night's Dream* and of *L'Allegro* and *Il Penseroso*.

Mention of *Il Penseroso* recalls the meditative tradition inherited from the seventeenth century which made the eighteenth so strong in elegy. The poetry of moods, of reflective states of mind, was a natural offshoot of the poetry of the passions. Contemplation, in the previous age a strenuous spiritual exercise leading to mystical union, became now a mild, detached rumination on landscape, the retired life, the vicissitudes of things. So in "The Contemplatist" John Cunningham writes of one who, detachedly observing the life of the village, notes how even there

> The Passions, a relentless train
> To tear the victim run,

and in his *Elegy on a Pile of Ruins*, which follows Gray's more masterly work, how

> There Contemplation, to the crowd unknown,
> Her attitude compos'd and aspect sweet,
> Sits musing on a monumental stone,
> And points to the Memento at her feet.

In Thomas Warton the Elder's poem *Retirement*, Contemplation takes a similar attitude when the poet seeks Joy in a vale

> Where haunts the lonesome nightingale;
> Where Contemplation, maid divine,
> Leans against some aged pine,
> Wrapt in stedfast thought profound,
> Her eyes fixt stedfast on the ground.

Such poets were the exponents of mild Melancholy or "Leucocholy", that pale agreeable cast of thought which had none of the sour bitterness of the Spleen. Its pleasures were described by Thomas Warton the Younger:

> Mother of musings, Contemplation sage . . .
> O lead me, queen sublime, to solemn glooms
> Congenial with my soul; to cheerless shades,
> To ruin'd seats, to twilight cells and bow'rs,
> Where thoughtful Melancholy loves to muse,
> Her fav'rite midnight haunts. . . .
>
> Few know that elegance of soul refined,
> Whose soft sensation feels a quicker joy
> From Melancholy's scenes, than the dull pride
> Of tasteless splendour and magnificence
> Can e'er afford. . . .

He suggests that Rousseau's Héloise,

> whose mind
> Had languish'd to the pangs of melting love,
> More genuine transport found, as on some tomb
> Reclined, she watch'd the tapers of the dead,
> Or through the pillar'd aisles, amid pale shrines
> Of imaged saints, and intermingled graves,
> Mus'd, a veiled votaress,

than any dazzling socialite could know in "the mazes of the festive ball". Here we are in the full tide of Sensibility, the habit of taking pleasure in rapidly changing emotions, in one's own sufferings and those of others.

"I love a tender sensation", said Sophia Western on reading a novel, "and would pay the price of a tear for it at any time." "Tender sensations" were at the heart of this literature, in which passions were reduced to delicate but piercing sentiments, a harmony was sought between man's and nature's moods, and the whole was suffused with a universal Benevolence. "There cannot be sympathy without benevolent affection", wrote Thomas Reid, in his *Essay on the Active Powers of Man* (1812). He defined the benevolent affections as including (1) Love between Parents and Children, (2) Gratitude to Benefactors, (3) Pity and Compassion towards the Distressed, (4) Esteem for the Wise and Good, (5) Friendship, (6) The passion of love between the sexes, (7) Public Spirit.

In developing thus the theory of Shaftesbury and Francis Hutcheson that man had an innate "sense of right and wrong", a "moral sense", which identified virtue with disinterested affection for the personal and social good of others, Reid was analysing affections which proved of supreme importance for the Romantic poets of the Revolutionary period. His classification corresponds closely to the types of person on whom the youthful Wordsworth, Coleridge, and Southey showered their poetic benevolence. But the sentiment of benevolence had long before been praised by Pope, and in 1745 Mark Akenside declaimed:

> Thron'd in the Sun's descending car,
> What pow'r unseen diffuseth far
> This tenderness of mind?
> What genius smiles on yonder flood?
> What god in whispers from the wood
> Bids ev'ry thought be kind?
> ("Ode against Suspicion")

In his best-known work, *The Pleasures of the Imagination* (1741), Akenside wrote one of many rambling discursive poems in which the poet's sensibility was encouraged to play round some sentiment or faculty. Important because it represents perhaps the first sustained and conscious use of the principle of association in verse, it anticipates some of Wordsworth's aims and methods in *The Prelude*.

Aristotle had recognized the associative activity and Descartes had briefly described it. In his *Leviathan* (Pt. I, ch. III), Hobbes had made a crude shot at accounting for what he called "the Consequence, or Trayne of Imaginations", declaring that "as wee have no Imagination, whereof wee have not formerly had Sense, in whole or in parts; so we have no Transition from one Imagination to another, whereof we never had the like before in our Senses". Although it happens "that in the Imagining of any thing, there is no certainty what we shall Imagine next; Onely this is certain, it shall be something that succeeded the same before, at one time or another". When our thoughts wander, with "no Passionate Thought, to govern and direct those that follow", the train of thought is "Unguided, without Designe", but even "in this wild ranging of the mind, a man may oft-times perceive the way of it, and the dependance of one thought upon another". In thought "regulated by some desire, and designe", we are seeking the connections between our thoughts, for instance, in remembrance. The mind then, like "a Spaniel ranges the field, till he find a scent". But "besides Sense, and Thoughts, and the Trayne of thoughts, the mind of man has no other motion".

The fear of undisciplined thought made Hobbes insist on the importance of Judgment to control and direct the "wild ranging" of Fancy. In a chapter added to his *Essay concerning Human Understanding* in the fourth edition (1700), Locke discussed the theory of association, but with grave suspicion of any notions not bound together by reason.

> ... there is another connexion of ideas wholly owing to chance or custom: ideas that in themselves are not at all of kin, come to be so united in some men's minds that it is very hard to separate them; they always keep in company, and the one no sooner at any time comes into the understanding, but its associate appears with it; and if they are more than two which are thus united, the whole gang, always inseparable, show themselves together (Bk. II, ch. XXXIII, sect. 5).

Such strong combinations of irrational ideas were a kind of madness responsible for our prejudices, obsessions, and false opinions. They hindered truth so much that educators ought "diligently to watch and carefully to prevent the undue connexion of ideas in the minds of young people". Locke would have thought *The Prelude* a proof that Wordsworth had been badly brought up!

David Hume treated associations more seriously than Locke and based his epistemology upon them when in his *Treatise of Human Nature* (1739) he insisted that our knowledge of the world outside us is built into order by the principle of Association, working through our perception of Resemblance, Contiguity in time or place, and Cause and Effect. Though "Objects have no discoverable connection together", our ideas of them have, and all our thoughts, whether rational or irrational, simple or complex, can be traced back to the mind's habit of associating its memories of impressions one with another. When we use our judgment correctly "avoiding all distant and high enquiries, [it] confines itself to such subjects as fall under daily practice and experience"; but "the Imagination of man is naturally sublime, delighted with whatever is remote and extraordinary, and running, without control, into the most distant parts of space and time in order to avoid the objects, which custom has rendered too familiar with it".[19] Again, in *An Inquiry concerning Understanding* (1742) after distinguishing thoughts or ideas from impressions (sensations or emotions): "The most lively thought is still inferior to the dullest sensation", Hume describes all mental experiences as bound together by custom ("the great guide of human life"), and tries to distinguish between fiction and belief:

> Nothing is more free than the imagination of man, and though it cannot exceed that original stock of ideas, furnished by the internal and external senses, it has unlimited power of mixing, compounding, separating, and dividing these ideas, in all the varieties of fiction and vision. It can feign a train of events with all the appearance of reality, ascribe them to a particular time and place, conceive them as existent, and paint them out to itself with every circumstance that belongs to any historical fact, which it believes with the greatest certainty (sect. 5, Pt. II).

Yet this is not belief: "We can, in our conception, join the head of a man to the body of a horse; but it is not in our power to believe that such an animal has ever existed." Belief "is something felt by the mind, which distinguishes the ideas of the judgment from the fictions of the imagination".[20]

Imagination was to Hume largely what Fancy had been to Hobbes, but his influence was more sympathetic to imaginative literature than his predecessor's had been. He did not decry fiction or try to limit it to the probable, and his exposition of the powers of the "associative principle", together with his reduction of cause and effect to "one event following another" assisted if they did not initiate the rise of a literature of associative rather than logical relationships, which produced Sterne's *Tristram Shandy*, the idiosyncratic essay, and the poetry of memory and fancy.

David Hartley gave an independent version of the association theory in his *Observations on Man* (1749), and based his perfectibilist view of mankind on it.[21] Starting from an attempt to combine Newton's doctrine of physical vibrations relating to sensation and motion (*Principia* and *Optics*) with the ideas about association found in Locke and other writers, Hartley discussed the associative traces left by the several senses, the nature of words and their power to communicate ideas or definitions. He had much to say about figurative language, e.g. analogies:

For the mind being once initiated into the method of discovering analogies, and expressing them, does by association persevere in this method, and even force things into its system by concealing disparities, magnifying resemblances, and accommodating language thereto.... Similes, fables, parables, allegories, &c. are all instances of natural analogies improved and set off by art. And they have this common to them all, that the properties, beauties, perfections, desires, or defects and aversions which adhere by association to the simile, parable or emblem of any kind, are insensibly, as it were, transferred upon the thing represented. Hence the passions are moved to good or to evil. Speculation is turned into practice, and either some important truth felt and realized, or some error and vice gilded over and recommended (Ch. III, sect. 1, Prop. LXXXII).

The passions were "no more than aggregates of simple ideas united by association". To analyse the affections, "by reversing the steps of the associations which concur to form them", was essential to learning "how to cherish and improve good ones", to transform sensuous into spiritual pleasures, and to form "motives to beneficent actions". Memory was vitally important, its rudiments being "laid in the perpetual recurrency of the same impression, and clusters of impressions".

It is to be observed, that as we think in words, both the impressions and the recurrence of ideas will be attended with words; and these words, from the great use and familiarity of language, will fix themselves strongly in the fancy, and by so doing bring up the associated trains of ideas in the proper order, accurately or nearly. And thus, when a person relates a past fact, the ideas do in some cases suggest the words, whilst in others the words suggest the ideas (Ch. III, sect. 4, Prop. XC).

But the memory of actual events may be crossed or confused with memory of preceding memories. In dreams there is "a great wildness and inconsistency", owing to the state of the body in sleep:

Thus a person who has taken opium, sees either gay scenes, or ghastly ones, according as the opium excites pleasant or painful vibrations in the stomach. Hence it will follow, that ideas will rise successively in dreams, which have no such connexion as takes place in nature, in actual impressions, nor any such as is deducible from association. And yet, if they rise up quick and vividly one after another . . . they will be affirmed of each other, and appear to hang together (Ch. III, sect. 5, Prop. XCI).

From sensuous associations Hartley passes to the "pleasures and pains of the imagination", which combine visual and auditory images with others, and spring from the beauty of the natural world, the arts and sciences, the beauty of human beings, wit and humour. Other intellectual functions are connected with ambition, self-interest, sympathy, theopathy, and the moral sense (ch. IV, sect. 1). By listing various pleasures and pains Hartley fostered a poetry of hedonistic catalogue which persisted for a century. His insistence on processes of thought and feeling made writers reflect on the nature of their own minds, and led ultimately (though his view was mechanistic) to an organic theory of the poetic imagination.

Hartley's term the "pleasures of the imagination" had been anticipated by Addison in his *Spectator* Essays (Nos. 411–21), as well as by Mark Akenside in *The Pleasures of the Imagination* (1741) which discussed the importance of association for education and poetry in the light of Hume's *Treatise*. Johnson, who ignored Akenside's philosophy, was bewildered by his imagery: "forms fantastically lost under superfluity of dress". But if, as the great critic said, "He remarked little, and laid hold on nothing", through trying to put too much in his poem, at least Akenside showed unusual interest in how the mind works, and went beyond Addison from whom he took the idea that "all the primary pleasures of the imagination result from the perception of greatness, or wonderfulness, or beauty, in objects".[22]

Early in his poem (I. 113–32) Akenside tells how

> Nature's hand
> To certain species of external things
> Attune(d) the finer organs of the mind:
> So the glad impulse of congenial pow'rs,
> Or of sweet sound, or fair-proportion'd form,
> The grace of motion, or the bloom of light,
> Thrills thro' Imagination's tender frame,
> From nerve to nerve; all naked and alive
> They catch the spreading rays; till now the soul
> At length discloses ev'ry tuneful spring,
> To that harmonious movement from without
> Responsive. Then the inexpressive strain
> Diffuses its enchantment; Fancy dreams
> Of sacred fountains and Elysian groves,
> And vales of bliss; the intellectual pow'r
> Bends from his awful throne a wond'ring ear,
> And smiles: the passions, gently sooth'd away,
> Sink to divine repose, and love and joy
> Alone are waking; love and joy serene
> As airs that fan the summer.

This affords an interesting if imperfect parallel to Wordsworth's Prospectus to *The Recluse*, in which he wished to make "groves Elysian ... A simple produce of the common day", and to celebrate "How exquisitely the individual Mind ... to the external world is fitted". Wordsworth went on to proclaim

> how exquisitely too—
> Theme this but little heard of among men,
> The external World is fitted to the Mind.

Akenside did not pursue this second theme, but he was aware of what "high capacious powers lie folded up in man", and "the mind's conscious determination of its own activity". He noted the "complicated joy" arising from the combination of several senses in natural pleasures, and saw, as Wordsworth and the Georgian poets were to do, how

> the various lot of life
> Oft from external circumstance assumes
> A moment's disposition to rejoice
> In those delights which at a diff'rent hour
> Would pass unheeded.
> (II. 84–9)

Introducing his account of the work of association Akenside asks

> Whence is this effect,
> This kindred pow'r of such discordant things?
> Or flows their semblance from that mystic tone
> To which the new-born mind's harmonious pow'rs
> At first were strung? Or rather from the links
> Which artful Custom twines around her frame?
> (III. 306–11)

He describes the concatenation of ideas and continues

> Such is the secret union when we feel
> A song, a flow'r, a name, at once restore
> Those long-connected scenes where first they mov'd
> Th'attention, backward thro' her mazy walks
> Guiding the wanton fancy to her scope,
> To temples, courts, or fields, with all the band

> Of painted forms, of passions and designs
> Attendant, whence, if pleasing in itself,
> The prospect from that sweet accession gains
> Redoubled influence o'er the list'ning mind.
>
> By these mysterious ties the busy pow'r
> Of Mem'ry her ideal train preserves
> Entire, or, when they would elude her watch,
> Reclaims their fleeting footsteps from the waste
> Of dark oblivion. . . .
>
> (III. 338–52)

Explaining that the poet makes use of association and memory, he proceeds to an account of the poetic process, in which the poet's "plastic powers" "labour for action", and are "with endless choice perplex'd", till "at length His plan begins to open, lucid order dawns". Here is a striking similarity to Wordsworth's account of his perplexity in Book I of *The Prelude*, and his discovery of his proper theme after making a tentative foray into his boyhood to reveal the dark

> Invisible workmanship that reconciles
> Discordant elements, and makes them move
> In one society.

In the uncompleted fourth book of his work as revised in 1770, Akenside introduced a series of reminiscences of his own youth in Northumberland above "solitary Wensbeck's limpid stream",

> When all alone, for many a summer's day,
> I wander'd thro' your calm recesses, led
> In silence by some powerful hand unseen

—another Wordsworthian touch. But "*Athenian Akenside*", the poetic physician, was no Wordsworth; his reach exceeded his grasp, and he never in his poem decided what he really wanted to write about. He saw the literary imagination as more than the trifling exercise which Hartley as well as Locke had made it: and he was interested in its origins and development. It is significant of the turn of his mind that in the year when he first published his poem Akenside got his doctorate at Leyden for a thesis on *The Origin and Growth of the Human Foetus*. Long afterwards, in the unfinished book (ll. 20-4), he expressed his intention

> the secret paths
> Of early genius to explore, to trace
> Those haunts where Fancy, her predestin'd sons,
> Like to the Demigods of old, doth nurse
> Remote from eyes profane . . . ;

which is precisely what Wordsworth did in *The Prelude*.[23] More will be said later about the effects of the "Association philosophy" on Wordsworth and on other Romantics. But it is easy to exaggerate Hartley's influence on the poet, great though that was in providing a first impetus towards an explanation of his own thought-processes and growth. Maybe Coleridge (who had also passed through a Hartleian phase) saved Wordsworth from becoming just a better Akenside, by developing his sense of the mind's creative activity, its "auxiliar light" which gave it a plastic power far greater and more organic than ever Akenside conceived.

Chapter Four ∽ ASSOCIATIONS, INTUITION, AND IMMORTAL LONGINGS IN THE NINETEENTH CENTURY

Between 1750 and 1900 psychology was dominated by an intensification of the conflict between mechanistic and organic theories of the mind, and this naturally extended to notions of the artistic imagination. Without always sharing the philosopher's systematized knowledge, many poets of the period were affected by his intellectual climate, and the differences between Augustan and Romantic literature and criticism are partly due to differences in the accepted assumptions about the mind's functions and mechanism.

From Hartley and Hume descended a long line of distinguished associationists, and the common sense school of Thomas Reid, Dugald Stewart, Thomas Brown, and Sir William Hamilton shared with the Utilitarians James and J. S. Mill the belief that thought was built up on sense-perception and association through such relationships as contiguity, similarity, contrast, cause and effect, and the habits set up by the frequency of certain associations. The idea that pleasure and pain determined all human behaviour was used to explain the phenomena of will and action, and to derive ethical ideas and motives from the primary and more complex associations; hence the term "psychological hedonism" given to the system. It was no accident that James Mill's *Analysis of the*

Phenomena of the Human Mind (1829) was published within ten years of Dalton's announcement of the atomic system of chemistry. For associationism was an atomistic theory: "The laws of the phenomena of the mind are sometimes analogous to mechanical, but sometimes also to chemical laws", wrote J. S. Mill. "When many impressions or ideas are operating in the mind together, there sometimes takes place a process of a similar kind to chemical combination . . . These therefore are cases of mental chemistry: in which it is proper to say that the simple ideas generate, rather than that they compose, the complex ones."[1]

In literature this "mechanical" element in psychology at first caused few misgivings. Associationism made some poets aware of the elements of their thinking. By pointing to the sensuous nature of the primary material of ideas it speeded the rise in the mid-eighteenth century of a poetry more "simple, sensuous and impassioned" than the Augustan mode. It helped to form the taste which made Thomson's *Seasons* influential and produced the great crop of what Wordsworth called "loco-descriptive poetry" as well as the many poems about the "Pleasures" of the mind. One questions whether most of the descriptive poets organized their material consciously in accordance with any psychological principles. Some indeed, like Dyer in *Grongar Hill*, thought rather in terms of landscape painting. But that Akenside used the principle of association we have already seen, and Samuel Rogers in his *Pleasures of Memory* praises "the sleepless energies of thought" which activate a savage or a Newton:

> Lulled in the countless chambers of the brain,
> Our thoughts are linked by many a hidden chain.
> Awake but one, and lo, what myriads rise!
> Each stamps its image as the other flies . . .
> Each thrills the seat of sense, that sacred source
> Whence the fine nerves direct their mazy course,
> And through the frame invisibly convey
> The subtle, quick vibrations as they play. . . .
> (Pt. I, ll. 71–86)

In Part I of his poem Rogers shows Memory evoking associations "in subservience to the senses"; in Part II he shows Memory colouring "all the prospects of life". "On her agency depends every effusion of the Fancy, who with the boldest effort can only compound or transpose, augment or diminish the materials which she has collected and still retains."

Certainly many descriptive poems from Thomson's *Seasons* to Cowper's *Task* and Byron's *Childe Harold* demonstrate how apt was Hartley's account of the pleasures derived from the beauties of nature:

> The pleasant tastes and smells, and the fine colours of fruits and flowers, the melody of birds, and the grateful warmth or coolness of the air, in the proper seasons, transfer miniatures of these pleasures upon rural scenes, which start up instantaneously so mixed with each other . . . as to be separately indiscernible. If there be a precipice, a cataract, a mountain of snow etc. in one part of the scene, the nascent ideas of fear and horror magnify and enliven all the other ideas, and by degrees pass into pleasures by suggesting the security from pain.

The grandeur and novelty of some scenes, by contrast with others, may greatly enhance the pleasure. "Uniformity and variety in conjunction . . . transfer part of the lustre borrowed from the works of art . . . upon the works of nature." Knowledge of poetry and painting, of country sports and pastimes, the contrast between town and country, all increase the pleasures of nature, and the sense of God's creative power in nature adds to them. "Inquisitive and philosophical persons have some others, arising from their peculiar knowledge and study of natural history, astronomy and philosophy in general."[2]

The tendency of the mind to wander under the influence of the emotions and ideas suggested by a particular object, scene, or situation became a major basis of late eighteenth-century art, whether in landscape painting or reflective poetry. As Whately wrote, when we meditate on nature

> We forget the particular object it presents, and, giving way to their effects,

we follow the track they have begun, to any extent which the dispositions they accord with will allow. It suffices that the scenes of Nature have power to affect our imagination and our sensibility: for such is the constitution of the human mind, that if once it is agitated, the emotion often spreads beyond the occasion . . . till we rise from familiar subjects to the sublimest conceptions, and are rapt in the contemplation of whatever is great or beautiful, which we see in nature, feel in man, or attribute to the Divinity.[3]

The analysis of mental processes into "trains of thought" greatly fostered that "diffused and flowing expression" which Hurd considered to be as valid as a "short and compact" style. It produced the long diffused poem of description or reflection. Dugald Stewart, writing in 1792, had some significant remarks on this kind of verse. In philosophical writing, he wrote, "we expect to see an Author lay down a distinct plan or method, and observe it rigorously". But "in that state of mind in which Poetry is read, . . . digressions are not only agreeable, but necessary to the effect; and an arrangement founded on the spontaneous and seemingly casual order of our thoughts, pleases more than one suggested by an accurate analysis of the subject".[4]

As an associationist, Stewart was interested in transitions in poetry. He shows how in Thomson's *Seasons* a digression in praise of Industry "arises naturally and insensibly from the view of a luxuriant harvest" and then a gentle return is made to the main theme. He finds that in Goldsmith's *Traveller* the "transitions are managed with consummate skill", and he illustrates the "associating principle of Contrast". Another transition "seems to be suggested by the accidental mention of a word". Elsewhere he points out that "similarity of sound" may cause associations, as in poetic alliteration; he cites Pope: "Puffs, Powders, Patches: Bibles, Billets-doux", and is offended (as Donne would not have been) when Pope writes that the Divine Power:

> Breathes in our soul, informs our mortal part,
> As full, as perfect, in a Hair, as Heart.

Had Stewart's taste been less conventional he might have made a real contribution to the development of literary criticism. But though he admired the elegant simplicity of Goldsmith, his ideas on poetic diction were conservative; he saw the need for a special traditional poetical diction, affecting the sensibility by ideas and music.

> Nor is it merely by a difference of words, that the language of poetry is distinguished from that of prose. When a poetical *arrangement* of words has once been established by authors of reputation, the most common expressions, by being presented in this consecrated order, may serve to excite poetical associations (p. 291).

A word which seems flat and prosaic by its familiarity may be excused; "but two such words coupled together in the order of conversation can scarcely be introduced into serious poetry without appearing ludicrous". This is directly opposed to Wordsworth's theory, but as we shall see later, in other respects Stewart had something in common with the author of *The Prelude*. The associationist doctrine produced at least one striking critical essay in Walter Whiter's *Specimen of a Commentary on Shakespeare* (1794), containing an "attempt to explain and illustrate various Passages on a new Principle derived from Locke's Doctrine of the Association of Ideas". This work anticipated modern analysis of the dramatist's use of image-clusters, but had to wait over a century for recognition.

The loose, diffused way of linking sensations and ideas was a godsend to Byron when in *Childe Harold* he jotted down his impressions of his Grand Tour, bringing to bear on the scenes he visited all the apparatus of associationism. The poet may not have read deeply in Hartley or his followers, yet that he had given some thought to the nature of poetical associations appears in his letter to John Murray on 7 February 1821, in which he answered the Reverend W. L. Bowles's strictures on Pope by asserting that nature becomes more poetical by the addition of some human object. Thus the sea needs a ship:

Even an old boat, keel upwards, wrecked upon the barren sand, is a "poetical" object (and Wordsworth, who made a poem about a washing-tub and a blind boy, may tell you so as well as I), whilst a long extent of sand and unbroken water, without the boat, would be as like dull prose as any pamphlet (i.e. Bowles's) lately published. Take away Stonehenge from Salisbury Plain, and it is nothing more than Hounslow Heath, or any other unenclosed down.

He goes on to list the buildings and statues which inspired *Childe Harold*, Canto IV, and declares them to be

as *poetical* as Mont Blanc or Mount Etna, perhaps still more so, as they are direct manifestations of mind, and *presuppose* poetry in their very conception.... The very Cloaca of Tarquin at Rome are as poetical as Richmond Hill; many will think more so.... The ground interests in Virgil because it *will* be *Rome*, and not because it is Evander's rural domain.

His belief that nature is poetic mainly because of the human associations connected with it was intimately related to Byron's own practice in descriptive writing.

Such early poems of Keats as "I stood tiptoe" and *Sleep and Poetry* follow the associationist fashion. Keats probably read little modern philosophy, but his friend Woodhouse mentions their discussing "the ideas derivable to us from our senses singly and in their various combinations", and there are numerous examples of free association in his letters, notably in those written from Teignmouth in 1818.[5] Thus after writing across as well as along the first page of his letter to Reynolds on May 3, he wrote: "This crossing a letter is not without its association—for chequer-work leads us naturally to a Milkmaid, a milkmaid to Hogarth, Hogarth to Shakespeare—Shakespeare to Hazlitt, Hazlitt back to Shakespeare —and thus by merely pulling an apron-string we set a pretty peal of Chimes at work."

To James Rice on 24 March he wrote that he could not "settle his thoughts": "I am obliged to run wild, being attracted by the Loadstone Concatenation"—which he exemplified at length. The fine verse-letter to Reynolds written next day began similarly, with recollections of the bizarre concatenations that had come before his eyes the previous night in bed, "that wonted thread Of Shapes and Shadows and Remembrances, That every other minute vex and please". He contrasts "these visitings" with the ordered beauty of Claude's painting "The Enchanted Castle", which starts him off on a long series of romantic fancies. The mood changes; he wishes that all his dreams could be derived from sensations, "the material sublime", yet (as in *Sleep and Poetry*) he knows that he must go further and he fears that "never will the prize, High reason, and the lore of good and ill Be my award". He knows that to give himself up to the associational habit is an escape from seriousness: "Things cannot to the will Be settled, but they tease us out of thought". But if his imagination is extended beyond sensations it becomes "Lost in a sort of Purgatory blind", since he has not as yet a proper standard of judgment whereby to reconcile the beauty with the sorrows of the world:

> It is a flaw
> In happiness to see beyond our bourn—
> It forces us in Summer skies to mourn:
> It spoils the singing of the Nightingale.

He goes on to illustrate the antithesis further, telling how one evening on the shore

> I saw
> Too far into the sea: where every maw
> The greater on the less feeds evermore:—
> But I saw too distinct into the core
> Of an eternal fierce destruction,
> And so from Happiness I far was gone.

He dismisses such "horrid moods" and promises from them "in new Romance Take refuge".[6]

To discipline the concatenations of associated ideas, to reconcile the life of sensations with that of thoughts, free-wandering fancy with exploration of life's miseries, was the task which Keats set himself and had not fully achieved when death took him so prematurely. Here I cannot trace his progress; but two examples may be cited to show his use of association for poetic transitions. The "Ode to a Nightingale" written a year after the verses to Reynolds might have been composed in answer to his line about the bird in that poem. For in it "concatenation" is fused with serious reflections upon human anguish. Its basis is a train of thought in which the song of the bird is contrasted and reconciled with ideas of sickness and death and darkness, all related to imagery of drugs and wine, Bacchus (in Titian's painting), the Poesy of nature and of death, the eternity of music. The use of the word "forlorn" in stanzas vii and viii is an instance of sound bringing associations which change with repetition:

> . . . faery lands forlorn.

> Forlorn! the very word is like a bell
> To toll me back from thee to my sole self!

As Professor Kenneth Muir has pointed out, "One kind of mastery displayed by Keats in this ode is . . . the continuous shifting of view-point." This shifting is due to the poet's surrender to a train of associations with a transition of contrast in stanza iv when the long chain of similar "drink" images is broken into by the image of the "viewless wings of Poesy". "The song of the bird is the song of the poet"[7]—but only for a short while before the chime of "forlorn" tolls him back to his "sole self". Whereas in the verse-letter he fled from harsh realities to fancy, he now recognizes that "the fancy cannot cheat so well As she is fam'd to do", and having relieved himself of his grief along with his fancies, he is left in suspense between vision and waking.

Another, less well-known, illustration of sound association appears in the "Ode on a Grecian Urn", stanza v, line 1, where the poet addresses the urn: "O Attic shape! Fair attitude!" Editors usually pass over the word "attitude" without comment. "The last stanza enters stumbling upon a pun", wrote Robert Bridges, and if the word "attitude" merely meant "posture" one might regret the weight laid on the exclamation. But for Keats and contemporary lovers of the antique the word recalled memories of Emma, Lady Hamilton, who in her youth as Sir William's mistress had become celebrated for the "Attitudes" in which she took up "variations of posture, mood and expression". "People who have seen her 'attitudes'", wrote Horace Walpole, "are mad about her expression."[8] A series of the "Attitudes" was engraved by Friedrich Rehberg and published in 1795. Maybe Keats had seen them, and also the painter Tischbein's engravings from the *Collection of Engravings from Greek Vases in the possession of Sir William Hamilton*, first published in 1791 (5 vols.) but reprinted twice later. Hamilton had died in 1803, Emma in 1815 (ten years after her lover Lord Nelson). But Keats must have known about Hamilton and his passion for Greek vases. Sir William had owned both the great Warwick Vase and the Portland Vase and was one of the most ardent popularizers of Greek art. So the word "attitude" summons up associations, of the dancing postures of that pleasant, ill-fated creature Emma whose warm love and "breathing human passion" had certainly left her "heart high-sorrowful" and whose lissom youth had turned to an obesity seized on by caricaturists; and of the apostle of Greek art whose collection may indirectly have helped to inspire the poem.

To regard Keats's odes merely as examples of the association psychology would be entirely to miss the heart of his poetic doctrine. He was a lover of Sensations (in the empirical usage of the word); he was also capable of asserting that "Poetry is not so fine a thing as philosophy". But when he exclaimed "O for a life of Sensations rather than of Thoughts", he was crying out against cold rationalism in favour of "the holiness of the Heart's affections and the truth of the Imagination—What the Imagination seizes as Beauty must be truth—whether it existed before or not" (*Letters*, Nov. 22, 1817). Moreover he declared that the imagination worked by sympathetic identification with the object contemplated: seeing a sparrow he could "take part in its existence and pick about the Gravel" (Nov. 22, 1817); when in a room with people, "the identity of every one in the room begins to press upon me that I am in a very little time annihilated" (Oct. 27, 1818). He found this power of empathy in Shakespeare and Chaucer, and regarded it as a feature of the "poetical Character... (I mean that sort of which, if I am any thing, I am a Member)", making the poet a being without identity (*ibid.*). Associated with this was the habit of "Negative Capability—that is, when a man is capable of being in uncertainties, mysteries, doubts, without any irritable reaching after fact and reason" (Dec. 21, 1817).

Keats's notion of Sympathy is obviously very different from that of Hartley, for whom it comprised the affections of "Sociality or the pleasure we take in the mere company and conversation of others", "goodwill and bevolence", and "compassion,... the uneasiness which a man feels at the misery of another".[9] All these are external in comparison with the immediate participation in the life of other beings which Keats implies. His intuition of sharing in the life of the sparrow may be illusory, but it is not the same as a feeling of companionship, similarity of interests, pity, love, or esteem. His delight in the creative immersion of Shakespeare in Iago or Imogen suggests a different view of the imagination from that of the empirical philosophers. It is nearer to Coleridge's view, and, indeed, it comes from Coleridge, probably through Hazlitt, whose 1818 lectures on Shakespeare Keats attended.[10]

In discussing "Negative Capability" Keats contrasted Shakespeare with Coleridge, who was always "reaching after fact and reason". The characterless poet he contrasted (Oct. 27, 1818) with "the wordsworthian or egotistical sublime". This brilliant phrase illuminates Wordsworth's genius, whose noble poetry depended largely on his egocentric exploration of his own mind in its absorption of the external world as it impressed itself upon his senses, memory, and intuitions of God. In human relations Sympathy meant for Wordsworth what it meant for Hartley. But he passed beyond the associationists in his creative view of memory and association and his very different attitude to the affections concerning God (Hartley's "Theopathy"). For Hartley "enthusiasm" was a "mistaken persuasion in any person, that he is a peculiar favourite with God", which gives "a reality and certainty to all the reveries of a man's own mind, ... cementing the associations in a preternatural manner".[11] For Hartley their "reality" was fictitious; for Wordsworth it was the highest imaginative experience of truth. The way in which Wordsworth both drew on and transcended associationism is indicative of the change which came over Romantic poetry in the Revolutionary period, and of a revolutionary change in the poets' attitude to the mind.

Wordsworth emerges in his early poems as the poet of sensibility, expressing in *An Evening Walk* a pensive melancholy akin to that of the Wartons. In *Descriptive Sketches* the sense of Nature's healing power is crossed by sentiments and sterner passions associated with Swiss scenery and history, terror, the sense of danger, superstition, fortitude, and independence, "Great joy by horror tam'd". The current cult of Benevolence and his acquaintance with the rustic poor in the north of England made him prefer incidents from village life. He was the poet of sentiment and the affections, of childhood and the moral decencies, of independence and duty.

At his best, however, Wordsworth is much more than this, and largely because of his interest in the operations of his own mind. In him and in Coleridge the self-consciousness implicit in Descartes's postulate found for the first time its full potential, with lasting effects on poetry.

Wordsworth's debt to Hartley has been exhaustively discussed by Professor A. Beattie.[12] The poet took over Hartley's scale of mental processes: simple sensations; "sensible" ideas, or ideas about sensations surviving in the memory; complex ideas composed by association, uniting clusters of simple ideas. Without copying Hartley's elaborate categories, Wordsworth made considerable use of the system in describing mental processes, and he showed his debt to associationism when in the 1800 Preface to *Lyrical Ballads* he declared that the poet

> considers man and the objects that surround him as acting and re-acting upon each other, so as to produce an infinite complexity of pain and pleasure; he considers man in his own nature and in his ordinary life as contemplating this with a certain quantity of immediate knowledge and with certain convictions, intuitions, and deductions, which from habit acquire the quality of intuitions.

His account of the method of communication which he hoped for in his poetry also shows the influence:

> our continued influxes of feeling are modified and directed by our thoughts, which are indeed the representatives of all our past feelings; and as by contemplating the relation of these general representatives to each other, we discover what is really important to men, so, by the repetition and continuance of this act, our feelings will be connected with important subjects, till at length, if we be originally possessed of much sensibility, such habits of mind will be produced, that, by obeying blindly and mechanically the impulses of those habits, we shall describe objects, and utter sentiments, of such a nature, and in such connection with each other, that the understanding of the Reader must necessarily be in some degree enlightened, and his affections strengthened and purified.

Wordsworth knew that his poetry might not "gratify certain known habits of association" formed in his readers by other men's verse. But he believed that human beings were fundamentally so alike that by depicting "incidents and situations from common life ... in a selection of language really used by men" he could make these interesting "by tracing in them, truly not ostentatiously, the primary laws of our nature; chiefly, as regards the manner in which we associate ideas in a state of excitement". By this he would improve his readers' minds without explicit didacticism.

In declaring that each of his poems had a purpose Wordsworth was striking at the somewhat dilettante fancy found in most previous poetry of association; indeed, he was guarding himself against a reproach commonly brought by later psychologists against the associationist school, that they described the mechanism of purely "reproductive" thought without regard for the directive influence of purposive thinking which selects associations in accordance with some "set of attention", or special "awareness".[13]

Wordsworth was rarely content with isolated associations, or with

> the shapes
> Of wilful fancy grafted upon feelings
> Of the imagination

such as he used in "The Daisy" (1802), though he saw the possibility of pursuing Fancy

> Through all her transmigrations, till she too
> Was purified, had learn'd to ply her craft
> By judgment steadied . . .

and the mind became

> satisfied
> And soothed with a conception of delight
> Where meditation cannot come, which thought
> Could never heighten.
>   (*The Prelude* [1805], XIII. 291–306)

His view of the imagination as not only pervasive but creative and visionary went far beyond anything in Hartley, Reid, or Dugald Stewart. To read Wordsworth along with these writers illuminates his relationship to eighteenth-century thought and his special contribution to the notion of mind. *The Prelude* might indeed be considered as an attempt to carry out a suggestion by Stewart, who in his *Elements of the Philosophy of the Human Mind* (1792) declared that individuals could be assisted in the culture of their minds

> if they were previously led to take a comprehensive survey of human nature in all its parts; of its various faculties and powers, and sources of enjoyment; and of the effects which are produced on these principles by particular situations. It is such a knowledge alone of the capacities of the mind, that can enable a person to judge of his own acquisitions.[14]

Stewart saw the limits of the mechanistic approach:

it is no less unphilosophical to attempt an explanation of perception, or of the association of ideas, upon mechanical principles, than it would be to explain the phenomenon of gravitation by supposing, as some ancients did, the particles of matter to be associated with principles of motion (p. 10).

The association of ideas (wrote Stewart) is "perfectly distinct from the power of the imagination" but "is immediately and essentially subservient to all its exertions.... It is obvious that a creative imagination ... implies a power of summoning up, at pleasure, a particular class of ideas: and of ideas related to each other in a particular manner; which power can be the result only, of certain habits of association which the individual has acquired" (p. 216). This leads Stewart to make a tentative distinction between Fancy and Imagination. After citing Reid's remark that "the part of our constitution on which the association of ideas depends was called, by the older English writers, the *fantasy or fancy*", he restricts the term "to that habit of association, which is subservient to poetical imagination" (pp. 216–17). Fancy is the "power of summoning up at pleasure the ideas so related"; its "office ... is to collect materials for the Imagination; and therefore the latter power presupposes the former, while the former does not necessarily suppose the latter" (p. 217). He does not explain *how* the imagination works, nor how it imposes selection upon the fancy. He uses the term "creative imagination" but does not show whether it differs from ordinary associative thinking. Both Wordsworth and Coleridge went further in emphasizing the power of imagination to suffuse the images of fancy with an overmastering and unifying emotional impulse. Yet there are other resemblances between Wordsworth and Stewart which show that in directing his self-examination towards the education he got from Nature, Wordsworth was not an isolated figure. For example, Stewart declares that perceptible objects are more potent in arousing and sustaining associations than ideas: "This influence of perceptible objects, in awaking associated thoughts and associated feelings, seems to arise, in a great measure, from their permanent operation as exciting or suggesting causes" (p. 212). This has something in common with Wordsworth's thanks to the "Wisdom and Spirit of the Universe", which has intertwined for him

> The passions that build up our human Soul,
> Not with the mean and vulgar works of Man,
> But with high objects, with enduring things,
> With life and nature, purifying thus
> The elements of feeling and of thought,
> And sanctifying, by such discipline,
> Both pain and fear, until we recognize
> A grandeur in the beatings of the heart.
> (*The Prelude*, I. 428-41)

Wordsworth's explanation of the "numinous" quality of his boyhood experiences likewise accords with Stewart's doctrine:

If the first conceptions . . . which an infant formed of the Deity, and its first moral perceptions, were associated with the early impressions produced on the heart by the beauties of nature, or the charms of poetical description, those serious thoughts which are resorted to by most men merely as a source of consolation in adversity . . . would recur spontaneously to the mind, in its best and happiest hours; and would insensibly blend with all its purest and most refined enjoyments (p. 31).

Compare Wordsworth's account (*The Prelude*, V. 608-29) of how the youthful "wanderer among the woods and fields" receives also

> enduring touches of deep joy
> From the great Nature that exists in works
> Of mighty Poets.

When Wordsworth at the end of the 1805 version of *The Prelude* wrote of himself and Coleridge as "United helpers forward of a day Of firmer trust", when "what we have loved Others will love; and we may teach them how";

> Instruct them how the mind of man becomes
> A thousand times more beautiful than the earth
> On which he dwells,
> (XIII. 438-48)

he was looking forward, as did the liberal Stewart (who was a supporter of the new "economical system" of Condorcet and Adam Smith), to a "happy aera" when, it might be, "all the prepossessions of childhood and youth were directed to support the pure and sublime truths of an enlightened morality" (p. 30). In such a state of society, the understanding

> instead of being obliged to struggle, at every step, with early prejudices, its office was merely to add the force of philosophical conviction, to impressions, which are equally delightful to the imagination and dear to the heart. The prepossessions of childhood would, through the whole of life, be gradually acquiring strength from the enlargement of our knowledge; and, in their turn, would fortify the conclusions of our reason, against the sceptical suggestions of disappointment or melancholy (p. 30).

In another passage Stewart expounds the aims and requirements of a good education:

> to watch over the associations which [children] form in their tender years; to give them early habits of mental activity; to rouze their curiosity, and to direct it to proper objects; to exercise their ingenuity and invention; to cultivate in their minds a turn for speculation, and at the same time preserve their attention alive to the objects around them; to awaken their sensibilities to the beauties of nature, and to inspire them with a relish for intellectual enjoyment; —these form but a part of the business of education; and yet the execution of even this part requires an acquaintance with the general principles of our nature, which seldom falls to the share of those to whom the instruction of youth is commonly intrusted (p. 18).

This is largely a statement of what Wordsworth sought to show he had done for himself, assisted by the presences of Nature, the "privileg'd world Within a world" of Cambridge, books, walking tours, London, French politics, disillusionment, "spots of time", his reverie on Salisbury Plain—all the

>   dark
> Invisible workmanship that reconciles
> Discordant elements and makes them move
> In one society.
>   (*The Prelude*, [1805], I. 352-5)

On the level of consciousness, the unifying principle within him was a growing apprehension of nature's part in man and of man's place in nature, of the divinity that works through all, and of the mind's ability to perceive this intuitively. It developed from his early animism to the meditation on Snowdon when he realized in the blue chasm below the moonlit vapours, "the Soul, the Imagination of the whole", and compared the domination which Nature oftentimes "Exerts upon the outward face of things", to the shaping spirit of the Imagination in "mighty minds":

> They from their native selves can send abroad
> Like transformations, for themselves create
> A like existence, and whene'er it is
> Created for them, catch it by an instinct;
> Them the enduring and the transient both
> Serve to exalt; they build up greatest things
> From least suggestions, ever on the watch,
> Willing to work and to be wrought upon,
> They need not extraordinary calls
> To rouze them; in a world of life they live,
> By sensible impressions not enthrall'd,
> But quicken'd, rouz'd, and made thereby more apt
> To hold communion with the invisible world.
> Such minds are truly from the Deity,
> For they are Powers; and hence the highest bliss
> That can be known is theirs, the consciousness
> Of whom they are habitually infused
> Through every image, and through every thought,
> And all impressions; hence religion, faith,
> And endless occupation for the soul
> Whether discursive or intuitive. . . .
>
> (*The Prelude* [1805], XIII. 66–119)

So the associationist psychology is transcended in a vision of the mind as approximating to the "primal unity", and holding all objects of thought in the "sense sublime Of something far more deeply interfused". This is the "creative imagination", described with greater power than even Coleridge ever managed to attain.

Wordsworth vindicated the power of the mind to apprehend directly the spiritual forces in the universe whether at moments when glimpses "like the flashing of a shield" seem to open up a new dimension or in reverie when

> with an eye made quiet by the power
> Of harmony and the deep power of joy
> We see into the life of things.

The fear of losing this faculty led him between 1802 and 1805 to enquire into the source of intuitive vision in the soul, and in the Ode on "Intimations of Immortality from Recollections of Early Childhood", as in his poem on Hartley Coleridge, he took over from Coleridge the idea of pre-existence and used it to explain the dim apprehensions of another life than sense and outward things, the "fallings from us, vanishings; Blank misgivings of a Creature Moving about in worlds not realis'd". These were due to reminiscences of the pre-natal life, as also were the unthinking joy of boyhood and the "joy within our embers" which recurs occasionally later. This Neo-Platonic idea was not a lasting part of Wordsworth's creed; it is a possible explanation which grips his imagination for the time being; and even in the Ode he turns from it to the more important consideration that the loss of the immediate heavenly vision can be compensated for by reflections based on experience, sympathy with suffering, "Thoughts that do often lie too deep for tears".

Towards the end of *The Prelude* Wordsworth realized the impossibility of permanently sustaining the mystical sense:

> Oh! who is he that hath his whole life long
> Preserv'd, enlarg'd, this freedom in himself?

He knew the tendency

> Of habit to enslave the mind, I mean
> Oppress it by the laws of vulgar sense,
> And substitute a universe of death
> (XIII. 120–43)

for "Reason in her most exalted mood". The vision waned, but even so he retained (poetically) more than Coleridge, in whom personal misery and the "abstruse research" of metaphysical speculation destroyed the "shaping spirit of imagination" along with the sense of a power in nature answering to the powers in man ("O Lady, we receive but what we give, And in our life alone doth Nature live!" ("Dejection")). For Wordsworth the "primal sympathy" implied the lifelong retention of at least a vestige of spiritual intercourse between the world and the imagination. So his poetry was not entirely ruined by the decline of spontaneous joy and mystical experience, even though he reverted to the kinds he had written in his early years and became again the poet of sentiments and affections, of topography and moral reflection.

If Wordsworth combined associationism with a vitalistic conception of imagination, Shelley more paradoxically combined a scepticism derived from Hume with Berkeleian immaterialism and Platonism. In the *Treatise of Human Nature* Hume, like Locke, rejected innate ideas and regarded knowledge as derived from impressions of sense and the "faint images" which afterwards remain to be used in thought. None of the relationships which we see in what we experience "can lead us beyond the immediate impressions of our memory and senses" (I. 390). Even the idea of causation is not absolute; it springs from the habitual association of successive experiences, and is a function of the imagination. We know nothing of things in themselves; we cannot prove the existence of a world outside us, or of our self, or of God. The self is "nothing but a bundle or collection of different perceptions, which succeed each other in an inconceivable rapidity and are in a perpetual flux and movement" (I. 534). Hume's scepticism about the powers of reason seems complete, but judgment is made to rest upon imagination and feeling. Reversing the customary belief that the reason should always be the master of the passions, he asserts that reason is "the slave of the passions" (II. 195). Moral principles originate in the feelings; and "Our most holy religion is founded on *Faith*, not reason".

After a short materialist phase in *Queen Mab*, where he declared mind to be a function of matter, Shelley accepted Hume's criticism of reason, though he confessed that "We are on the verge where words abandon us, and what wonder if we grow dizzy to look down the dark abyss of how little we know." The negative quality of such scepticism left a vacancy which he sought to fill in different ways.[15] The poetry which he first wrote under its influence between *Queen Mab* and "Mont Blanc" was saddened by the insubstantiality of all things human:

> We are as clouds that veil the midnight moon . . .
> Naught may endure but Mutability. . . .
>
> This world is the nurse of all we know,
> This world is the mother of all we feel. . . .
> ("On Death")

In 1819 he wrote in his essay *On Life*:

Nothing exists but as it is perceived. The difference is nominal between those two classes of thought, which are vulgarly distinguished by the names of ideas and external objects.[16]

This idea recurs in *Hellas* (1821) in which Ahasuerus declares that the universe of phenomena

> Is but a vision;—all that it inherits
> Are motes of a sick eye, bubbles and dreams;
> Thought is its cradle and its grave; nor less
> The Future and the Past are idle shadows
> Of thought's eternal flight—they have no being;
> Nought is, but that which feels itself to be.
> (ll. 780-5)

It is easy to understand how the conception fitted the poet's moods of despondency. But Shelley was not content with it. The power, intensity, and quickness of his mind, his ability to frame and hold ideas, made him erect on his disbelief in a material world a universe of thought. So Ahasuerus continues, to allay Mahmud's "Doubt, insecurity, astonishment":

>   Thought
> Alone, and its quick elements, Will, Passion,
> Reason, Imagination, cannot die;
> They are what that which they regard appears,—
> The stuff whence mutability can weave
> All that it hath dominion o'er,—worlds, worms,
> Empires, and superstitions. What has Thought
> To do with time, or place, or circumstance?
>   (ll. 795–802)

In the light of this we may answer the question at the end of "Mont Blanc" when, after describing the "Remote, serene and inaccessible Power" suggested by the mountain, he asks

> And what were thou, and earth, and stars, and sea,
> If to the human mind's imaginings
> Silence and solitude were vacancy?

The qualities apprehended by the human mind are not illusions; they exist. And Shelley found in the idealism of the Platonists and perhaps Berkeley the further support he needed to develop a substitute for materialism or scepticism. In *Adonais* (1821) he expressed with some assurance the unity of partial ideas in eternity:

> The One remains, the many change and pass;
> Heav'n's light for ever shines, Earth's shadows fly. . . .
> That Light whose smile kindles the Universe.
> That Beauty in which all things work and more,
> That Benediction which the eclipsing Curse
> Of Birth can quench not, that sustaining Love
> Which through the web of being, blindly wove
> By man and beast and earth and sky and sea,
> Burns bright or dim, as each are mirrors of
> The fire for which all thirst. . . .
>   (Stanzas lii, liv)

Shelley's "Platonism" is not dialectically attained, nor is it true Platonism,[17] but rather an intuitive, emotional flight over the gulf of man's ignorance about all but his own mental states.

In *Alastor* Shelley had traced the tragedy of the sensitive idealist who, attempting "to exist without human sympathy", "images to himself the Being whom he loves" and seeks its prototype not in the world of men but in intellectual solitude. In the "Hymn to Intellectual Beauty" he had vowed himself to just such a search, but the Spirit of Beauty now suffused the mutable universe as well as his own mind. His later work had been preoccupied with the question whether and how far the ideas in the human mind had correspondences in the world without. In *The Revolt of Islam* good and evil seem to be twin powers coexistent with the universe. *Prometheus Unbound* was a daring experiment in a drama whose characters were mainly either projections of the human mind or dim figures of the unknown universe. In this, however, good seemed to be the eternal force and evil a creation of the human imagination. So Jupiter the tyrant is an invention of Prometheus ("I gave all he had"), and the evil tormentors take their shape "from their victim's destined agony". Demogorgon seems to be Necessity, not the Necessity of *The Revolt of Islam* (IX. xxvii)

> whose sightless strength forever
> Evil with evil, good with good must wind
> In bands of union which no power may sever,

but the law by which evil—in reality a shadow—perishes by its own negative qualities as soon as Prometheus unsays his curse and becomes perfect. On the other hand, Asia ("Shadow of beauty unbeheld") represents a universal principle too vast to be apprehended by the imperfect mind of man. Beauty, Truth, and Goodness unite in the universal perfection and the mind attains them not by the stages of the Platonic dialectic, but only by love and suffering.

In his own attempts to attain to mystical union whether in love or religion Shelley often fails. In him desire kills contemplation; ecstasy is not an expansion of the self into the other, but a swooning dissolution. "I die, I faint, I fail", he cries in the "Indian Serenade", and this is not, as in *Epipsychidion*, because (ll. 588-91)

> The wingèd words on which my soul would pierce
> Into the height of Love's rare Universe,
> Are chains of lead around its flight of fire—
> I pant, I sink, I tremble, I expire!

The consummation of spiritual desire brings on the "little death" of physical lovemaking; the overwrought nerves cause not a unitary bliss but a chaos of sensibility.

When all the phenomena of the universe are reduced to thoughts, the poetic imagery describing them must lose concreteness. Shelley's febrile emotionalism accentuated this, so his imagery is kinaesthetic, shot through by vivid contrasts, fluent and restless as the world itself,

> Where nothing is but all things seem
> And we the shadows of a dream.

His use of symbols—boats, streams, isles, clouds, winds, leaves, caves, apparitions, veils—accords with the struggle of a mind torn between a sense of mutability and a longing for some permanent stay, a paradisal home; and whereas most poets clarify abstractions by using images from concrete objects, Shelley's procedure is often the opposite;

> He wanders, like a day-appearing dream
> Through the dim wildernesses of the mind.

The process is natural for one for whom the poet in *Prometheus Unbound* (I. 741-2)

> feeds on the aërial kisses
> Of Shapes that haunt thought's wildernesses

and whose song "Peopled with thoughts the boundless universe". But the failure to pin ideas down by concrete, stable similitudes makes Shelley's poetry difficult for earth-bound spirits;

> Alas, our thoughts flow on with streams, whose waters
> Return not to their fountain—Earth and Heaven . . .
> All that we are or know, is darkly driven
> Towards one gulf. . . .
>   (*Revolt of Islam*, IX. xxxv)

Nevertheless, the attempt to extend the bounds of poetry by making its substance not so much sensations as ideas of sensations, thoughts about thoughts, social sympathies and science, was a noble one. In his intuitive flight from doubts of man's ability to see beyond the grave ("The deep truth Is imageless") to an assertion of some form of immortality, Shelley anticipated the poets of the next generation in whom we find the same protest against the dissolution of the soul with its instruments:

> Shall that alone which knows
> Be as a sword consumed before the sheath
> By sightless lightning?
>
> (*Adonais*, xx)

But neither Browning nor Tennyson could so courageously accept the soul's absorption into the Soul of the World.

The associationist psychology shifted attention from social activities and needs to the machinery of the individual mind. Poetry followed suit and moved from the *Essay on Man* to *The Pleasures of the Imagination* and of *Memory*. Romantic poetry from Wordsworth onwards took a further step, and whether the "formal principle", as Professor R. S. Crane has called it,[18] was to show "a man in an evolving state of passion interpreted for him by his thought (as in the *Ode to a Nightingale*)" or "a man adjusting himself voluntarily to an emotionally significant discovery about his life (as in the *Ode on Intimations of Immortality*)", or—we may add—a man projecting his own self-criticism or his secret desires (as in *Alastor* and *Epipsychidion* respectively), the result was the same: an exploration by the poet of his own personal nature. This self-exploration is carried out with reference to the mysterious world outside the mind, but especially by subordinating senses, associations, and complex thoughts to a pervasive emotional drive and an intuitive consciousness of reality.

In the stage of development reached before his death Keats's sensuousness and his unmetaphysical immersion in "the strife And agonies of human hearts" restricted his attention to the earthly here and now. Wordsworth and Shelley on the other hand regarded the self as, however fleetingly, participant in and capable of apprehending the Divine power or Ideas, as needing for its fulfilment an immortal life. For neither of them at his best was the life after death a constant poetic preoccupation. But in *The Excursion* (1814) when the Wanderer, a Christian optimist, disputes with the Solitary, a despondent sceptic (Books II–IV), the poet, admitting that the "fervent raptures" of mystical vision are ephemeral, seeks not only to remember "What visionary powers of eye and soul" were his in youth, but also to fix

> A satisfying view upon that state
> Of pure imperishable blessedness
> Which reason promises, and holy writ
> Ensures to all believers....
> I cannot doubt that they whom you deplore
> Are glorified; or, if they sleep, shall wake
> From sleep, and dwell with God in endless love.
>   (Bk. IV, 157–90)

Any hope less than this is inconsistent with belief in God's infinite mercy and perfect wisdom. In the discussion between Faith and Doubt in *The Excursion* and in the particular reasons he gives for believing in the immortality of the soul, Wordsworth foreshadows the conflicts of the Victorian age.

The Wanderer in Book IV, after discussing the myths in which the "bewildered Pagans of old time" looked above and beyond their own natures, cannot believe that modern scientists will do worse:

> Shall men for whom our age
> Unbaffled powers of vision hath prepared,
> To explore the world without and world within,
> Be joyless as the blind?...
> And they who rather dive than soar, whose pains
> Have solved the elements, or analysed
> The thinking principle—shall they in fact
> Prove a degraded Race?
>   (IV. 944–54)

Yet he fears the analytic temper, "Viewing all objects unremittingly In disconnection dull and spiritless", and prefers to think of man as like a child listening to a seashell:

> Even such a shell the universe itself
> Is to the ear of Faith; and there are times
> I doubt not, when to you it doth impart
> Authentic tidings of invisible things.
>   (IV. 1141-4)

The achievements of science and philosophy must not endanger "the imaginative Will".

In the main the study of the mind took the rationalistic direction deplored by the poet. John Stuart Mill so far modified his father's theories in the light of his own experience of Wordsworth's poetry as to admit that though the most complex thoughts and feelings are generated by association, yet "the effect of concurring causes is not always precisely the sum of the effects of those causes when separate, not even always an effect of the same kind with them". Mill drew his analogies from the natural sciences, likening the blending of simple ideas to make complex ones to the mixing of the seven colours of the spectrum to make white; "these are cases of mental chemistry", he wrote, and "the laws of mind may be derivative laws resulting from the laws of animal life, and . . . their truth therefore may ultimately depend on physical conditions". A science of human nature was for him a possibility, but he refused "to reject the resources of psychological analysis and to construct the theory of the mind solely on such data as physiology at present affords". Psychology he thought further advanced than physiology when he wrote his *System of Logic* in the eighteen-forties.[19] Unlike many other Utilitarians he did not despise the cultivation of the feelings:

the imaginative emotion which an idea, when vividly conceived, excites in us, is not an illusion but a fact, as real as any of the other qualities of objects; and, far from implying anything erroneous and delusive in our mental apprehension of the object, is quite consistent with the most accurate knowledge and most perfect practical recognition of all its physical and intellectual laws and relations (*Autobiography*, ch. v).

This commonsense conclusion might be regarded as a reply to Wordsworth's fears of modern science, but the poet's doubts would not have been dispelled had he lived to read the essays on Descartes (1870 and 1874) in which T. H. Huxley declared his belief "that the human body is a machine, all the operations of which will, sooner or later, be explained on physical principles. I believe that we shall sooner or later arrive at a mechanical equivalent of consciousness, just as we have arrived at a mechanical equivalent of heat." Considering Descartes's hypothesis "That animals are automata", Huxley asserted,

The soul stands related to the body as the bell of a clock to the works, and consciousness answers to the sound which the bell gives out when it is struck....

It follows that what applies to brutes holds equally of men; and, therefore, that all states of consciousness in us, as in them, are immediately caused by molecular changes of the brain-substance.[20]

The relationship of mind to matter, consciousness to physical energies, was much debated at this time. Henry Maudsley in his *Physiology and Pathology of Mind* (1867) considered consciousness a by-product of activity in the brain. Others were not so downright. Alexander Bain developed the theory of "psycho-physical parallelism" to avoid postulating purely physiological causes, and Samuel Butler in *Unconscious Memory* cited the physiologist Ewald Hering who denied that necessarily

matter and consciousness stand in the relation of cause and effect, antecedent and consequence, to one another. For on this subject we know nothing. The materialist regards consciousness as a product or result of matter, while the idealist holds matter to be a result of consciousness, and a third maintains that matter and spirit are identical.[21]

There was much confusion, not removed by such statements as Huxley's, that "matter and spirit are but names for the imaginary substrata of natural phenomena".[22] Belief in the independent existence of the soul, and in its immortality, was shaken among many good men, while others were shocked by the publication of

John Tyndall's presidential *Address delivered before the British Association assembled at Belfast* in 1874, which marked a climax in "materialistic" thinking.[23] In this brilliant paper Tyndall surveyed the history of ideas about the relation of body and soul, showing how in the modern world the part played by soul has become more and more nebulous since Gassendi detached the soul from the body ("though to the body he ascribes an influence so large as to render the soul almost unnecessary"), and since Bishop Butler drew "the sharpest distinction between our real selves and our bodily instruments", and went so far as to assert that "our organised bodies are no more a part of ourselves than any other matter around us". This position Tyndall thought to demolish by referring to experiments and accidents to the brain. He admitted that the Bishop would be right if he asked the Lucretians: "Are you likely to extract Homer out of the rattling of dice, or the Differential Calculus out of the clash of billiard-balls?" No materialistic theory could explain the nature of sensation. Yet Tyndall declared that modern physics, comparative anatomy, and physiology had shown that "the activity of each animal as a whole was proved to be the transferred activity of its molecules", while Herbert Spencer's *Psychology* had demonstrated on the one hand how "the organism is played on by the environment, and is modified to meet the requirements of the environment", and, on the other, that "in its inherited organization are registered all the powers which it displays at birth". After summarizing various solutions (all unsatisfactory) to the problem of our knowledge of the outside world, he concluded, "Man the *object* is separated by an impassable gulf from man the *subject*." So long as there remained mystery and wonder about ourselves and the universe, there would be a place for religion:

Each succeeding age must be held free to fashion the Mystery in accordance with its own needs.... I would affirm this to be a field for the noblest exercise of what, in contrast with the *knowing* faculties, may be called the *creative* faculties of man.

M

This relegation of religion to a place outside the sphere of knowledge met with great disapproval, and Clerk Maxwell wittily satirized the "materialist" position in his verse "Notes of the President's Address to the British Association":

> they did not abolish the gods, but they sent them well out of the way,
> With the rarest of nectar to drink, and blue fields of nothing to sway.[24]

The defenders of faith and the knowledge above associative reason were not silent. The influence of the Cambridge Platonists had been carried on by the botanist John Ray who in 1691 attacked the Cartesians in *The Wisdom of God Manifested in the Works of the Creation*, agreeing with Cudworth that God's shaping power perpetually moulds the forms of plants using "the Subordinate Ministry of some Inferior Plastick Natures, as in his Works of Providence he doth of Angels". Newton and Bentley saw gravitation and sensation as evidence of Divine activity, and Samuel Clarke protested against the deist view that the universe was a machine "going on without the assistance of a clockmaker".[25]

This revulsion against the coldness of a mechanical universe was accompanied by a revival of mystical religion. John Wesley denied that faith was "a speculative rational thing ... a train of ideas in the head". It was a spiritual rebirth: "About three in the morning as we were continuing insistent in prayer, the power of God came mightily upon us, insomuch that many cried out for exceeding joy, and many fell to the ground." Religion for the Methodists and others became, as the late Monsignor Ronald Knox wrote, "identified with an experience".[26] The works of Jakob Boehme were studied by Newton, Blake, and William Law. Law answered the proponents of "natural religion" by asserting that man "has a Spiritual Nature or Principle in him entirely distinct from his rational Nature, and which, receiving its Life and Power from the Spirit of God, has alone the Power of owning, knowing, and receiving Jesus Christ our Lord".[27] The elevation of this "Light or Instinct of the Heart or Attraction to God" was an important factor in countering excessive rationalism. The traditions of religious intuition and poetic inspiration combined in a special way in the thought of William Blake in his attacks on the age of "Bacon, Newton, Locke". He loathed the separation of secondary from primary qualities, and the conception of the imagination as a mechanical compound of associations drawn from nature. He disliked Wordsworth's attempt to show "How exquisitely the individual mind . . . to the external World Is fitted". "You shall not bring me down to believe such fitting and fitted", wrote Blake, for "Natural objects always did and do now weaken, deaden and obliterate Imagination in me". Against the epistemology of Locke and Hartley he set the practice of direct intuitive vision: "All Forms are Perfect in the Poet's Mind, but these are not Abstracted nor compounded from Nature, but are from Imagination."[28]

In the nineteenth century several lines of thought converged in the campaign against rationalism. J. H. Newman in an Oxford sermon admitted: "All that we know, strictly speaking, is the existence of the impressions our senses make on us", but he escaped from scepticism somewhat as did Dean Mansel and J. B. Mozley, who in their Bampton Lectures (1848 and 1865) used Hume's attack on reason to argue for the acceptance of Revelation.[29] Newman asserted that, despite our fallibility, we know our own existence, and that the external world exists. This subjective assurance, which he called the "Illative sense", makes us receive as certain

the informations of sense and memory, of our intellectual instincts, of the moral sense, and of the logical faculty. It is on no probability that we receive the generalizations of science, and the great outlines of history. There are certain truths . . . and so as regards the world invisible and future, we have a direct and conscious knowledge of our Maker, His attributes, His providence, acts, works and will.[30]

The "Illative sense" makes him accept revealed religion as he accepts other forms of knowledge, but even more fully, "as absolutely certain knowledge, certain in a sense in which nothing else can be certain, because it comes from Him who neither can deceive nor be deceived".[31]

The Romantics, for whom the "Illative sense" was a commonplace, were mainly preoccupied with its imaginative value for life on earth. For many Victorians, however, the worth and happiness of this life depended on the probability of a life after death. It was an age of intellectual ferment. Biblical critics were doubting the plenary inspiration of Scripture. Evolutionary theorists were suggesting that man was not a special creation marked off from lower nature by his soul, but a descendant of the higher apes, who became human by chance through natural selection. Some scientists, as we have seen, were denying the soul's existence either in or apart from the body. Moreover it was an age of individualism, when education, the social order, culture, and religion itself were regarded as working for the improvement, enrichment, and preservation of the particular personality; an age of philanthropy when the well-to-do were uneasily conscious of how little *this* life had to offer the suffering poor—the starving Irish peasants, the Hindu widows, the Oliver Twists and crossing-sweepers of real life. Accordingly not only were all the old potent arguments in favour of immortality still valid, but egoism and altruism combined to show its necessity if the universe were benevolent. For robust optimists whose belief in perpetual social progress implied belief in perpetual progress for the individual mind, for earnest seekers anxious to preserve the superiority of soul over matter, for the bereaved who in that period of fertility and high death-rate had lost their loved ones, the issue was crucial. Not surprisingly, in some Victorian poets the romantic intuition is focused upon the spiritual progress of the individual and the species and upon the likelihood of the survival of consciousness after death.

Browning's early work exemplifies this trend. In *Pauline* (1833), a poem which John Stuart Mill thought revealed "a more intense and morbid self-consciousness than I ever knew in any sane human being", the poet proposes an autobiographical self-analysis akin to Shelley's self-projection in *Alastor*, promising to unravel his mind's first elements,

> not as they struggled forth
> In infancy, nor as they now exist,
> When I am grown above them and can rule—
> But in that middle stage when they were full,
> Yet ere I had disposed them to my will;
> And then I shall show how these elements
> Produced my present state, and what it is.

He then makes what is perhaps the clearest assertion in the period of the romantic Ego in its psychological aspect:

> I am made up of an intensest life,
> Of a most clear idea of consciousness
> Of self, distinct from all its qualities,
> From all affections, passions, feelings, powers;
> And thus far it exists, if tracked, in all:
> But linked, in me, to self-supremacy
> Existing as a centre to all things,
> Most potent to create and rule and call
> Upon all things to minister to it;
> And to a principle of restlessness
> Which would be all, have, see, know, taste, feel, all—
> This is myself; and I should thus have been
> Though gifted lower than the meanest soul.

His growth was fostered not by external nature but by his own imaginative activity, his yearning for God, his hero-worship of great men (he "lived with Plato"), the pleasures of feeling, the desire for knowledge. He boasts of the power of his imagination to call up scenes and situations; he has

> lived all life
> When it is most alive, where strangest fate
> New-shapes it past surmise . . .

and he approaches the Keatsian empathy,

> I can live all the life of plants, and gaze
> Drowsily on the bees that flit and play, ...
> I can mount with the bird ...
> Or like a fish breathe deep the morning air
> In the misty sun-warm water.

Later in the poem the hero realizes the ill-effects of his egoism:

> I have too trusted my own lawless wants,
> Too trusted my vain self, vague intuition,

and tells how, to him as to Tennyson in "The Palace of Art",

> As by an inspiration life seemed bare
> And grinning in its vanity; while ends
> Foul to be dreamed of, smiled at me as fixed
> And fair, while others changed from fair to foul
> As a young witch turns an old hag at night.

Through the rather incoherent Shelleyan idealism two features stand out: the poet's firm sense of personal identity, and the pleasure he takes in identifying himself with other creatures and tracing their situations and lives. This latter is significant for students of Browning's poetry, for henceforth, shrinking from self-confession in public, he found expression through forms of dramatic writing into which he could yet introduce his own views and vision of the world.

In *Paracelsus* he discusses the superiority of love over intellect, and the need for a union of the two. Paracelsus himself has the Faustian longing for knowledge. But he is self-obsessed: "I go to prove my soul". He lacks love; he believes "Truth is within ourselves", innate, and his goal will be

> Discovering the true laws by which the flesh
> Accloys the spirit.
>
> (Pt. I)

The inordinate, noble aim of the Renaissance scientist is set over against Aprile's gospel of love, to be expressed in the several arts:

LONGINGS IN THE NINETEENTH CENTURY

> Every passion sprung from man, conceived by man,
> Would I express and clothe in its right form,
> Or blend with others struggling in one form,
> Or show repressed by an ungainly form.
>
> (Pt. II)

Aprile has denied Knowledge as Paracelsus has denied Love; the two are "halves of one dissevered world".

Though acclaimed at Basle for his cures and experiments, Paracelsus has failed to find the secret he sought. The most he can claim is to be before his age and to foreshadow a better future:

> 'Tis in the advance of individual minds
> That the slow crowd should ground their expectation
> Eventually to follow. . . .
>
> (Pt. III)

He turns against the intellect:

> Love, hope, fear, faith—these make humanity . . .
> And these I have lost.
>
> (*Ibid.*)

At the last, in a sublime flash of insight Paracelsus sees man as part of God's order and he adds to the microcosmic view of the Renaissance the modern view of an evolving organism, the

> Imperfect qualities throughout creation,
> Suggesting some one creature yet to make,
> Some point where all those scattered rays should meet
> Convergent in the faculties of man.
>
> (Pt. V)

These faculties are three, not yet perfect: Power—to be used with care, inspired or checked by hope and fear; Knowledge—"not intuition, but the slow Uncertain fruit of an enhancing toil, Strengthened by Love"; and Love—described in terms reminiscent of Shelley's *Prometheus Unbound*. But

> these things tend still upward, progress is
> The law of life, man is not Man as yet,

till "all the race is perfected alike As man";

> But in completed man begins anew
> A tendency to God.

So in 1835 was foreshadowed the evolutionary idea of man's progress which at the end of the century produced the Utopian dreams of Wells and Shaw.

Such an extravagant vision of human potentialities was not permanent in Browning. Mainly he was content to describe the lower realms of human effort, though usually with the insistence that the mind of man should look beyond this world, which is a testing place for character:

> Leave *Now* for dogs and apes! Man has for ever!
> ("Grammarian's Funeral")
>
> Ah, but a man's reach should exceed his grasp
> Or what's a heaven for?
> ("Andrea del Sarto")
>
> ... progress, man's distinctive mark alone,
> Not God's, and not the beasts': God is, they are;
> Man partly is, and wholly hopes to be.
> ("Death in the Desert")
>
> On the earth the broken arcs; in the heaven, a
>   perfect round.
> ("Abt Vogler")

Scores of these familiar aphorisms could be given. Such a faith is founded not on science but on a personal intuition of the kind justified by Newman in *A Grammar of Assent*. Browning may owe something to Bishop Joseph Butler, whose *Analogy of Religion* (1736) asserted "the general doctrine of religion, that our present life is a state of probation for a future one" (ch. IV). In defiance of creeping intellect—though he could admire the dead Grammarian who "Gave us the doctrine of the enclitic *De*, Dead from the waist down"—Browning was for the big bold gesture in faith as in love. The human faculties were meant to be exercised, and he admired men who used them to the full "Though the end in sight be a crime, I say". This helps to explain the excellence of his studies of violent and criminal characters in situations bringing out their essential natures. The gospel of effort is found in Fichte and Carlyle, and the puritan sage may have influenced Browning. Later the doctrine of tensions and struggle enters the evolutionary psychology of Herbert Spencer ("The impression of resistance is the primordial, the universal, the ever-present constituent of consciousness").[32] For Browning, apparent failure was the inevitable result of the human mind's incapacity to fulfil its desires in act.

> What hand and brain went ever paired?
> What heart alike conceived and dared?
> What act proved all its thought had been?
> What will but felt the fleshly screen?
> ("The Last Ride Together")

The discrepancy was an earnest of human progress and divine recompense.

In "Christmas Eve" and "Easter Day", speaking in his own person, Browning defended his belief in religious intuition, and showed his tolerant understanding of Protestant and Catholic points of view with which he could not agree. For instance, although he was repelled by the harsh unloveliness of the chapel-salvationists, he recognized, as Matthew Arnold did not, their motivating love and aspiration, and was content to take the will for the deed. Preferring to trust insight before logic, he rejected the German biblical critic who undermined one by one the evidence's of Christ's divinity. He attacked the modern mechanists. Since God made man

> Able, His own word saith, to grieve him
> But able to glorify Him too,
> As a mere machine could never do,
> That prayed or praised, all unaware
> Of its fitness for aught but praise and prayer,
> Made perfect as a thing, of course.
> Man therefore stands on his own stock
> Of love and power as a pin-point rock. . . .
> (v)

He recognizes God as like himself. "And I shall behold thee face to face", he asserts, confident in the possession of an innate consciousness of God.

> We are made in His image to witness Him;
> And were no eye in us to tell,
> Instructed by no inner sense,
> The light of Heaven from the dark of Hell,
> That light would want its evidence.
>
> (xvii)

Later, in a passage (xxii) which throws much light on his own dramatic work Browning asserts the mingled state of human nature, aspiring to good yet blemished by the world. In "Easter Day", anticipating the fate of Eustace in Aldous Huxley's *Time Must Have a Stop*, the ultimate punishment for the man who has chosen the senses instead of the spiritual plenitude of which they form a part will be to be doomed eternally to live in the senses. But most men have a glimmer of the Inner Light, and in much of his work Browning sought to portray various approximations in different ages, sects, ways of life—Saint, Savage, Sage—to the knowledge of God suited to their condition. So Cleon and Karshish, on the threshold of Christianity, have an inkling of what they miss, David in "Saul" has a fuller vision of praise, Caliban is the savage of contemporary anthropology giving his view of a capricious demon-deity, yet behind it something other—the Quiet. Insight takes many forms—it may strike the erring, whimsical monastic painter Fra Lippo Lippi with the realization that to "paint the souls of men" he must paint their bodies with all their imperfections, and catch

> The beauty and the wonder and the power,
> The shapes of things, their colours, lights and shades,
> Changes, surprises;—and God made it all.

It may come to the cynical Bishop Blougram when he asserts that just when we feel safest in our unbelief

> there's a sunset-touch
> A fancy from a flower-bell, some one's death,
> A chorus-ending from Euripides,
> And that's enough for fifty hopes and fears ...
> To rap and knock and enter in our soul,

with intimations of "the grand Perhaps".

His witty harangue to the bewildered journalist Gigadibs may be considered a *divertissement* on Bishop Butler's argument in *The Analogy of Religion* that "if upon consideration of religion the evidence of it should seem to any persons doubtful in the highest supposable degree; even this doubtful evidence will, however, put them into a general state of probation in the moral and religious sense", and "the apprehension that religion may be true does as really lay men under obligations as a full conviction that it is true" (ch. vi).

Even the abominable Mr. Sludge, the exposed medium, is at times

> ready to believe my very self
> That every cheat's inspired, and every lie
> Quick with a germ of truth.

Browning hated short-cuts to knowledge of the hereafter of the kind attempted in Spiritualism, which the poet had experienced, with his wife, at a *séance* given by D. D. Home in 1855. But the subject fascinated him both by the flashes of truth it might reveal and by the moral and intellectual trickery it fostered. He was also briefly interested in mesmerism, which was much discussed in the forties and fifties. F. A. Mesmer's "animal magnetism" had been discredited before its discoverer died in 1815, but John Elliotson, professor of the practice of medicine at University College, London, had experimented on patients in University College Hospital, and in 1838 resigned his chair when the college council forbade "the practice of mesmerism or animal magnetism within the Hospital". In his Harveian Oration in 1846 Elliotson urged his audience to carry on the work. Meanwhile in Manchester

James Braid had coined the term "Hypnotism" for the sleep caused by sensory fixation.[33]

In his poem "Mesmerism" Browning imagines a man drawing the woman he loves from her room and house by concentrating on the image of her within his mind until his will enters hers and she is forced to do his bidding and come to him:

> I, still with a gesture fit
>   Of my hands that best
>   Do my soul's behest,
> Pointing the power from it
> While myself do steadfast sit.

The piece ends with a prayer against the misuse of the dangerous power. It was probably written in 1853 after the Brownings met Bulwer-Lytton's son Edward, who was "inclined to various sorts of spiritualism, and given to the magic arts".[34] It shows no acquaintance with Braid's new approach, but follows the popular notion, derived from Reichenbach, that a man endowed with peculiar powers of "animal magnetism" could impose his will on others. Du Maurier's Svengali in *Trilby* was a later, more sinister, embodiment of the same belief.

From his two *Madhouse Cell* poems of 1836 Browning kept an interest in unusual mental states: "Johannes Agricola" was a study in religious Antinomianism; in "Porphyria's Lover" the man strangles his mistress to keep her for ever at the moment when she is his. In more normal cases Browning loved to trace the approaches of souls, the setting up or breaking down of barriers, moments of spiritual awareness in love. Describing, in "Two in the Campagna", the failure of two people to come wholly together, he sees it as symbolic of "Infinite passion, and the pain Of finite hearts that yearn". In "The Last Ride Together" the failed lover has a temporary illusion of harmony. In "By the Fireside" a genuine fusion of souls is brought about in the Italian woods at twilight:

> A moment after, and hands unseen
> Were hanging the night around us fast;
> But we knew that a bar was broken between
> Life and life; we were mixed at last
> In spite of the mortal screen.

Such an intuitive awareness of union in love is the nearest equivalent in human relationships to the mystical knowledge of God.

It was easy for Browning to see good in the scientific theories of evolution which took England by storm after 1859, though he leaned more to Lamarck's insistence on Will than to Darwin's "natural selection". When "modern Science" in *Prince Hohenstiel-Schwangau* (1871) expects the prince to be shocked at the thought (not very accurately representative of what science was claiming):

> That mass man sprung from was a jelly-lump
> Once on a time; he kept an aftercourse
> Through fish and insect, reptile, bird and beast,
> Till he attained to be an ape at last,
> Or last but one,

the prince replies,

> I like the thought He should have lodged me once
> I' the hole, the cave, the hut, the tenement,
> The mansion and the palace; made me learn
> The feel o' the first, before I found myself
> Loftier i' the last, not more emancipate.
> From first to last of lodging, I was I.

Browning was in fact only adding an evolutionary treatment to the "microcosmic" theories of the Renaissance which he had studied in his youth;

> for many a thrill
> Of kinship I confess to, with the powers
> Called Nature: animate, inanimate,
> In parts or in the whole, there's something there
> Man-like that somehow meets the man in me,

and he insists on the continuity of the life through the process, for God "dwells in all".

Greatly though Browning esteemed man's intellectual aspirations, as time went on he emphasized much more the limitations of the mind. In the elegy "La Saisiaz" (1878) on his dead friend Ann Egerton-Smith, carrying on discussions he had had with her about a series of articles in the *Nineteenth Century* called "The Soul and Future Life", he argued for the goodness of life from an initial position of Cartesian scepticism.

> I have questioned and am answered. Question, answer presuppose
> Two points: that the thing itself which questions, answers—*is*; it knows;
> As it also knows the thing perceived outside itself— . . .
> Call this—God then, call that—soul, and both—the only facts for me

From these two certitudes all else follows, but he frankly admits that his reasoning is true for himself alone, since

> Knowledge stands on my experience: all outside its narrow hem
> Free surmise may sport, and welcome! Pleasures, pains affect mankind
> Just as they affect myself? Why, here's my neighbour colour-blind;
> Eyes like mine to all appearance: "green as grass" do I affirm?
> "Red as grass!" he contradicts me: which employs the proper term?
> Were we two the earth's sole tenants, with no third for referee,
> How should I distinguish? Just so God must judge 'twixt man and me.
> To each mortal peradventure earth becomes a new machine,
> Pain and pleasure no more tally in our sense than red and green; . . .
> What though fancy scarce may grapple with the complex and immense
> "His own world for every mortal?" Postulate omnipotence.

Postulate an omnipotent Deity and all grows simple; postulate further "that after body dies soul lives again", and Reason can build a fabric of hope.

> So I hope—no more than hope, but hope—no less than hope, because
> I can fathom, by no plumb-line sunk in life's apparent laws.

There is no breach in the law of life and order, and we are entitled to trust the larger hope. Since this accords with Browning's instinctive sense of natural relationships, he trusts his intuition. The Pope in *The Ring and the Book* expresses the poet's belief that the human mind, though limited, is illuminated by a vision of the real:

> O Thou—as represented here to me
> In such conception as my soul allows,—
> Under Thy measureless, my atom width!—
> Man's mind, what is it but a convex glass
> Wherein are gathered all the scattered points
> Picked out of the immensity of sky,
> To reunite there, be our heaven for earth,
> Our known unknown, our God revealed to man?
> (X. 1308-15)

So the end is not doubt but the certainty of a mind

> Within whose circle of experience burns
> The central truth, Power, Wisdom, Goodness,—God.
> (X. 1632-3)

The scepticism about human mind which at times saddened Browning was more habitual to Tennyson, partly through an inherited tendency to melancholy and his sorrowful upbringing, partly through his greater participation, from his early days at Cambridge, in the intellectual discussions of the time.

Much has been written about Tennyson's interest in the "evolutionary" sciences—astronomy, geology, embryology, physiology—for before 1832, when he wrote the first draft of *The Palace of Art*, he had studied Laplace on the nebular hypothesis, Cuvier on species, and Tiedemann on the theory of recapitulation in the developing embryo. Small wonder, for his tutor was William Whewell, who in the Third Bridgewater Treatise in 1833 showed how, under the guidance of God's "Creative intelligence", "The laws of material Nature ... operate at all times, and in all places; affect every province of the Universe and involve every relation of its parts".[35] Robert Chambers's *Vestiges of the Natural History of the Creation* (1844) came as no great shock to a mind so well prepared for evolutionary ideas. Of specific learning in current *psychological* books there is, however, no great evidence in Tennyson's poetry; he speculates freely from a fund of general reading and mainly on four topics: the evolution of the race, the development of the individual, dreams and insanity, and man's immortality.

Mr. E. D. H. Johnson has recently explored Tennyson's interest in dreams and visions, declaring that his poems "show a knowledge of dream psychology unique in the period and such as could only have been acquired through autoanalysis".[36] From the first he was a careful expositor of states of mind, often with a philosophical or religious implication. In "The Mystic" he described moods which, though not really mystical, show his ability to achieve a "still serene abstraction" in which

> He often, lying broad awake, and yet
> Remaining from the body, and apart,
> In intellect and power, and will, hath heard
> Time flowing in the middle of the night,
> And all things creeping to a day of doom.

The frequency of dreams and visions in the poems is an indication of Tennyson's curiosity about what happened when the conscious will was asleep. This interest became more important after Hallam's death, and *In Memoriam* contains several pieces in which sleep is explored (e.g., IV, LXVIII, LXIX, LXXI). In his mature work there are echoes of the notion that all life is a dream which in the early poem οἱ ῥέοντες he linked with the Heraclitean flux:

> All thoughts, all creeds, all dreams are true,
>   All visions wild and strange;
> Man is the measure of all truth
>   Unto himself. All truth is change.
> All men do walk in sleep, and all
>   Have faith in that they dream—
> For all things are as they seem to all,
>   And all things flow like a stream.

"The Two Voices" shows him obsessed by mistrust of the mind's power to achieve any certainty. The voice within that tempts him to suicide argues from the insignificance of the individual, the fallibility of senses and reason—all the old sceptical objections. He is saved by an innate love of life and the thought of a well-ordered Christian life of simple piety.

Much of Tennyson's trouble during the years of *In Memoriam* sprang from doubting the validity of rational judgments, especially about the place of man in nature, and the life after death. He never lost completely his belief in immortality; but Tennyson was a man of moods, and *In Memoriam* bears witness to the way in which he studied the manifold unprovable possibilities suggested by modern thought about the mysteries of nature, always with the stipulation:

> My own dim life should teach me this,
> That life shall live for evermore,
> Else earth is darkness at the core,
> And dust and ashes all that is.
>
> (XXXIV)

In him Browning's general assurance gave place to a queasy questioning. What happens to the mind after death? Hallam was always spiritually ahead of him, so Tennyson will be "evermore a life behind" (XLI); yet he hopes that he may still reap "A truth from one that loves and knows" (XLII). On the other hand, if the dead sleep till the Last Day, then he will not have lost his friend

> And love will last as pure and whole
> As when he loved me here in Time,
> And at the spiritual prime
> Rewaken with the dawning soul.
>
> (XLIII)

Perhaps the dead, though forgetful in the main of their earthly life, still have at times "A little flash, a mystic hint" of the past. Perhaps the growth of the child as he

> ... learns the use of "I" and "me"
> And finds "I am not what I see,
> And other than the things I touch"

is justified only if man has not "to learn himself anew Beyond the second birth of death" (XLV). Tennyson's desire for personal immortality makes him reject Averroes's doctrine that we fall "Remerging in the general Soul" of the world. The desire for immortality derives "from what we have The likest God within the Soul". Yet modern science shocks him with its suggestion that Nature conserves neither the individual nor the species (LV, LVI). This makes him all the more eager to believe that despite such waste, individual life persists "behind the veil" (LVI). He clings to the trust

> That nothing walks with aimless feet;
> That not one life shall be destroyed
> (LIV)

and although he knows himself "an infant crying in the night",

> I stretch lame hands of faith, and grope,
> And gather dust and chaff, and call
> To what I feel is Lord of all,
> And faintly trust the larger hope.
> (LV)

The confident intuition of Wordsworth and the early Browning has vanished. Yet *In Memoriam* does not end here. The poet revives; he expresses a hope that as man has risen from the ape and tiger, he will evolve into a "higher race" if he will control his destiny (CXVIII). He turns against science, declaring that knowledge must walk "With wisdom, like the younger child" (CXIV). He rejects the mechanical theory of human behaviour (CXX):

> I trust I have not wasted breath:
> I think we are not wholly brain,
> Magnetic mockeries . . .
> . . . .
> Not only cunning casts in clay:
> Let Science prove we are, and then
> What matters Science unto men,
> At least to me? I would not stay.

And he concludes (CXXIV) that if in his poem he *has* been a child crying in the night,

> Then was I as a child that cries,
> But, crying, knows his father near.

So the end is in faith and the love of God (CXXVI). But the faith is rooted in desire, not in proof, for as the Ancient Sage in a later poem declares

> Thou canst not prove the Nameless, O my son,
> Nor canst thou prove the world thou movest in,
> Thou canst not prove that thou art body alone,
> Nor canst thou prove that thou art spirit alone,
> Nor canst thou prove that thou art both in one:
> Thou canst not prove thou art immortal, no,
> Nor yet that thou art mortal . . .
>   wherefore thou be wise,
> Cleave ever to the sunnier side of doubt,
> And cling to Faith beyond the forms of Faith!

The argument might have pleased Bishop Blougram, and it expresses Tennyson's conclusion about the mind's limitations and man's right to choose what brings life rather than death.

His delicate poise on the knife-edge between belief and unbelief was not possible to all in his age. Arthur Hugh Clough, with a mind less tough than Tennyson's, portrayed in his poetry some of the despondency and incapacity for action described by Froude in his *Nemesis of Faith* and by other doubters of the soul's certainties such as Mark Rutherford.

In Clough's early poem *The Human Spirits* the questioning spirit urges more ordinary human spirits to question as he does, but they are unresponsive, being satisfied to take life as it comes:

> Dost thou not know that these things only seem? [he asks]
> "I know not, let me dream my dream."
> Are dust and ashes fit to make a treasure?
> "I know not, let me take my pleasure."
> What shall avail the knowledge thou hast sought?
> "I know not, let me think my thought."

Another spirit speaks of duty: he will do that though he knows nothing. The questioning spirit is unabashed. Finally he whispers to the one spirit that believes but needs not know—having faith:

> I also know not, and I need not know,
> Only with questionings pass I to and fro,
> Perplexing these that sleep, and in their folly
> Imbreeding doubt and sceptic melancholy;
> Till that, their dreams deserting, they with me
> Come all to this true ignorance and thee.

That is, faith and hope come only when questioning and doubt have stirred men from self-satisfaction and thoughtless habit to divine discontent. In a sequel written two years later Clough imagines these spirits as like "The maimed and halt, diseased and impotent" by the five porches (senses?) at the Pool of Bethesda, awaiting the miraculous visitant;

> But what the waters of the pool might be,
> Of Lethe were they, or Philosophy,

and whether the miracle was ever worked, the poet does not know.

In Clough's verse-novel *Amours de Voyage* the practical weakness of the questioning soul is fully revealed and the end is futility. In this story of an abortive love affair in Italy during the stirring days of the 1848 revolution, a highbrow young Oxfordian, Claude, writes home to a friend about his visit to Rome where he meets the three Misses Trevelyan whose father is in business and whose mother "Grates the fastidious ear with the slightly mercantile accent". More in Claude than his ear is fastidious; he falls in love with Mary but he believes from the start that he has no chance, since woman

> Ever prefers the audacious, the wilful, the vehement hero;
> She has no heart for the timid, the sensitive soul; and for knowledge,—
> —Knowledge O ye Gods!—when did they appreciate knowledge?
> (II. xiv)

As Georgina Trevelyan says "he really is too *shilly-shally*". Detached from life, he suffers from a disease of thinking which lessens his hold on identity: "All that is Nature's is I, and I all things that are Nature's". Like Keats or Whitman he can identify himself with other creatures:

> I am the ox in the dray, the ass with the garden-stuff panniers;
> I am the dog in the doorway, the kitten that plays in the window.
> (III. vii)

Yet he fears human passion:

> Life is beautiful, Eustace, entrancing, enchanting to look at; . . .
> Even so beautiful Earth; and could we eliminate only
> This vile hungering impulse, this demon within us of craving,
> Life were beatitude, living a perfect divine satisfaction.
> (III. viii)

He refuses to bind himself to any person, admits no obligation to the woman he has approached, yet he hates the self-consciousness which torments him so.

> *Hang* this thinking, at last! What good is it? oh and what evil?
> Oh what mischief and pain! like a clock in a sick man's chamber,
> Ticking and ticking, and still through each covert of slumber pursuing.
> What shall I do to thee, O thou Preserver of Men? Have compassion;
> Be favourable, and hear! Take from me this regal knowledge;
> Let me, contented and mute, with the beasts of the field, my brothers,
> Tranquilly, happily lie,—and eat grass, like Nebuchadnezzar!
> (III. x)

The last line, with its evocation of the insane tyrant become a beast, gives away his disgust at his own pathological revulsion.

His friends urge him to propose to Mary; he answers

> Action will furnish belief?—but will that belief be the true one?
> This is the point you know. However, it doesn't much matter.
> (V. ii)

Disgusted with his dilatoriness Mary's family take her away; he tries half-heartedly to follow, but then he asks

> After all, do I know that I really cared so about her?
>
> ... Indeed, should we meet, I could not be certain.
> All might be changed you know. Or perhaps there was nothing to be changed.
>
> (V. viii)

And so, with the bewildered girl shocked and trying to cover her humiliation, we leave him in fatalistic mood, "I will go where I am led, and will not dictate to the chances."

It is a story of weakness in passion, of the Questioning Spirit turned inward, of the ultimate scepticism about life. This is what happens to the Romantic self-consciousness when faith fails and reason eats up the affections, with too much looking before and after. The Victorian age of action produced people like this in real life—one thinks of Edward FitzGerald who could not bring himself to propose to the woman he loved; of Amiel's *Journal intime* which Arnold admired so much.

I cannot here trace the footsteps of others who went further than Clough into the Slough of Despond—James Thomson for whom the symbol of a godless world was the "Melancolia" of Dürer, or Thomas Hardy who came to feel, like Schopenhauer, that the mind of man was an upsurge of the unconscious Immanent Will of the universe, that his Gods were illusions of his own creation, and his "mountings of mindsight" were an error of nature, in which all went well till "the disease of feeling germed And primal rightness took the tinct of wrong". Hardy's moods of gloom were caused, not by mistrust of man's reason, but by a suspicion that the process of evolution had casually produced "a Consciousness To ask for reasons why", who had learned to "Use ethic tests [God] never knew Or made provision for". The development of percipience, sensibility, and reflection had brought tragedy into the world.

Such a view was an extreme reaction against the Romantic vision of the mind's union with God or Nature. But it was not characteristic of the later nineteenth century. Against it may be set the faith of a G. M. Hopkins who rejoiced to devote his self-consciousness to the service of God:

> Man was created to praise, reverence and serve God Our Lord, and by so doing to save his soul. And the other things on the face of the earth were created for man's sake, and to help him in the carrying out of the end for which he was created. Hence it follows that man should make use of creatures so far as they help him to attain his end, and withdraw from them so far as they hinder him from so doing.[37]

Accordingly, his poetry shows that the structure of natural things, the individual "inscape" of leaves and clouds and men, and the delighted exercise of his own imaginative and verbal dexterity were for him an exciting proof of the diversity of the Divine energy and a symbol of the Divine order.

Hopkins's friend Robert Bridges was also opposed to the pessimism of Hardy, and his long philosophical poem *The Testament of Beauty* (1928) was a tribute to the evolutionary view of mind. Bridges thought little of Browning's ideas ("You could not get a better example of a perfectly confused mind") or of Shelley's ("too childish or unconsidered for serious treatment"),[38] yet his poem belongs to the same tradition of philosophic poetry: it is an argument for religious faith and the power of man to perceive the unity of the world. Among his masters were Plato, Aristotle, Lucretius. Indeed, at first he called the poem *De Hominum Natura* with reference to the Epicurean's *De Rerum Natura*.

The primary feature of human life is the sense of Beauty which includes Truth and Goodness, and the poet seeks to trace the rise of this sense in the race and the individual, and its expansion into all beneficent activities. As Oliver Elton put it:

> He thinks of a driving force that presses for ever upward through the atom, through the organism, and then through all human experience, sensuous, aesthetic, rational, and spiritual. In this process beauty becomes, ever more and more consciously, *valued*, as well as perceived and expressed.[39]

Bridges fuses Platonism with the notion of "emergent evolution". Every man is

>   a unique creature, a personality
> in whom we broadly distinguish body and mind,
> and talk readily of either tho' inseparable
> and mutually dependent, together or apart
> and created expression of Universal Mind.
> And of the body I think as the machinery
> of our terrestrial life evolving towards conscience
> in the Ring of Reality; and thence of the mind
> as thatt evolved conscience, the which in every-one
> is different, as the body differeth also in each.
>   (IV. 883–92)

Man's intellect is formed "of the essential Ideas" in so far as he has come into contact with them; it is the

>   ultimat issue
> of the arch-creativ potency of Being, wherefrom
>   the senses took existence.
>   (IV. 902–4)

Individual minds are like the colour-bands in the spectrum whose combination makes white light. In art the artist tries to express "the Ideas which thru' the senses have found harborage" in him, bringing order into their "promiscuous company" as reason does in her different sphere.

The poem tells—as if in answer to Hardy—

> How the mind of man from inconscient existence
> cometh thru' the animal by growth of reasoning
> to'ard spiritual conscience. (IV. 1065–7)

From the first the soul's chariot has had two horses (like the steeds in Plato's *Phaedrus*), but these are both good if rightly used (II. 36). They are Selfhood and Breed. The "Self-regarding instinct", as others have called the first, perhaps began "in atom or molecule", and pushed life up the long ladder of plant and animal to man. It is early restrained by Breed, which shows itself in the parental instinct. Selfhood knows pain and suffering but may gain power through conflict. It produces aggressiveness and war. As the mind grows to reason, man is aware of "reality in

LONGINGS IN THE NINETEENTH CENTURY 185

the appearance of things", yet creates religion when "stirr'd by influences that intreating Reason Kindled unknown desires". Plato's Ideas should be renamed "Influences", since these are

> eternal Essences that exist in themselves,
> supreme efficient causes of the thoughts of men.
> (II. 838-9)

> Beauty is the highest of all these occult influences,
> the quality of appearances that thru' the sense
> wakeneth spiritual emotion in the mind of man.
> (II. 842-4)

Bridges traces the evolution of Breed as well as of Selfhood, showing how sex

> from like degrading brutality at heart,
> distilleth in the altruism of spiritual love
> to be the sublimest passion of humanity,
> (III. 209-11)

though in base natures it finds "parallel corruption". In love the soul should have first place, then the body, and lastly the intelligence. The differences between the sexes, springing from their functions, make women intuitive since in them spirit is incarnate, whereas man is led more by reason.

So the poet reveals the ladder of evolution, but the interrelationship between the parts of the universe is better imaged as a ring, since all comes from

> God, the Universal Mind,
> whither all effect returneth whence it first began.
> (IV. 121-2)

There are obvious reminiscences of Wordsworth in the poet's "belief that childhood has the purest, if not the surest, hold on the vision of beauty",[40] and also in the conception of duty as corresponding in the moral world to order in the physical world:

> Thru'out all runneth Duty, and the conscience of it
> is thatt creativ faculty of animal mind
> that, wakening to self-conscience of all Essences,
> closeth the full circle, where the spirit of man

> escaping from the bondage of physical Law
> re-entereth eternity by the vision of God.
>
> (IV. 125 ff.)

There were Victorian writers who declared that the doctrine of evolution could add nothing to the study of the human mind. As James Martineau coarsely put it: "If Darwin describes the inward conflict of an extinct baboon, he paints a picture of what remains for ever without witness", and "Nothing can be more chimerical than prehistoric psychology."[41] Bridges does not lay himself open to such objections. Nor does he venture into the deep waters of the Unconscious, though he realizes the importance of the racial heritage and the motivation of instinct. Indeed he attacks the psychoanalysts who

> impute precocious puberty
> to new-born babes, and all their after tumble in life
> to shamefast thwarting of inveterat lust.
>
> (III. 949-51)

Writing in the 1920's this 85-year-old man who was born in the year of *Vestiges of the Natural History of the Creation* makes use of modern social psychology as well as of the evolution theory in his noble assertion of man's growth to a state when

> In truth "spiritual animal" wer a term for man
> nearer than "rational" to define his genus.
>
> (IV. 1132-3)

His latter-day reconciliation of Platonism with science and Christianity depends not on reason so much as on man's intuitive realization that we are

> aware of . . . existences crowding
> mysterious beauties unexpanded, unreveal'd,
> phantasies intangible investing us closely,
> hid only from our eyes by skies that will not clear . . .
> And every divination of Natur or reach of Art
> is nearer attainment to the divine plenitude
> of understanding, and in moments of Vision
> their unseen company is the breath of Life.
>
> (I. 679-91)

A bold if not completely successful attempt at a philosophical poem, the *Testament of Beauty* thus sums up in a theory of "emergent evolution" the nineteenth century's exploration of self-consciousness and its debts to biological and racial forces. For this reason it may fitly close our survey of a century of hopes and fears about the scope of the human mind.

Chapter Five ↝ THE INDIVIDUAL AND THE RACIAL IMAGE IN MODERN POETRY

Previously the study of the mind had been inextricably bound up with the history of philosophy, from which in the seventeenth and eighteenth centuries it drew correspondences with the prevalent interest in mathematics and mechanics; but in the nineteenth century psychology became ever more closely associated with the new sciences of the living organism.[1] In 1843 John Stuart Mill could deplore any close dependence upon physiology on the ground that "imperfect as is the science of mind, ... it is in a considerably more advanced state than the portion of physiology which corresponds to it" (*Logic*, ch. IV, §2). But in the latter half of the century experimental physiology gave birth to experimental psychology. It would be irrelevant here to survey early developments in "physiological psychology", since few poets showed any acquaintance with the work of Sir Charles Bell, Magendie, Hall, Claude Bernard, or Helmholtz, and until the First World War literature was mainly conceived in terms of the old faculty-psychology and associationism. During the past forty years, however, the acceptance of experimental psychology as a "respectable" study in the universities, the spread of psychoanalytic theory and practice, and the popularization of psychological ideas by press and radio have coincided with the rise of a new "intellectual" poetry and of a belief that the poet should show his awareness of current science. In considering what poets have thought about the mind since 1880 we may perceive differences in the particularity and depth of scientific influence during the first and second halves of the period.

The spread of evolutionary thought and the ever-increasing realization of the close connection between the mind and the physiological activities of brain and nerves made psycho-physical relationships a perpetual theme of controversy. The soul was by no means banished, but its operations seemed more and more tenuous because not open to objective experimental check. Some enquirers came to agree with T. H. Huxley that "all states of consciousness in us, as in [animals], are immediately caused by molecular changes of the brain-substance". It was no big step from this to the more recent assertion of Berman: "The chemistry of the cell is the chemistry of the soul"; "The grey walls of the brain, the glands of internal secretion, the pituitaries, the pineal, the thymus, the thyroid and parathyroids, the liver and the pancreas, the adrenals and the sex-glands, constitute the core of our personality, because they are the mediators between the individual and the environment."[2] The influence of this modern doctrine can be traced in the earlier novels of Aldous Huxley, who at one time took a horrified pleasure in pointing out the biological origins of man's highest emotions.[3] The later Victorian poets were rarely interested in the apparatus of psycho-physical processes, but many were affected by the apparent implications of a mechanistic explanation of behaviour which sapped belief in free will and the absolute validity of religious intuition.

That the "Decadent" or "Aesthetic" school was moved thus is apparent from Walter Pater's "Conclusion" (1868) to *The Renaissance*, which may be regarded as the manifesto not only of the New Hedonism but also of Impressionism in British art. Pater's essay applied to ethics and artistic taste doctrines which went back to Hume's statement:

I venture to affirm of the rest of mankind that they are nothing but a bundle or collection of different perceptions which succeed each other with an inconceivable rapidity and are in a perpetual flux and movement. The mind is a kind of theatre where several perceptions successively make their appearance. . . . The comparison of the theatre must not mislead us; they are the successive perceptions only that constitute the mind.[4]

In France the Abbé de Condillac, Étienne Bonnot, in his *Treatise on the Sensations* (1754) had derived a psychology from the sensations alone, imagining that a statue endowed with them and with memory could achieve reflection and morality, since no man knows anything about objects save through his senses: "But it matters little to know with certainty whether these objects truly exist or not. I have pleasant or unpleasant sensations and they affect me as much as if they expressed the very qualities of the objects to which I am driven to attribute them. I see myself, I touch myself, in a word I sense myself, but I do not know what I am." "To live is properly to enjoy, and that man lives longest who is most proficient in multiplying the objects of his enjoyment."[5]

More recently J. S. Mill had declared (*Logic*, ch. III, § 7–8):

. . . of the outward world, we know and can know absolutely nothing, except the sensations which we experience from it. . . .

All which we are aware of, even in our own minds, is (in the words of James Mill) a certain "thread of consciousness"; a series of feelings, that is, of sensations, thoughts, emotions, and volitions, more or less numerous and complicated. There is something I call Myself, or, by another form of expression, my mind, which I consider as distinct from these sensations, thoughts, &c. . . . But what this being is, though it is myself, I have no knowledge, other than the series of its states of consciousness.

Mill did not stop here. In his *Examination of Sir William Hamilton's Philosophy* (1865) he based the psychological belief in an external world not only on the sensations of the moment but also on "a countless variety of possibilities of sensation" of whose potentiality the mind is aware. "These various possibilities are the important thing to me in the world. My present sensations are generally of little importance, and are moreover fugitive: the possibilities, on the contrary, are permanent" (ch. XI).

Pater probably did not know Condillac's *Treatise*, but he admired Hume and Mill. Ignoring the latter's later theory, and the important traces of past experience, he drew parallels between the flux of atoms in physical life and that of thought: "What is the whole physical life in [any] moment but a combination of natural elements to which science gives their names? . . . Our physical life is a perpetual motion of them." In the mind the things which seem so solid around us are dissipated on reflection:

> Each object is loosed into a group of impressions—colour, odour, texture—in the mind of the observer. And if we continue to dwell in thought on this world, not of objects . . . but of impressions, unstable, flickering, inconsistent, which burn and are extinguished with our consciousness of them, it contrasts still further; the whole scope of observation is dwarfed to the narrow chamber of the individual mind. . . . Every one of those impressions is the impression of the individual in his isolation, each mind keeping as a solitary prisoner its own dream of a world.

Instead of driving Pater into despair, this limitation of the mind acts as a stimulus. Our aim in life should be to make the most of the passing sensations and ideas.

> Not the fruit of experience, but experience itself, is the end. . . . How shall we pass most swiftly from point to point, and be present always at the focus where the greatest number of vital forces unite in their purest energy? To burn always with this hard gemlike flame, to maintain this ecstasy, is success in life. . . . While all melts under our feet, we may well catch at any exquisite passion, or any contribution to knowledge that seems by a lifted horizon to set the spirit free for a moment, or any stirring of the senses, strange dyes, strange colours, and curious odours, or work of the artist's hands, or the face of one's friend.[6]

A life of "curiously testing new opinions and courting new impressions", of refusing to form habits, must lead to eclecticism. Pater like Mill recognizes that sensations have different intensities and refinements and that altruistic behaviour is one form of self-titillation, but he finds in art the most satisfactory form of experience: "For art comes to you professing frankly to give nothing but the highest quality to your moments as they pass, and simply for those moments' sake."

In after years Pater modified somewhat his ethical ideas, but his early doctrine affected Oscar Wilde and others whose work reached a climax in the Yellow Book phase of the nineties. Wordsworth's aim had been to keep his eye on the object, and Arnold had preached the need in art and criticism "to see life steadily and see it whole". To the Aesthetes such an ideal was illusory. Engaged in a struggle to extract from the passing moment an intense thrill, to enjoy and set down the flickering patterns of life's phantasmagoria, they disdained or despaired of all attempt at impersonality, and saw in art not the transcript of an objective ideal but the projection of the moment's experience, without moral or religious *arrière pensées*, but in enduring form. To Pater's disciples art was a perpetuation of sensations, emotions, moods, and personalities, and since after the Franco-German war there was a vast increase in cultural interchange between France and England, the influence of Gautier and of the *Symbolistes* came together with that of French Impressionist painting.

The Impressionists combined with their scientific use of the palette to excite visual vibrations blending colours in the eyes of the spectators, an insistence on instantaneous vision and effects of evanescent light. "There is only one true way", wrote Manet, "to set down at one go what one sees. When that's done, all's done. When it isn't, one starts again. All the rest is humbug." And, "What I should have liked would have been to set down women like yourself in the greenery, among the flowers, on the beaches, there where the air eats away the edges, but where all is fused and confused in the splendours of the light."[7] After Whistler with his twilight effects and colour compositions the New English Art Club, with Shannon, Sickert, McEvoy, and Wilson Steer, followed the French example with varying degrees of boldness.

We must not confuse Impressionism in painting with that in

literature—but both had in common a desire to capture the moment's sensations, to see the world through the eye, to give oneself up to what entered sensation and feeling from the outer world, and to be accurate in delineating and discriminating the interplay of sense-impression and emotion. The community of aim explains the considerable influence of Impressionist painting on English poetry in the last quarter of the century. This influence is apparent in the work of W. E. Henley and Arthur Symons. Impressionism inspires the *London Voluntaries* (1890-2) in which Henley tries to catch (as Shelley had done in the Euganean Hills) the atmospheric changes through the day, the play of light and colour dissolving objects into evanescent shiftings of shape. For him "the golden end of afternoon" in the Strand shimmers like a "Symphony in Gold" by Whistler: and dawn is

> the Wizard Hour!
> His silent, shining sorcery winged with power!
> Still, still, the streets, between their carcanets
> Of linking gold, are avenues of sleep.
> But see how gable ends and parapets
> In gradual beauty and significance
> Emerge! . . .
>   And behold
> A rakehell cat—how furtive and a-cold!
> A spent witch homing from some infamous dance—
> Obscene, quick-trotting, see her tip and fade
> Through shadowy railing into a pit of shade! . . .
> What miracle is happening in the air,
> Changing the very texture of the gray
> With something luminous and rare?

Henley was not always a good poet, but he was trying to do something significant here, to catch the flow of sensations as they went by, to snare iridescence, the atoms of light and feeling, yet without departing from fact.

In making his verse a moment's monument Arthur Symons often emulates the work of contemporary painters of light and colour. At Dieppe, then the painter's paradise, he sketches in the manner of his friend Wilson Steer:

> The sea lies quieted beneath
>   The after-sunset flush,
> That leaves upon the heaped grey clouds
>   The grape's faint purple blush.
>
> Pale, from a little space in heaven,
>   Of delicate ivory,
> The sickle moon and one gold star
>   Look down upon the sea.
>
>   ("After Sunset")

Like Manet, Degas, and Toulouse-Lautrec he loves the city, haunting theatres and bars to catch fleeting glimpses by light of oil or gas of an Absinthe Drinker, Emmy the shameless innocent in a Berlin music-hall, Javanese Dancers, Behind the Scenes at the Empire:

> The little painted angels flit,
> See, down the narrow staircase, where
> The pink legs flicker over it!
>
> Blonde, and bewigged, and winged with gold,
> The shining creatures of the air
> Troop sadly, shivering with cold. . . .

But Symons is a victim of the world he describes. Life is but a dream, a puppet-play of eternal recurrence.

> The modern malady of love is nerves.
> Love, once a simple madness, now observes
> The stages of his passionate disease,
> And is twice sorrowful, because he sees
> Inch by inch entering, the fatal knife.
>
>   ("Nerves")

He explores many moods of love, from affection for a child or a cat to the light encounters of the night, his raging passion for a bought woman, and "the desert of virginity" in Bianca's body, "Rigid with sterile ecstasies".

He was frankly a "decadent", exploring not only "strange dyes, strange colours, and curious odours" but also all kinds of strange experiences and abnormal passions. In this he was typical of a whole generation of artists whose work has been related by Professor Mario Praz in his brilliant study, *The Romantic Agony* (1933), to a long Romantic tradition of sadism, masochism, satanism, and other perverse fantasies in several literatures. The artistic tradition was accentuated in the later nineteenth century by the scientific study of psychopathology. This may be said to have begun with F. J. Gall's work on the brain, which he pursued in prisons and lunatic asylums as well as among ordinary people before writing *Les Fonctions du Cerveau* (1822). Unfortunately he was chiefly remembered for his erroneous phrenological doctrines —which influenced Hugo, Balzac, and Dickens. After Gall, Prosper Lucas showed the importance of heredity among criminals; B. A. Morel ascribed habitual criminality to "degeneration", which he defined as "a morbid deviation from the normal type of humanity" (*Les Dégénérescences*, 1857), and P. C. Despine in his *Psychologie Naturelle* (1868) discussed instinctive criminality as "the insanity of the sane". In England H. Maudsley and J. Nicholson contributed to an understanding of irresponsibility in lunatics and law-breakers; but the greatest step in criminal psychology was taken in Italy when Cesare Lombroso at the University of Pavia found in Darwin's *Origin of Species* (1859) a biological basis for the study of mental aberrations, and in his *L'Uomo Delinquente* (1876–89) used anthropometry to support psychology and stressed the effects of mental and physical atavism and diseases such as epilepsy. To some extent he was preceded by the early work of R. von Krafft-Ebbing.

Not only criminality but also genius came to be regarded as a deviation from the norm. The old idea of the poet as an inspired prophet was not ousted by Wordsworth's conception of him as "a man speaking to men" and like his fellows save for a more refined and an intenser organization of his faculties. Schiller had described the genius as either naïve and instinctive or sentimental and self-conscious. Now however fresh truth was found in Dryden's maxim, "Great wits are sure to madness near allied". Magnan wrote of the "higher degenerates", Maudsley of "borderland dwellers", Lombroso of "mattoids" (not quite insane) and "graphomaniacs" (semi-insane persons with an itch to write). Highly gifted degenerates, declared the Italian alienist, might by their special attainments be valuable (though inconvenient) members of society. According to Legrain, "The degenerate may be a genius"; according to Guérinsen, "Genius is a disease of the nerves". Francis Galton stated: "Great men may be even indebted to touches of madness for their greatness; the ideas by which they are haunted, and to whose pursuit they devote themselves, and by which they rise to eminence, having much in common with the monomania of insanity."[8] Havelock Ellis cited Verlaine as a type of criminal mind with a "curious power of expressing the most delicate *nuances* of sentiment side by side with the crudest, most unabashed impulses of cynical depravity, self-revelations of sexual perversity" (*The Criminal*, 1890, pp. 187–90). J. F. Nisbet studied these phenomena in *The Insanity of Genius* (1891).

Such was the scientific thought which, percolating through press and public opinion, helped to transform the Bohemianism of Victorian artists from the happy-go-lucky youthfulness depicted in H. Murger's *Vie de Bohème* (1845) to a cult of deliberate abnormality which encouraged poets to accentuate their oddities and give free rein to their wildest cravings. If genius were abnormal, to be abnormal might be a proof of genius. The exploitation of psychopathic states was of course not mainly caused by science. It was due also to the breakdown of orthodox faiths, to a protest against Victorian convention; due also to a desire to extend the frontiers of art so as to include the whole of life frankly and naturalistically. Moreover a growing awareness of the cultural gulf between art and the philistine public fostered a self-conscious separation, the cultivation of shocking aberrations, of drink or drugs, as if the artists were resolved to live up to the opinion of them held by alienists and puritan moralists.

In accordance with this fashion, Symons wrote a poetry of felons and harlots, of Baudelairean "Flowers of Evil", of conscious sinning against God and self. He is *Amoris Victima*, a betrayer of innocents, haunter of brothels. He writes "Studies in Strange Sins (After Beardsley's Designs)" celebrating Priapus (with his "god's virility, With woman's breasts that passionately rise") and the perversions of Salome. In "Ballad of the Café Royal" he notes, "Here comes a girl with disenchanted eyes, Close followed by another, shamelessly." He writes of Huysmans' Des Esseintes morbidly attracted by eyes, "Eyes of the morbid morphine-drunk women whose gazes Drag at one's senses, drift in one's veins . . ." Imagining a young woman "Of the beast pernicious, malicious, in bestiality" he aches to possess her. He hints at the madness which periodically overtook him when, in "The Body", he describes "his nature's twists", where "Strange creatures shake and dance that never trod Earth's floor, Nor ever entered in nor shut the door". Such febrile stuff is valuable chiefly as a case-history. There was too much of it in the nineties, but it has considerable historical significance since it brought to public notice moods and manners previously regarded as unsuitable for poetic expression: this Symons recognized when he wrote: "The moods of men! There I find my subject, there the region over which art rules: and whatever has once been a mood of mine, though it has been no more than a ripple on the sea, and had no longer than that ripple's duration, I claim the right to render, if I can, in verse" (*London Nights*, 1897 ed., Preface).

Hospital poems were not infrequent in a period when so many poets became patients in them, and when their development brought them to popular as well as scientific notice. Henley wrote journalistically of his impressions "In Hospital". Symons made his "Jezebel Mort", like so many heroines of the French naturalistic novel, end

in hospital grey, whose walls were built by no priest,
Where a white glare shines on one's very self in one's bed,
Drifting over one's skin, touching the hair on one's head.

More sentimentally Dowson wrote "To One in Bedlam", envying his delusions, his "long laughing reveries". For the Irish poets insanity at large had a more Wordsworthian quality as in Yeats's early "Ballad of Moll Magee", or was associated with the old tradition of the wisdom of the innocent fool, careless of modern science.

The fashion for "decadent" poetry was short-lived and never very widespread in England. It received its death-blow with the disgrace of Oscar Wilde, but attacks on it had been frequent, and the translation from the German of Max Nordau's *Degeneration* (1895), which went into eight editions within a year, contributed to its disgrace. Dedicating his work to Lombroso, Nordau declared that his intention was to carry the master's method into the domain of art and literature in order to warn the age against the corrupting influence of much modern art. Aspiring to a "really scientific criticism" based on "the psycho-physiological elements from which [art] sprang", he argued that Rossetti, Baudelaire, Wagner, Ibsen, Zola, Tolstoy, Maeterlinck, Hauptmann, and the French Symbolists and Impressionists were all "degenerates" in the strict sense of the word, and their work worthless. Crude and violent though the onslaught was, it appealed to the conservative in art and the conventional in morals. There was a revulsion among publishers and poets towards tradition and respectability.

In the "Georgian" poets of 1900-20, Impressionism turned away from the hothouse febrility, the gaslit realism of the nineties, and went out into the open air, to produce a simple poetry of observation and self-analysis, reworking Romantic themes such as the pleasures of nature, pity for animals, delight in the child mind. It was still a poetry of the fleeting moment, but there was an endearing freshness about it, though it avoided much discussion of moral or religious questions. The tramp-poet W. H. Davies, who could describe lodging-house life realistically, preferred to sing with Elizabethan naïvety of the sensuous pleasures of idleness:

> If it be summer time, then what care I
> For naked feet and flesh through tattered garb?
> ("The Jolly Tramp")

He loved "to stand and stare", to capture the joy of some unexpected concatenation:

> A rainbow and a cuckoo's song
> May never come together again;
> May never come
> This side the tomb.
> ("A Great Time")

The ex-sailor John Masefield swung between moods of realism, Yeatsian nostalgia, and swashbuckling gaiety:

> Laugh, for the time is brief, a thread the length of a span,
> Laugh and be proud to belong to the old proud pageant of man.

He catches the grace of a sailing ship leaving port, or returning after a long voyage. In "Biography" he recalls memorable moments of his life at sea and on land, when the "gleams were golden":

> O Time bring back those midnights and those friends,
> Those glittering moments that a spirit lends.
>
> When I am buried, all my thoughts and acts
> Will be reduced to lists of dates and facts,

he asserts, but what matter to him are

> Those hours of life that were a bursting fount
> Sparkling the dusty heart with living springs.

So he concludes

> Best trust the happy moments. What they gave
> Makes man less fearful of the certain grave.

Masefield is fully aware of the implications of atomism for mortality. In *Lollingdon Downs*, a sonnet sequence, he accepts the thought that death will destroy "The million cells that made a good man wise" (xxxiv); yet

> It may be, that the million cells of sense
> Loosed from their seventy years' adhesion, pass
> Each to some joy of changed experience,
> Weight in the earth, or glory in the grass.
> It may be that we cease; we cannot tell.
> Even if we cease, life is a miracle. (xxxvi)

He marvels at the life in himself, "A thing of watery salt Held in cohesion by unresting cells" (xxxvii), and wonders (to no avail) which is the master cell that governs his activities (xxxviii–xxxix):

> What is the atom which contains the whole,
> This miracle which needs adjuncts so strange,
> This, which imagined God and is the soul,
> The steady star persisting amid change?

Insisting that "There is no God, as I was taught in youth", he is yet a pantheist:

> There is no God; but we, who breathe the air,
> Are God ourselves, and touch God everywhere.

Another poet of the Moment was Rupert Brooke, who in pieces like "The Great Lover" might seem merely a seeker of sensations as he catalogues his pleasures

> the rough male kiss
> Of blankets, grainy wood, live hair, that is
> Shining and free, blue-massing clouds, the keen
> Unpassioned beauty of a great machine,
> The benison of hot water; furs to touch. . . .

He pursues passing moods of joy, sadness, mockery in love. On the other hand, he likes to imagine an instant of time suspended, crystallized, as in "Dining-Room Tea", when suddenly "I saw the immortal moment lie";

> I saw the marble cup; the tea,
> Hung on the air, an amber stream;
> I saw the fire's unglittering gleam,
> The painted flame, the frozen smoke . . .
> I saw the stillness and the light,
> And you, august, immortal, white,
> Holy and strange; and every glint,
> Posture and jest and thought and tint
> Freed from the mask of transiency,
> Triumphant in eternity,
> Immote, immortal.

Then Time began to speed once more. "The bodies moved. The drifting petal came to ground" and experience became normal again.

The desire of the fluctuant mind for a changeless harmony recurs in "Thoughts on the Shape of the Human Body" (so different from the religious pæan sung long before by Traherne on the same subject), where Brooke shows the influence of the Jacobean poets he loves as he regrets that

> No perfection grows
> 'Twixt leg, and arm, elbow, and ear, and nose,
> And joint, and socket; but unsatisfied
> Sprawling desires, shapeless, perverse, denied . . .
> How can love triumph, how can solace be,
> Where fever turns toward fever, knee toward knee?
> Could we but fill to harmony, and dwell
> Simple as our thought and as perfectible . . .
> Grow to a radiant round love, and bear
> Unfluctuant passion for some perfect sphere!

The Heraclitean flux and the life of transient passion cannot satisfy for long. In his 1914 war sonnets he writes of the dead soldier as being "A pulse in the eternal mind", and as moving from the world of quick sensations into a frozen world of clarity and stability:

> Frost with a gesture, stays the waves that dance
> And wandering loveliness. He leaves a white
>   Unbroken glory, a gathered radiance,
> A width, a shining peace, under the night.

Such Georgian impressionists were not, after all, content with moments of quickened consciousness. The best of life did not consist in passing (in Pater's words) "most swiftly from point to point". They wished also for some permanent stay in the perpetual process and made tentative explorations of the mind's power to achieve it. The poets of this period made little attempt to follow the novel in experiments with the "stream of consciousness" technique. Occasionally, as in Henley's "In Hospital" sequence, Masefield's "Wild Duck", and Robert Nichols's "Into Battle", a swift staccato method is employed to jot down the impressions as they speed past.

> Twilight. Red in the West.
> Dimness. A glow in the wood.
> The teams plod home to rest.
> The wild duck come to glean . . .
> Wings linked. Necks a-strain,
> A rush and a wild crying. . . .
>   ("The Wild Duck")

In the main they use traditional syntax and verse forms, as Symons had done.

The interest in birds and animals shared by the Georgians with poets such as D. H. Lawrence and Rex Warner makes relevant some enquiry into the relations between modern poetry and the science of animal (or "comparative") psychology. The nineteenth century inherited the Cartesian separation of man with his immortal soul from the animals who had no souls; in considering this, "little distinction was made between a soul and a mind" (Boring). Examples of animal "intelligence" were however discussed, especially by humanitarian observers, and the evolutionists sought to establish elements of likeness and continuity between the animal and the human mind. Darwin explained certain emotional gestures (such as the sneer) as vestiges of animal behaviour (baring the teeth in rage), and his friend George John Romanes, accumulated anecdotes of animal behaviour[9] tending towards an anthropomorphic view of animals. Romanes used associationist terms to argue that "simple ideas" are found in some animals, and that "notional ideas" (abstractions and generalizations) are peculiar to man.

This neat scheme was opposed by C. Lloyd Morgan who laid down the principle that no action should be interpreted in terms of a higher psychological faculty "if it can be interpreted as the outcome of the exercise of one which stands lower in the psychological scale".[10]

Comparative psychology became fully experimental when E. L. Thorndike began to use puzzle-boxes in 1898. The careful study of bees, wasps, and ants by observers such as Sir John Lubbock, J. H. Fabre, and A. Bethe brought divided opinions about the intelligence of such insects.[11] In "Behaviourism", J. B. Watson and others tried to make a psychology which ignored consciousness, and the experiments of Jacques Loeb and those of Pavlov on "conditioned reflexes" have suggested that many of the mental activities of men as well as of dogs might be explained in mechanistic terms. Obviously it is difficult for man not to regard the psychology of animals as analogous to his own in so far as their external behaviour resembles his. But it is generally agreed that "with gross differences in structure, human and animal behaviour differ so greatly that it is not possible to penetrate the animal's consciousness by way of analogy" (Boring, *History of Experimental Psychology*, p. 551).

Poets, like other amateur observers, have always tended to interpret animal behaviour by analogy, but the last half-century has seen a great decrease in anthropomorphism. The Romantics selected those elements of animal behaviour most like our own. For them the animals retained the characteristics they had in the old fables. So Wordsworth in "Fidelity" tells the story of the dog who for three months watched over the dead body of his master on Helvellyn:

> How nourished there through such long time
> He knows, who gave that love sublime;
> And gave that strength of feeling, great
> Above all human estimate!

In "Incident Characteristic of a Favourite Dog" he told how the "loving creature"—a bitch—tried to save another dog which fell through the ice when chasing a hare; and in a "Tribute" to the same animal he celebrated in it

> some precious boons vouchsafed to thee
> Found scarcely anywhere in like degree!
> For love, that comes wherever life and sense
> Are given by God, in thee was most intense;
> A chain of heart, a feeling of the mind,
> A tender sympathy, which did thee bind
> Not only to us Men, but to thy Kind:
> Yea, for thy fellow-brutes in thee we saw
> A soul of love, love's intellectual law.

The humanitarianism found in Sterne's account of his meeting with a donkey recurs in Coleridge's "Lines to a Young Ass tethered near its Mother", with its regrettable exclamation, "I hail thee Brother", which gave so excellent an opening for satire by *The Anti-Jacobin* and Byron.

Of course many Romantic poems on birds and animals have nothing to do with animal psychology. "Bird thou never wert", writes Shelley to his Skylark, which is indeed merely a nucleus round which to spin a rhapsody of joy, and when he cries

> Teach us, Sprite or Bird,
>   What sweet thoughts are thine,

he ascribes to it all the happiness, love, and knowledge which he himself finds lacking on earth. The Georgian poets combined humanitarianism with rather more attention to likelihood. Keenly aware of the suffering of the creatures, they sympathized with dancing bears, "little hunted hares", and the "rabbit in a snare". Typical of the Georgian attitude is Ralph Hodgson's portrait of "an old unhappy bull Sick in soul and body both", defeated and left by the herd to die. Here the anthropomorphic analogy is exaggerated for pathos and to suggest parallels with human ingratitude, and throughout the poem observation is combined with biographical fancy. Thus the bull "dreams" of his past youth and growth, his battles, triumphs, and leadership. He is a "dupe of dream" as he imagines himself young again. He wakes and the swarm of flies round his eyes scatters as the vultures begin to swoop,

> Flocking round him from the skies
> Waiting for the flesh that dies.
> ("The Bull")

Masefield in *Reynard the Fox* reduces the analogies with human introspection to a minimum. The objectivity of Chaucer's "Prologue" is applied to animals as well as men; thus the hounds had

> noses exquisitely wise,
> Their minds being memories of smells; ...
> Their flesh was sinew knit to bone,
> Their courage like a banner blown ...
> Their joy to push him out of cover,
> And hunt him till they rolled him over.

The limitations of a fox's view of life are accepted:

> The fox's nose tipped up and round,
> Since smell is a part of sight and sound.
> Delicate smells were drifting by,
> The sharp nose flaired them heedfully ...
> A faint rank taint like April coming,
> It cocked his ears and his blood went drumming,
> For somewhere out by Ghost Heath Stubs
> Was a roving vixen wanting cubs ...
> He cocked his ears, he upped his brush,
> And he went up wind like an April thrush.

The effect of his passing upon other animals is not missed and the description of his reactions in the hunt as he makes for the land he knows fifteen miles away is a *tour de force*. Compare the method used by Rupert Brooke in two poems about fish. In "Heaven" Brooke uses the analogy between man and other creatures to jest at man's anthropomorphic conception of the after-life:

> Fish say they have their Stream and Pond;
> But is there anything Beyond?
> This life cannot be All, they swear,
> For how unpleasant, if it were!
> One may not doubt that, somehow, good
> Shall come of Water and of Mud.

Their God is a fish,

> Squamous, omnipotent, and kind;
> And under that Almighty Fin,
> The littlest fish may enter in,

while the fishy Heaven abounds in

> Unfading moths, immortal flies,
> And the worm that never dies.
> And in that Heaven of all their wish,
> There shall be no more land, say fish.

In another poem, Brooke tries more seriously to describe the fish's sensual equipment.

> In a cool curving world he lies
> And ripples with dark ecstasies . . .
> Those silent waters weave for him
> A fluctuant mutable world and dim. . . .
> ("The Fish")

Instinct is a "dark fire" in his blood:

> Dateless and deathless still,
> The intricate impulse works its will. . . .
> Sans providence, sans memory
> Unconscious and directly driven,
> Fades to some dank sufficient heaven.

There is a suggestion that the fish is aware of

> The myriad hues that lie between
> Darkness and darkness!

But the fish has little or no sense of hearing ("the secret deeps are whisperless") and its chief pleasure is tactual, in the rhythms of water,

> And joy is in the throbbing tide
> Whose intricate fingers beat and glide
> In felt bewildering harmonies
> Of trembling touch; and music is
> The exquisite knocking of the blood.

Obviously analogy is at work here again, for the final bliss—corresponding to human mysticism—is where under the mud

> The lights, the cries, the willows dim
> And the dark tide are one with him.

It is possible that Rupert Brooke had been reading, or listening to scientists discussing, recent work on animal behaviour. M. F. Washburn, in her text-book *The Animal Mind* (1908), had discussed the sensations of fishes, pointing out the importance for them of tactual experience. Many fishes have "lateral-line canals" along their sides through which they seemed to react "when the water in the aquarium was made to vibrate slowly" (p. 117). Some have "terminal buds", structures resembling taste buds, distributed over the skin, and are "sensitive to food stimulation applied to different regions of the skin" (p. 102). "For fishes the distinction between smell and taste becomes obscure" (p. 102). Their sensitivity to noise may reside mainly in the skin (p. 115), which is also sometimes sensitive to light (p. 140). There were various opinions about the fishes' power to discriminate colours, but general agreement on their ability to distinguish tones. To assume that Brooke had any direct knowledge of these findings would be far-fetched. His poem may well have been simply an exercise in Keatsian empathy.

D. H. Lawrence's poems on the creatures show less assumption of knowledge about their inner lives. In "Fish", for instance, he wonders at its strange sex-life, at the simple consciousness which knows only

> Himself,
> And the element,
> Food of course . . .
> Fear also!
> He knows fear! . . .
> Food and fear, and joie de vivre,
> Without love.

He imagines its watery pleasures and isolation—"A magnetism in the water between them only". But then he remembers how, watching a pike in a lake, he realized

> I had made a mistake, I didn't know him, . . .
> I didn't know his God,
> I didn't know his God. . . .
>
> And I said to my heart, *there are limits*
> *To you, my heart;*
> *And to the one God.*
> *Fish are beyond me.*
>
> Other Gods
> Beyond my range . . . gods beyond my God. . . .

Watching other creatures usually gives Lawrence a sense of alien lives, incomprehensible to man. He accepts them as they are, horrible though some seem ("Bats must be bats!"). Encountering a poisonous snake in Sicily he is "honoured" to meet "one of the lords of life", and feels petty when he has thrown a stick at the reptile. In six poems about tortoises he admires while he laughs at the cumbrous mechanism of their life and love-making. When he hears the

> Strange, faint coition yell
> Of the male tortoise at extremity,
> Tiny from under the very edge of the farthest far-off horizon of life,

he regards it as the death-cry of creative surrender—

> The same cry from the tortoise as from Christ, the Osiris-cry of abandonment,
> That which is in part, finding its whole again throughout the universe.

For the most part Lawrence is content to observe the qualities and behaviour of the creatures with humorous detachment and no pretence at understanding their minds. Nevertheless, he cannot avoid drawing an analogy in one respect, for in the independence and inscrutability of the wild creatures he finds a quality akin to the exclusive individuality he desires for men and women, especially in sexual life. Characterizing the animals in terms of his own ideal of an ultimate privacy and of a communion below the level of intellect and words, he sets them up as examples for human beings to emulate. He writes several poems about the need for men and women to keep their personalities intact in marriage (e.g., "Manifesto"), and in "She said as well to me" he warns his wife not to invade his private pride with excessive fondness and caresses:

> Don't touch me and appreciate me.
>
> It is an infamy.
> You would think twice before you touched a weasel on a fence
> As it lifts its straight white throat
> Your hand would not be so flig and easy. . . .

For Lawrence the mystical union of sex is a descent into the primordial dark of animal creativeness. In his work we see an effort, not to conceive animals in human terms, but rather to get human beings to admit and develop qualities and powers which they share with other creatures but which are obscured by civilization.

In his prophetic vein Lawrence's poetry moves away from Impressionism, for he was too much the preacher, too full of ideas about the age's failings and the need for a new way of life, to give himself up habitually to the flux of sensation. He was an isolated figure, glorying in his nonconformity, but he owed something to the movement of opinion, which had emerged in the eighties, that an artist has a right and a duty to impose the pattern of his own personality, or at least his intellect, on his experience.

With D. H. Lawrence indeed we leave the Impressionist phase for one which in the visual arts, for want of a better term, was often called Post-Impressionism. In French painting this included the work of the "Fauves" and the Cubists, of Gauguin, Matisse, Douanier Rousseau, Cézanne, Braque, and Picasso, all of whom rebelled against the pseudo-scientific "divisionist" technique of Seurat and Signac, and against the servility of the Impressionists to external sensations, asserting that the painter must organize his material selectively and structurally in accordance with his own creative vision. This creative vision was usually either lyrical (as in the Fauves) or mathematical (as in the Cubists). In either case it was associated with a sense of alienation from naturalism. So Van Gogh (a lyrical painter) wrote: "The struggle with nature has sometimes something in common with what Shakespeare calls 'Taming the Shrew', that is, to overcome courageously and willy-nilly whatever resists us." And Georges Braque (a mathematical painter) declared: "One must not imitate what one wishes to create"; yet also, "I love the rule which corrects the emotion"; while Cézanne asserted that his aim was "To treat nature in the light of the cylinder, the sphere, the cone, all placed in perspective".

In England James MacNeill Whistler had issued the first manifesto of "modernist" art, of the movement towards arbitrary design, in his "Ten O'clock Lecture" in 1885. Puckishly protesting against Naturalism and Ruskin, Whistler declared that, far from being always right and to be copied exactly,

> Nature is usually wrong . . . that is to say, the condition of things that shall bring about the perfection of harmony worthy a picture is rare, and not common at all.

> Nature contains the elements, in colour and form, of all pictures, as the keyboard contains the notes of all music. But the artist is born to pick and choose, and group with science, these elements, that the result may be beautiful—as the musician gathers his notes, and forms his chords, until he bring forth from chaos glorious harmony.
>
> To say to the painter, that Nature is to be taken as she is, is to say to the player, that he may sit on the piano.

This vindication of the artist's creative will opened the way to all the dazzling experiments in which the painter adapts, distorts, transforms what he has seen, in accordance with his own constructive impulses. But because the lecturer was an eccentric, the significance of his words was not seen for twenty-five years.

Whistler was no metaphysician, but a student of Velasquez and Japanese prints, who learned from what they had done. But it is no mere coincidence that Post-Impressionism became fashionable in England when there was a revulsion against scientific determinism which showed itself in the Nietzschean cult of the Will, in the philosophic Pragmatism of William James and John Dewey, and in a growing interest among psychologists in patterns of Apperception. Nietzsche's dictum, "Nothing is true; all is permissible" sprang from his belief in the primacy of the Ego, in the right of the natural aristocrat to shape the world to his own desires. William James, while despairing of absolute truth, asserted the formative energy of the human mind:

> In our cognitive as well as in our active life we are creative. We *add*, both to the subject and to the predicate part of reality. The world stands really malleable, waiting to receive its final touches at our hands. Like the kingdom of heaven, it suffers human violence willingly. Man *engenders* truths upon it.[13]

John Dewey too insisted on the organizing power of the mind when he made "inquiry" rather than knowledge the heart of logic: "Inquiry is the controlled or directed transformation of an indeterminate situation into one that is so determinate in its constituent distinctions and relations as to convert the elements of the original situation into a unified whole."[14]

Here Dewey was extending the application of the unifying activity first called Apperception by Leibnitz, taken over by Herbart and Wundt and defined by Carl Lange as "that psychical activity by which individual perceptions, ideas, or idea-complexes are brought into relation to our previous intellectual and emotional life, assimilated with it, and thus roused to greater clearness, activity and significance". Of course to call the Post-Impressionist period the age of Apperception would be grossly to overload the psychological term; but the period of Cubism and Ezra Pound's *Cantos* was certainly one in which Impressionist "pointillisme" and "stream of consciousness" were superseded by the eager exploration of diverse methods of organizing the chaotic medley of experience into formal patterns, with reference to the potentialities of the several artistic media.

It would be possible to give many correspondences between painting and poetry in the Post-Impressionist period. There is Cubism in Edith Sitwell—her "Aubade" about the servant girl Jane creaking down the stairs to light the fire. But in her early work she usually conceived her themes in terms of a private imagery derived often from her enclosed domestic life at Renishaw, from her reading of the French symbolists, or from the Russian ballet, especially the ballet of puppets (*Petrouchka*). D. H. Lawrence may be likened to Van Gogh at times in the broad vitalistic gestures of his landscapes and the sense of vibrant energy bursting through the bright tints.

The struggle of the Impressionist artists to preserve a pattern in the flux had always been difficult, and the career of Virginia Woolf was a series of experiments during which—as in *Orlando* and *The Waves*—one can see her imposing a design on refractory material. Joyce's use of the Ulysses myth and of various styles in his account of twenty-four hours of Dublin life is another example.

In the *Cantos* of Pound and Eliot's *The Waste Land* we see the poet deliberately forcing his material into a set scheme. *The*

Waste Land, with its varying viewpoints, its attempt to see the theme from several angles in the shortest possible time—to compress what might have been a long didactic or satiric poem into a few lines—might be likened to those "simultaneous" analytic compositions of Braque and Picasso in which several facets of a human figure or a musical instrument are seen from various sides or opened up within, and all these are put together to form an ingenious, often very satisfying design.[15] Certainly Pound and Eliot introduced into England a new principle of psychological effect. Previously poets had been warned that easy transitions were necessary to good style. Alison's *Taste* (1790) had illustrated from the Augustan poets; a hundred years later John Addington Symonds declared, "The art of transition and connection has quite as much to do with veracity of thought as with elegance of expression".[16] Quite so. Symonds was all for ease and perspicuity; but what if veracity of thought involved violent contrast, if progression of thought were by a series of explosions in the mind like those of the recently invented internal combustion engine? "Shock is creative", wrote Braque. William James expounded the disjunctive nature of thought, though less violently, when in his chapter on "The Stream of Consciousness" he declared: "Like a bird's life, it seems to be an alternation of flights and perchings. . . . The resting places are usually occupied by sensorial imaginations of some sort . . . the places of flight are filled with thoughts of relations."

It could be argued that *The Waste Land* and the *Cantos* were attempts to make poetry by representing the "perching places", the "sensorial imaginations", leaving the reader to supply the "places of flight", the "thoughts of relations". But the main influences on Eliot and Pound were literary, for both were strongly affected by French poets such as Mallarmé who depended on the mind's power to unify apparently disparate images, and sought to evoke an idea "without actually mentioning it, by allusive words, never by direct words" (*Divagations*). The reader must blend the brief contrasted images in his own mind somewhat as the viewer of a "pointilliste" painting must blend the touches of colour. Connecting links, reflective and abstract passages, were reduced to a minimum. Involved also in the theory of the new "imagist" poetry was the idea common among psychologists but expressed in 1839 in Edgar Allan Poe's essay on "The Poetic Principle" (1850), that moments of heightened consciousness were inevitably short, that intense emotion could be only briefly sustained, and that "a long poem does not exist": what were called long poems consisted of passages of intense feeling strung together on a thread of lower-toned descriptive or discursive matter. *The Waste Land* was the quintessential equivalent of a "long poem". The theory (like Pater's) ignored the poetic as well as the psychological importance of phases of lowered tension, the alternations of which William James wrote, the rise before and the recuperatory fall after the moment of "hard gemlike flame". Nevertheless, by his practical proof that poetry could work by the shock of conflicting images brought into rapid juxtaposition, Eliot revitalized English poetry and gave a new instrument to association in literature; a dangerous instrument, however, in so far as its effect must depend on community of interests, and of reading, between poet and reader. This "disjunctive music" of Mr. Eliot's was natural to him because even in his sceptical phase before 1922 he had a horror of the atomic solipsism of Pater and, following F. H. Bradley, on whom he wrote a Ph.D. thesis for Harvard University, he regarded the worship of the self as a delusion.[17] In his essay on Bradley (1926), he commended that philosopher for changing his mind when, after speaking in *Ethical Studies* "of the awareness of the self, the knowledge of one's own existence is indubitable and identical", he confessed in *Appearance and Reality* "that no one 'fact' of experience in isolation is real or is evidence of anything". In Eliot's poetry the presentation of "facts" of experience in isolation is a sign of unreality, of living in a world of illusions. For some time Eliot seems not to have been able to apprehend fully in his poetry Bradley's consequent doctrine that appearance forms part of reality and can be subsumed in a transcendental pattern, that the "finite centres" of our consciousness are united in the Absolute.[18] By the time he wrote the essay, he could quote with understanding, out of a fuller knowledge of its religious implications, Bradley's assertion that the imperfect private ego must die to itself:

> You must resolve to give up your will, as the mere will of this or that man, and you must put your whole self, your entire will, into the will of the divine. That must be your one self, as it is your true self; that you must hold to both with thought and will, and all other you must renounce.[19]

This opposition of the individual to the Absolute, of the part to the whole, is associated in Eliot's writings with a swing from the fragmentary to the total order. Often he thinks in a way not unlike that described in the Gestalt ("structural" or "pattern") psychology adumbrated by Christian von Ehrenfels in 1890 (who used the term "Gestalt" or "form quality") and developed by Wertheimer, Köhler, and Koffka between 1912 and 1920. In contrast to the conventional analysis of mental states into associative elements this movement emphasized the concept of wholeness, asserting that we strive to see things not in their individual details but as unitary structures in which the whole is more than the sum of the parts (as a tune has a form quality of its own apart from the notes it contains), and also that "the change of any part changes the whole, and conversely".[20]

Mr. Eliot's love of pattern and habit of seeing all things in terms of it is obvious in both poetry and criticism. Mr. Prufrock in his incoherent self-depreciation—which recalls Claude in Clough's *Amours de Voyage*—cries accurately enough

> It is impossible to say just what I mean!
> But as if a magic lantern threw the nerves in patterns on a screen.

This passage may help in the interpretation of the "heap of broken images" in "Gerontion" and *The Waste Land*. There the poetic intention is to induce the reader to synthesize a succession of apparently unrelated details under the pressure of an overmastering emotional apprehension of life. How carefully considered the structure of *The Waste Land* was is clear even without the corroboration provided by the Pound-Eliot letters.[21] But in places the design of the poem seems intellectually imposed rather than inevitably implicit in, and emergent from, the central conception. Thus the introduction of the short fourth section, "Death by Water", translated from an earlier poem in French, is useful to balance the key idea of life through water and the Spirit with an instance of pagan death, but was it *poetically* necessary? And the part played by Tiresias, who is not introduced until line 218 yet is (we are told in a note) "the most important personage in the poem, uniting all the rest", remains a puzzle. "What Tiresias *sees*, in fact, is the substance of the poem": here is an instance where a new detail involves a re-ordering of the whole Gestalt. This can be achieved, maybe, if we identify Tiresias, the unheeded prophet, with the poet. But there is real danger in this "spasmodic" method of treatment that the poem will finally remain no more than a kaleidoscope of shifting patterns.

In his critical writing Mr. Eliot started with the idea of dominant pattern, declaring that the history of European literature should be regarded as a unity, and that tradition is a dynamic order which influences every new writer and is itself changed not only in detail but in totality by each new work of art. Art implies self-limitation to a convention outside which the artist should not go. Drama is a ritual, and in recognizing this the Greek dramatists and Racine were superior to the Elizabethans, even to Shakespeare, who would not keep within any one convention. Mr. Eliot's own practice of drama was deeply affected by such ideas, and his plays (after *Murder in the Cathedral* where he mixed several conventions) are almost too skeletally conceived in his desire for economy, propriety, and concentration.

The *Four Quartets* provide a unique example of variations upon a design at once intellectual and poetic. The clarity and depth of the poet's apprehension of the several themes which move through the poems appear all the more remarkable when we realize that these pieces were written over a period of six years, that *Burnt Norton* (1935) "grew out of fragments discarded from a draft of *Murder in the Cathedral*; only in writing *East Coker* did Eliot envision the set of four".[22]

It would be a mistake to regard Eliot as simply a disciple of the Gestalt psychologists. His interest in the science was considerable, and he took what he liked from various schools, but he related it always to metaphysics and theology and especially to the practice of piety which was increasingly the impulse of his writings. A brief summary of *Four Quartets* will indicate their complexity. *Burnt Norton* begins with a metaphysical speculation about the interpenetration of past, present, and future—before passing on to discuss an experience in which *what might have been* and *what was* were inextricably interwoven, and unseen presences seemed near in a garden. He ends the first section by insisting—though not as Pater would have done—on the reduction of past, future, and the might-have-been to the present in which they are imagined. Section II revives the microcosm-macrocosm idea of our first chapter. The rhythms of the physical universe,

> The dance along the artery
> The circulation of the lymph
> Are figured in the drift of stars
> Ascend to summer in the tree.

The poet turns to consideration of the point of rest within the ceaseless movement. This point of rest corresponds to the moment out of time and space when

> I can only say, *there* we have been: but I cannot say where.
> And I cannot say, how long, for that is to place it in time.

Psychologically the experience involves

> The inner freedom from the practical desire,
> The release from action and suffering, release from
>   the inner
> And the outer compulsion, yet surrounded
> By a grace of sense, a white light still and moving.

This approaches awareness of the ultimate, but "human kind Cannot bear very much reality" and the breaking of time into past, present, and future is a salutary effect of our physical limitations—they prevent consciousness of the Absolute, yet we can approach this realization only through our experience and memory of the fleeting moments of heightened perception.

Section III comments on London life in which the breaking-up of eternity into "time before and time after" brings "distraction" and "tumid apathy". He describes the way from this to perception of the timeless reality in terms reminiscent of the mediaeval mystics and St. John of the Cross; it is the *via negativa* which involves shutting off the instruments of the soul in order that new life may enter—a descent into

> Internal darkness, deprivation
> And destitution of all property,
> Desiccation of the world of sense,
> Evacuation of the world of fancy,
> Inoperancy of the world of spirit.

In Section V the poet turns to the crystallization of shifting thought in art. At best art attains a sort of timelessness and dynamic stillness analogous to that sought in religion. He regrets that in poetry this is less attainable than in a Chinese jar which "Moves perpetually in its stillness", and he ends by distinguishing Desire, which involves movement towards the beloved, and Love, which "is itself unmoving, Only the cause and end of movement" although it may not seem so to us. But we can have moments of vision such as he had in the garden, and these make what went before and after seem ridiculous and empty. So in *Burnt Norton* the main topic is the moment of illumination in ordinary life, religion, and art, and the problem of its relation to past and future and the need of the soul to perpetuate it.

In *East Coker*, suggested by a visit to the ancestral home from which the Eliots went out to America in the seventeenth century, the meditation shifts from succession of experience to the links of beginning and ending: the starting-point of the family and its later history; the cycle of birth and death; the rhythm of the seasons and of human life, the dancers

> Keeping the rhythm in their dancing
> As in their living in the living seasons.

He turns from this to the personal problem of the ageing mind still open to "the disturbance of the spring". The "long hoped for calm, the autumnal serenity And the wisdom of age" do not come, or if they come are little better than decrepitude. The knowledge of former experience falsifies new experience, "For the pattern is new in every moment" and old men learn not wisdom but "fear of fear and frenzy . . . fear of possession".

> The only wisdom we can hope to acquire
> Is the wisdom of humility.

In Section III the keynote is darkness: the darkness of materialism known by the world; the darkness of death; and the dark night of the soul which we must know before Divine Grace can illuminate the mind. He cites from St. John of the Cross the paradoxes of learning through ignorance, possessing by dispossession, etc.

In the last section, the mind's liability to be tyrannized over by the patterns it has erected (as in Section II) is applied to poetry

> Because one has only learnt to get the better of words
> For the thing one no longer has to say, or the way in which
> One is no longer disposed to say it.

So every new poem is an attempt to make a new pattern out of the words which will not stay still, and from "undisciplined squads of emotion". There is no evolutionary progress in art; other men have done it all before,

> There is only the fight to recover what has been lost
> And found and lost again and again.

But this does not imply despair: "For us, there is only the trying". And though we may regret the past, and always find the pattern of life more complicated as we grow older, we should see that life is not merely a succession of intense isolated Paterian moments but a focusing of the whole of past experience on the present. For the old, the here and now should matter less than this pattern, and the effort to explore a timeless state of being, "a further union, a deeper communion", pursued in the bleakness of age, symbolized in "the dark cold and the empty desolation" of the sea.

In *The Dry Salvages* the sea image, representing the mystery of the universe about us, is counterpointed with that of the river which represents the darker mystery within us, the untamed wildness in human nature which, like the Mississippi, breaks out every so often—and is ever

>   implacable
> Keeping his seasons and rages, destroyer, reminder
> Of what men choose to forget.

Section II returns to the problem of growing old without an objective, when life is simply "the trailing Consequence of further days and hours", with "the failing Pride or resentment at failing powers". In age the pattern of life past seems to be made up of the "moments of happiness", which recall Masefield's—but their "sudden illumination" takes on a new glory if, looking back, we can perceive their meaning; and

> the past experience revived in the meaning
> Is not the experience of one life only
> But of many generations—

and also of something more, "probably quite ineffable". Although Eliot discounts the easy popular misconception of inevitable evolution, we all share in the inheritance of the race, which shows itself not only in the happy moments but also in "the backward half-look Over the shoulder, towards the primitive terror". Moments of joy and of agony are equally permanent, for "Time the destroyer is time the preserver". Yet on the other hand we are changing every moment as each new experience makes the whole of our life into a different pattern:

> You are not the same people who left that station
> Or who will arrive at any terminus.

In a sense it is vain to think of a goal, or of escape from the past. We must just "Fare forward", irrespective of where we arrive. This is true of the world of time, but what of the timeless world which we seek in religion or its substitutes? The saint may "apprehend The point of intersection of the timeless". Our nearest approach to that is "only the unattended Moment, the moment in and out of time", the moment of sudden illumination —as in *Burnt Norton*—when we cease to live to ourselves, which is to be followed by "prayer, observance, discipline, thought and action".

Little Gidding is set in midwinter when a spring-like, pentecostal fire, a blossom-like scattering of snow light the cold. The church where Nicholas Ferrar practised his seventeenth-century mysticism and was twice visited by Charles I, in prosperity and defeat, is a place of prayer and for communication with the dead, a place to experience "the intersection of the timeless moment". This last poem in the series emphasizes the element of fire, aptly since it was written during the German air-raids on London in 1940, which are touched on in the Dantesque Section II; but fire means purification, and this is applied both to religion and to language when the poet meets the "familiar compound ghost" of those who like himself have striven

> To purify the dialect of the tribe
> And urge the mind to aftersight and foresight.

Perhaps with Yeats in mind the speaker discloses the penalties of old age—"the cold friction of expiring sense", the impotent rage at human folly, and the living over of the past in bitter self-realization. This decline is inevitable

> unless restored by that refining fire
> Where you must move in measure, like a dancer.

Turning to the historic lesson of Little Gidding, the poet distinguishes between attachment to things and persons, indifference, and detachment; he points out the influence of time as we look back on the civil strife of the seventeenth century, and on the participants now "folded in a single party". We pray for ourselves that our motives be purified, and "All shall be well" in God's Grace, as Dame Juliana of Norwich wrote. Section IV puts with beautiful economy the paradoxes of love and fire. We are saved from the burning city of the senses by the fire of purgation, the torment devised by God's love. Such a death is a beginning, a new birth, and in Section V the poet discusses the circular movement of life, in which "The end is where we start from"; similarly in the achievement of good style, every poem is an epitaph to an experience in time, a timeless moment, and history itself is "a pattern Of timeless moments". So the *Quartets* conclude as the explorers return to

> where we started
> And know the place for the first time,

and a series of ejaculations sum up the states of eternity—the timeless moment of *Burnt Norton*, the complete surrender which brings Grace, and the promise of full paradisal union when "the fire and the rose are one".

There are at least six chief centres of poetic thought in the *Quartets* mainly connected with discussions of Time: (i) the idea of Place, each poem radiating out from recollections of a visit to some place or places, with indications of things seen entering into the imagery and meditation; (ii) the problem of Time, its nature and our relation to it; the connection between past, present, and future; the nature of memory, and of history; (iii) Timelessness or eternity and the human mind's power of attaining that state; (iv) arising from (ii) and (iii), comments on the time-ridden life of our workaday world, and assertions about the method of achieving the timeless state of Grace; (v) religious prayers and hymns; (vi) application of the wish to escape from Time in art, with special reference to language and poetry.

A philosophic preoccupation with Time was noticeable in the first half of the twentieth century, which produced Einstein's theory of relativity and works by J. A. Gunn, H. Bergson, J. M. E. McTaggart, S. Alexander, and J. W. Dunne.[23] Mr. Eliot may have been acquainted with several of these discussions, but probably Henri Bergson's *Creative Evolution* has most bearing on the poems, which may indeed be considered as meditations on Bergsonian Duration in the light of Bradley's idealism and Christian mysticism. To discuss this adequately here is impossible; a few passages from Bergson must suffice.[24]

Creative Evolution starts from the supposition that the human intellect, which "feels at home among inanimate objects", cannot present the true nature of life, and its separation from intuition limits our consciousness. If theory of knowledge and theory of life could unite, "they would substitute for the false evolutionism of Spencer . . . a true evolutionism". Mr. Eliot is little concerned with evolution, creative or otherwise, but his reference to "superficial notions of evolution" (*Dry Salvages*) may reflect agreement with Bergson's attack on Spencer.

Defining Duration, Bergson insists "that we change without ceasing, and that the state itself is nothing but change". "The apparent discontinuity of the psychical life is then due to our attention being fixed on it by a series of separate acts. . . . [Yet] each is only the best illuminated point of a moving zone which comprises all that we feel or think or will." Our Ego is "an artificial bond" on which we thread the psychic states we set up as independent entities.

"Duration is the continuous progress of the past which grows into the future and which swells as it advances . . .; the past is preserved by itself, automatically. In its entirety, probably, it follows us at every instant; all that we have felt, thought, and willed from our earliest infancy is there, leaning over the portals of consciousness that would fain leave it outside [Cf. *The Elder Statesman*.] Doubtless we think with only a small part of our past, but it is with our entire past, including the original bent of our soul, that we desire, will and act. Our past then, is made manifest to us in its impulse. . . . From this survival of the past it follows that consciousness cannot go through the same state twice. The circumstances may be the same, but they will act no longer on the same person, since they find him at a new moment of his history. . . . That is why our duration is irreversible. . . . [Compare Eliot's "All time is unredeemable" (*Burnt Norton*, I), and "time is no healer: the patient is no longer here"; "You are not the same people who left that station . . ." (*Dry Salvages*, III).]

"Each of the moments of our life is a kind of creation . . . each of our states . . . modifies our personality, being indeed the new form that we are just assuming. [Cf. Gestalt; and "the pattern is new in every moment", etc. (*East Coker*, II).] The present moment of a living body does not find its explanation in the moment immediately before, . . . *all* the past of the organism must be added to that moment, its heredity—in fact, the whole of a very long history. [Cf. "the past experience revived in the meaning Is not the experience of one life only But of many generations . . ." (*Dry Salvages*, II).]

"Life . . . progresses and endures in time. Of course, when once the road has been travelled, we can glance over it, mark its direction, note this in psychological terms, and speak as if there had been pursuit of an end. . . . But of the road which was going to be travelled, the human mind could have nothing to say, for the road has been created, *pari passu* with the act of travelling over it, being nothing but the direction of this act itself." [Cf. "Fare forward, travellers! not escaping from the past Into different lives, or into any future", etc. (*Dry Salvages*, III).]

Like Bergson, Eliot is aware of the war between intuition and intellect, and realizes the limitations of the latter, which, "preoccupied before everything with the necessities of action, is, like the senses, limited to taking, at intervals, views that are instantaneous and by that very fact immobile of the becoming matter" (Bergson). He would also agree that "in order to advance with the moving reality, you must place yourself within it". But the reality which Eliot seeks is not Duration, not the ceaselessly evolving change in the *élan vital*, but the Absolute which he identifies with the Christian God. For him there are moments of rest, "at the still point of the turning world", which are not just an artificial convenience for the kinetic intellect, but occasions of Timelessness, premonitions of Eternity. Although he adapts ideas from Bergson, and even images (e.g., rail-travel, and the river in *Dry Salvages*; cf. Bergson, p. 284), he rejects Bergson's major doctrine. The latter turned away from the notion of an immutable Absolute, a stable equilibrium in which "Things re-enter into each other. What was extended in space is contracted into pure form. And past, present and future shrink into a single moment, which is eternity." But this was in fact Eliot's goal.

The following passage in Bergson may also serve to show the poet's divergence from the French philosopher:

It must not be forgotten that the force which is evolving throughout the organized world is a limited force, which is always seeking to transcend itself and always remains inadequate to the work it would fain produce. The errors and puerilities of radical finalism are due to the misapprehension of this point. It has represented the whole of the living world as a construction, and a construction analogous to a human work. All the pieces have been arranged with a view to the best possible functioning of the machine. Each species has its reason for existence, its part to play, its allotted place; and all join together, as it were, in a musical concert, wherein the seeming discords are really meant to bring out the fundamental harmony. In short, all goes on in nature as in the works of human genius, where, though the result may be trifling, there is at least perfect adequacy between the object made and the work of making it.

Nothing of the kind in the evolution of life. There, the disproportion is striking between the work and the result. From the bottom to the top of the organized world we do indeed find one great effort, but . . . even in its most perfect works, though it seems to have triumphed over external resistances and also over its own, it is at the mercy of the materiality which it has had to assume. It is what each of us may experience in himself. . . . The most living thought becomes frigid in the formula that expresses it. The word turns against the idea. The letter kills the spirit (*Creative Evolution*, pp. 133-4).

Eliot pursues *le mot juste* with the scrupulous integrity of Flaubert. He is the heir of the nineties in his martyrdom to the word. In the *Four Quartets* he uses the same analogy as Bergson between the struggle for expression in nature and man, and especially in words (cf. *Burnt Norton*, v; *East Coker*, II and v). But whereas Bergson attacks "radical finalism" for regarding the world as like the construction of a mind, Eliot (though he would not like the "machine" image) prefers the Mind of God to the *élan vital*, and believes that in a world of goodness and in good art a harmony should exist that Bergson declares impossible; hence his delight in

> every phrase
> And sentence that is right (where every word is at home,
> Taking its place to support the others, . . .
> The complete consort dancing together . . .)

The concord of language is parallel to the peace achieved by those who are "redeemed from fire by fire". In *Burnt Norton* Mr. Eliot's ideal for art is the formal balance of flowing line and volume in a Chinese jar:

> Only by the form, the pattern
> Can words or music reach
> The stillness, as a Chinese jar still
> Moves perpetually in its stillness.

And he laments the imprecision of words, their refusal to be and do what the poet would wish. In *Little Gidding* he has become reconciled to his medium, and the image of the dance suggests the special virtue of poetry with its constantly shifting patterns of interwoven verbal thought.

Such discussions touch on what is currently an important philosophical as well as a psychological problem; the relation between words and thought, the value of language as an instrument. This has exercised several younger poets, notably Elizabeth Jennings and Kathleen Raine, who explore the delicate recesses of the mind where words and feeling meet.

I must move on to my last topic, some effects of the "psychology of the Unconscious" on modern poetry. The existence of mental energies below the level of consciousness was recognized in the nineteenth century, but they were generally regarded as untappable. John Stuart Mill wrote of

Something I call Myself, or ... my mind ... a something which I conceive to be not the thoughts, but the being that has the thoughts, and which I can conceive as existing for ever in a state of quiescence, without any thoughts at all. But what this being is, though it is myself, I have no knowledge, other than the series of its states of consciousness.[25]

Dean Mansel flatly declared "I exist in so far as I am a Person; and I am a person in so far as I am conscious".[26] On the other hand, Coleridge's *Notebooks* bear witness to his realization that much went on below the conscious mind, and when he jotted down trains of thought which floated up from below, he recognized that they were often interrelated by some emotional impulse. The study of abnormal states of mind and the development of hypnosis; Charcot's work on hysterical patients; his pupil Pierre Janet's cure of a hysterical coma by taking the patient back to the time when she received the shock and suggesting to her under hypnosis that the shock was harmless; Josef Breuer's discovery (1880–2) that severe cases could be cured by making the patients conscious of the root causes of their trouble—these bore fruit in

1893-5 when Breuer and Freud in *Studies in Hysteria* laid down most of the principles of psychoanalytic method, showing the importance of (*a*) dreams as symbolic visions, (*b*) the repression of painful ideas, (*c*) the sexual content of repressed ideas, (*d*) the use of free association by which the patient pours out everything that comes to mind on to his physician, who perceives (*e*) the relationship between the images used in the "unloading" and the repressions and complexes below.[27]

Ere long, professional psychologists writing on psychoanalysis discussed the nature of dream-symbols and showed their relationship to the overt symbolism found in mythology, religion, everyday metaphorical language, and literature. The arts were declared to arise by the sublimation of unconscious impulses, and poems and dramas were analysed to trace in them the complexes and inhibitions individual to their authors. Much of this study was extraneous to literary criticism, yet as Sir Herbert Read writes (with particular reference to *Hamlet*), "any explanation that psychology can offer for the complicated strands of poetic creation tends to quicken our general sensibility".[28] Sir Herbert's several essays on the nature of poetry and the nature of criticism provide a judicious exploration of the ways in which poetry makes use of symbols allied to dream and myth, how it organizes the wild impulses of the Id under the discipline of the Ego, and how far psychoanalysis sheds light on the creative mind in the creative process.

English literature was little affected by the "new psychology" before the end of the First World War, and considerable resistance to Freudian interpretations of the mind was exerted by poets then writing. Two examples may be mentioned, marked by a similar reaction. In a short poem, "Psychoanalysis", W. J. Turner lamented that "Dragons and hippogriffes and centaurs all Have fled the mind" and become mere symbols of unconscious cravings. A lovely tree no longer evokes a wood nymph or a painting by Pissarro or Sisley—

> Nay,
> Some *libido* whose name you dare not say
> Expresses thus itself standing symbolical.
> Here is no cause for tears. Ascend a bus,
> And if you find your mother on it, know
> That you are face to face with Œdipus.
> Daphne did not into a laurel grow
> Quicker than will a wish, eluding us,
> Take on a strange, terrible incognito.
> *(New Poems, 1928)*

Walter de la Mare in a late piece ("Dreams") expressed at greater length his disapproval of the psychologists who

> have decreed
> Dreams the insidious wiles of sex.

He describes a Greek statue of Hypnos, father of Dream:

> Not ours these follies. We haunt instead
> Tropical jungles drear and dun,
> And see in some fetish of fear and dread,
> Our symbol of dream—that brooding head!
> And deem the wellspring of genius hid
> In a dark morass that is dubbed the Id.

With little understanding of the psychoanalytic theory of art, de la Mare considers Mozart's music and Shakespeare's drama as creations of waking dream, and cries,

> O Poesy of well-spring clear,
> Let no sad Science thee suborn,
> Who art thyself its planisphere.

By 1920, however, the "sad Science" was making its positive influence felt in imaginative literature. Perhaps the first British poet to make extensive use of the idea of the Unconscious was Robert Graves.

Coming back from the First World War bitter and almost broken in mind, Mr. Graves used poetry as a means of recuperation and brought the repressed anguish of recent experience into the open by means of lyrics and anecdotes suffused with a quality of nightmare. The poetry of this phase probably owes something to that of Walter de la Mare, but is distinguished by a harsher note and by a realization of the Freudian nature of the release afforded. In "Incubus" he describes the Body lying on the bed and the nightmare Incubus settling upon it.

> Asleep, amazed, with lolling head,
> Arms in supplication spread,
> Body shudders, dumb with fear;
> There lifts the Moon, but who am I,
> Cloaked in shadow wavering by,
> Stooping, muttering at his ear?

Morning brings deliverance:

> "O morning scent and tree-top song
> Slow-rising smoke and nothing wrong!"

But there *was* something wrong, and we owe a number of fine poems expressive of the troubled mind to it. Startled at night by owls and bats he writes of them, in "Outlaws", as vampires, evil deities:

> Old gods, tamed to silence, there
>   In the wet woods they lurk,
> Greedy of human stuff to snare
>   In webs of murk. . . .
> For though creeds whirl away in dust,
>   Faith dies and men forget,
> These aged gods of power and lust
>   Cling to life yet—
> Old gods almost dead, malign
>   Starving for unpaid dues,
> Incense and fire, salt, blood and wine,
>   And a drumming muse.*

The "unclean muse" reappears in "The Haunted House", in

* Revised form as in *Collected Poems 1959*. In *Poems (1914–1926)*, "And an unclean muse."

which the poet, asked to sing a song, catalogues the "clouded tales of wrong And terror" he can offer:

> Of a night so torn with cries,
>   Honest men sleeping
> Start awake with rabid eyes,
>   Bone-chilled, flesh creeping . . .
> Of lust frightful, past belief
>   Lurking unforgotten,
> Unrestrainable endless grief
>   In breasts long rotten.

The guilt-complex basic to Christianity is expressed in "Reproach" where the poet sees a grieving moonlight face crowned with thorns reproachfully looking down "through the forest of my fears" and protests that "Straining in memory, I can find No cause why you should weep". Yet the incomprehensible reproach goes on—"Unkind, untrue"—till he cries out against the persecution:

> Speak, speak, or how may a child know
>   His ancestral sin?

In "Lost Love" he imagines the effect of grief in quickening a man's senses so that

> He can watch a grass or leaf
> Every instant grow; . . .
> The woodlouse or the maggot's weak
> Clamour rings in his sad ear.

(This little exercise in hyperaesthesia was drawn out to full novel length by Walter de la Mare in *Memoirs of a Midget*.)

In time Graves passed out of this phase and perhaps his cure came from realizing the causes of his trouble and from writing openly about it. He believed that the best poetry—the ballads, Shakespeare's—had always used material welling up from the Unconscious and that modern poets should seek this underground spring of Helicon.[29] His amusing skit "The Marmosite's Miscellany" (in *Poems 1914-1926*) attacked recent literature:

> We serve a lost cause: does any pride remain
> In prolonging tradition beyond its due time,
>   Giving it lip-service, mumbling and vain,
> With a measured metre and expected rhyme?
> Morning and evening our ancient bells chime,
>   Yet the whole congregation could sit in one pew,
>   The sexton, the verger, and old folk one or two, . . .
>
> The beginning of wisdom is laughter and song,
> The furtherance of wisdom, scholarship and groans.
>   Between first and second, reactions are strong;
> The disputants wrangle in no playful tones,
> Dream against waking, blood against bones.
>   Let poetry, then, enter on its third degree,
>   In grammar of unreason marching close and free.

The poetry of unreason would draw on both the conscious and the unconscious levels, be witty and reverberant.

The Surrealist writers of the thirties took the "poetry of unreason" to its extreme limit, assuming that "automatic writing", a trancelike transcription of a free flow of images, must produce a work of art.[30] Freudian psychologists had helped to recharge literature with psychic energy by revealing how in dreamlike states the mind can pour out images symbolical of repressed fears and desires. Under their influence critics explored the reverberatory effect of Shakespeare's *Hamlet*, Coleridge's poetry, and the prose of Poe and De Quincey. It seemed easy to write poetry in which powerful upsurges of emotion from the unconscious would ejaculate series of significant images unified by their common source in the poet's private life.

In England, as in France, some Surrealists had considerable success in evoking a nightmare mood:

> today is the day when the streets are full of hearses
> and when women cover their ring fingers with pieces of silk
> when the doors fall off their hinges in ruined cathedrals
> when hosts of white birds fly across the ocean from america
> and make their nests in the trees of public gardens

> the pavements of cities are covered with needles
> the reservoirs are full of human hair
> flames of sulphur envelop the houses of ill-fame
> out of which bloodred lilies appear.
>
> across the square where crowds are dying in thousands
> a man is walking a tightrope covered with moths.
> (David Gascoyne, "And the Seventh Dream is the Dream of Isis")

Here the ominous message of death and disorder is plain enough. But often the symbolism of the Surrealist is peculiar to the poet, and the effect is merely to startle and bewilder.

To startle and bewilder was one aim of these poets, who, tired of the commonplace or intellectual imagery of their predecessors, sought (as Ernst put it) "to intensify the irritability of the mental faculties" by such bizarre conjunctions as Lautréamont's "chance encounter of a sewing-machine and an umbrella on a dissecting-table". This is not in itself an artistic activity.

Sigmund Freud gave a neat criticism of Surrealism when, asked by André Breton to contribute to an anthology of dreams, he replied: ". . . a mere collection of dreams without the dreamer's associations, without knowledge of the circumstances in which they occurred, tells me nothing, and I can hardly imagine what it could tell anyone". Freud was doubtless thinking chiefly of the dream as a projection of the dreamer's inner life. Organized in verse it may conceivably evoke a response, not identical indeed with the impulse which inspired it, yet aesthetically satisfying. In such art, "what is being shared is not specific contents but what [psychologists] call dynamic processes, and so we should perhaps not speak of communication but of resonance. . . . In this reverberation the private meaning is all but swallowed up."[31]

This, however, is usually an accidental occurrence, and such happy accidents are rare in Surrealist poetry. The early work of Dylan Thomas displays the incoherence caused by a private use of sexual and religious imagery (e.g., in "Our Eunuch Dreams" and "Altar-wise by Owl-light"). Till the last he was not altogether free of obscurity, but much of his later poetry was more communicative in that the imagery was less private to himself. Moreover he was a rigorous craftsman, and although he worked by the juxtaposition of images which at first seemed disparate, at his best he organized the associations rising from the two or three main images of each poem into a strong moving pillar or spiral of meaning.

W. H. Auden showed much closer acquaintance with the work of modern psychologists, not only of Freud himself but also of others who disagreed with Freud's insistence on narrowly sexual interpretations and moved outside the clinical field into regions of social and religious speculation.[32] Without becoming exclusively a disciple of any one psychoanalyst the poet drew eclectically on the teaching of Carl Jung, Homer Lane, J. Layard, Alfred Adler, and others. His early work may indeed be regarded as an attempt to make poetry a satiric educational force in transforming Capitalist society. The "new psychology" much more than revolutionary Marxism was the motive force in the poems he wrote before 1942.

Auden's key ideas included the belief that love, the Freudian Eros, is the creative energy in all human life, operating not only in obvious sexual relations but throughout all private and social behaviour. He accepted Freud's theory that men's wishes are not free but are conditioned by unconscious memories from infancy and childhood: "their fate is for the most part arranged by themselves and determined by infantile influences". Sexual deviations, hysterical symptoms, tics, obsessive acts, are connected with the history of the personality and often symbolical of the original cause. Eccentricities of manner, neurotic behaviour, may be devices of escape, means of obtaining sympathy, or ways of masking a hidden weakness. Not surprisingly therefore Auden's poetry was much concerned with "perverted lovers", narcissism, self-abuse, homosexuality, all the failures in self-adjustment which make people anxious, sickly, morbidly introspective, shy, aggressive, wearers of masks. Thus in the 1930 *Poems* he describes "the one whose part it is to lean, For whom it is not good to be alone" (III), and the nonchalant young gallant who is not really a "returning conqueror"

> But poised between shocking falls on razor-edge
> Has taught himself this balancing subterfuge
> Of the accosting profile, the erect carriage.
>
> (IV)

In a score of such brief, brilliant portraits he sketches what he calls, in "Happy New Year", "the dingy, difficult life of our generation". The difficulties are the result of sexual disturbances going back to infancy, but they are augmented by the difficulties of growing up in a family, by relations with parents, brothers, and sisters, by effects of school and other environmental influences, and by the climate of society into which men are born. Auden's Marxist reading fostered a sociological attitude and directed his attention to the middle class in which he was born and bred, but he soon came to admire the writings of Gerald Heard (*The Ascent of Humanity*, 1929; *The Emergence of Man*, 1931; *This Surprising World*, 1932) which lent support to his belief in an evolving society in which a "higher consciousness" might control the lower. Thus the Marxist dialect of social change might be spiritualized by a "sublimation" akin to Freud's, to achieve a "love outside our own election" which "holds us in unseen connection" ("A Communist to Others"). By 1941 the revolutionary element had almost vanished from his thought, to be replaced by a Christian faith in which "sublimation" took on new meaning.

For Auden society always existed for individual man, not man for society. In this respect he may have owed something to Alfred Adler, the founder of Individual Psychology, and "the legitimate father of the inferiority complex".[33] For Adler, as for Hobbes and Nietzsche, the major factor in emotional life was the will to dominate the environment, including one's fellows. If a man has a weak organ he strives to compensate for it; thus speech impediments produced Demosthenes, Mirabeau, Burke; shortness of stature produced Napoleon, Lloyd George, and other leaders. From the very beginning of our lives we start to make a "life-plan" in relation to our own bodies and minds and our family-constellation. Each makes his own "scheme of apperceptions": "his interpretation of life ... is his own masterpiece". This is related to the three spheres, communal life, work, and love.

The goal of personal superiority is such that it invariably magnifies one of the three problems of life out of all proportion. We find that a person's ideal of success becomes unnaturally limited to social notoriety, business success, or to sexual conquests. Thus we see the social careerist, fighting and jealous, the business magnate, extending his interest at the expense of others, and the amorous intriguer, the would-be Don Juan. Each disturbs the harmony of his life by thus leaving many necessary demands unsatisfied, and then tries to compensate by still more frantic strivings in his narrowed sphere of action.[34]

Diseases are often the result of neurotic needs; "the organic functions are dominated by the style of life". (Hence Auden's cruel ballad of "Miss Gee".) Health can be achieved only when the individual is in harmony with himself and with society.

Auden's view of the poet's function was that he should expose the errors of individuals and society and point the way to improvement. A schoolmaster himself, he regarded the poet as a combination of teacher and psychotherapist. In an early poem he prays to God as a heavenly psychoanalyst who will forgive everything except the "negative inversion" of the will:

> Send to us power and light, a sovereign touch
> Curing the intolerable neural itch,
> The exhaustion of weaning, the liar's quinsy,
> And the distortions of ingrown virginity.
> Prohibit sharply the rehearsed response
> And gradually correct the coward's stance;
> Cover in time with beams those in retreat
> That, spotted, they turn though the reverse were great;
> Publish each healer that in city lives

> Or country houses at the end of drives;
> Harrow the house of the dead; look shining at
> New styles of architecture, a change of heart.
>
> *(Poems, 1930, XXX)*

Images of the healer, the miracle-worker, diviner, augur, and preacher occur often in Auden's work (e.g., "In War Time"), which is largely a poetry of diagnosis as with clinical detachment he points out the evils of the age and of his own class with an unerring eye for the significant symptom. He would agree with Professor Mark Baldwin that in the modern world "Aristotle's 'Man is a social animal' becomes 'Man is a society individualised' ". For Auden the individual was a mirror of the society which produced him, and one reason for desiring a social revolution was that capitalist and *bourgeois* society produced "ruined boys" and "compulsory touchers", and those who find refuge from human suffering in a half-life:

> Who, thinking, pace in slippers on the lawns
> Of College Quad or Cathedral Close,
> Who are born nurses, who live in shorts
> Sleeping with people and playing fives. . . .
>
> *(Poems, 1930, XXIX)*

The maladjusted society has produced also the religious yearning which makes us in difficulties invoke the life

> That shapes the individual belly and orders
>   The private nocturnal terror . . .
>   Intervene. O descend as a dove or
> A furious papa or a mild engineer: but descend!
>
> *(Spain, 1937)*

As he wrote later:

> Beloved, we were always in the wrong,
> Handling so clumsily our stupid lives,
> Suffering too little and too long,
> Too careful even in our selfish loves:
> The decorative manias we obey
> Die in grimaces round us every day.
>
> ("In Sickness and in Health")

The need of healing is present everywhere; in "Journey to Iceland"

> On the bridle path down by the lake
> The blood moves also by crooked and furtive inches,
> Asks all our questions: "Where is the homage? When
> Shall justice be done? O who is against me?
> Why am I always alone?"

All men are moved by pride, self-pity, and loneliness. From these spring the deadly sins of the modern world.

In *New Year Letter*, written at Christmas 1940, the poet of the divided mind sees psychological integration as the great problem of our day:

> To set in order, that's the task
> Both Eros and Apollo ask.

Art
> cannot be
> A midwife to society,
> For art is a *fait accompli*,

presenting a formula for experiences already completed, yet art and life agree in seeking an unconscious harmony, a tensionless pattern,

> A true *gestalt*, where indiscrete
> Perceptions and extensions meet.

Unfortunately we find it hard "To live according to our station"; hard to face the fact that

> each great I
> Is but a process in a process
> Within a field that never closes.

We hate the relativist truth, "That we are changed by what we change", preferring to live in a familiar pattern;

> we'd rather
> Be perfect copies of our father,
> Prefer our fixed ideas to be
> True of a fixed Reality;

hence the eccentricities in people who

> Unwilling to adjust belief
> Go mad in a fantastic grief
> Where no adjustment need be done.

We cling to relationships already established, and love, "not friends, or wives But certain patterns in our lives". The Devil is this inner enemy of facing changing facts, the enemy of logic and intelligence, of Cartesian clarity. He loves mingled states of mind, doubts, the "False Association" which makes men identify their ideals with faulty hopes and then swing violently into other errors when disillusioned (e.g., Wordsworth's flirtation with the French Revolution or the modern Leftists' with Marxism). The remedy is reasonableness, love, and humility.

By 1940 the educational psychologist in Auden had triumphed over the revolutionary and in appealing again to God he regarded Him still as the divine healer, but chiefly as the teacher of social justice, the "Source of equity and rest":

> Instruct us in the civil art
> Of making from the muddled heart
> A desert and a city where
> The thoughts that have to labour there
> May find locality and peace,
> And pent-up feelings their release.

A year later Auden announced his acceptance of Christianity, with its doctrines of Original Sin, the Incarnation of Christ, Redemption, and Divine Grace. The guilt, loneliness, pride, frustration which he had always perceived in himself and others were now ascribed to a different origin, and to be cured by a different course of treatment. Mr. Auden moved nearer to Mr. Eliot, though he kept his own poetic approach. In the poems written since 1941, the sense of a lost vision of wholeness and truth colours his view of man, who lives in a subjective, relative world, exiled from reality:

> When he had finished looking at them, there
> Were helpless images instead of things
> That had looked so decided; instead of earth
> His fatherless creation; instead of truth
> The luckiest convention of his eyes.
> ("Kairos and Logos")

Man's regress from God brings a diminution in which it seems,

> The order of the microcosmic spaces . . .
> Has lost all interest in our confusion.
> (*Ibid.*)

Whereas Pascal was terrified by the silence of the infinite spaces of the stars,

> The sub-atomic griefs confront our lives
> With the cold stare of their eternal silence.
> (*Ibid.*)

Obviously Auden yearns for the symbolic harmony of the mediaeval universe. Yet even in his darkest moments he sees a possibility of psychological and moral order among men, and he sets over against the chaos of pride and fear the idea of an Elect, the Just, the "fair, the faithful and the uncondemned", who

> Set against the random facts of death
> A ground and possibility of order,
> Against defeat the certainty of Love.
> (*Ibid.*)

Growth into religion has merely rechannelled his belief in the unifying force of love. It has also given new force to his belief in the power of art to portray, and by so doing, to heal the divisions in the mind.

He praises the composer because music is not "a criticism of life":

> Only your notes are pure contraption,
> Only your song is an absolute gift;
> ("The Composer")

yet he loves poetry because

> Rummaging into his living, the poet fetches
> The images out that hurt and connect;
> <div align="right">(<i>Ibid.</i>)</div>

and he celebrates the novelist as one who immerses himself in the experiences of others, who must

> Among the Just
> Be just, among the Filthy filthy too,
> And in his own weak person, if he can,
> Must suffer dully all the wrongs of man.
> ("The Novelist")

Several brilliant portraits of individual writers describe their conflicts and their success or failure in resolving them. Notable examples are "Voltaire at Ferney", a picture of the old rationalist ("The night was full of wrong, Earthquakes and executions"), sure that he would be remembered for his poetry!; Pascal in the night of vision when his "isolation had been utterly consumed, And everything that could exist was holy"; Edward Lear, the "dirty landscape painter who hated his nose", till "Guided by tears he successfully reached his Regret",

> And children swarmed to him like settlers. He became a land.

Matthew Arnold, whose "gift knew what he was—a dark, disordered city", but who, in order to be like his father, "thrust his gift in prison till it died".

The elegy "In Memory of Sigmund Freud" is not a good poem, but it contains a valuable indication of the revolution in men's minds started by the great psychologist. Freud

> Showed us what evil is: not as we thought
> Deeds that must be punished, but our lack of faith,
>   Our dishonest mood of denial,
>   The concupiscence of the oppressor.

He taught us to admit things in ourselves from which we had always shrunk:

> Games we had thought we must drop as we grew up,
> Little noises we dared not laugh at,
> Faces we made when no one was looking.

Freud wished for justice too,

> But he would have us remember most of all
> To be enthusiastic over the night
> Not only for the sense of wonder
> It alone has to offer, but also
> Because it needs our love.

The present age, which has shown the utmost individualism in art and produced poetry of intellectual and emotional privacy, has also seen various attempts to reach beyond the individual and to make artistic use of levels of experience shared by all men. Wordsworth had tried to do this by appealing to the elemental passions through a depiction of incidents and persons affected by a rural setting. A modern method is to make use of the theory that the human mind ceaselessly repeats certain basic patterns of mood, belief, and imagery, and that the survival of some stories and dramatic situations (e.g., the Oedipus theme, the wandering Ulysses theme, the visit to the Underworld, the fight against the dragon) survive and are reworked over in diverse lands and centuries because they have a peculiar resonance, a symbolic significance, for mankind.

In modern poetry we can trace three phases of this notion. W. B. Yeats represents what may be called the "Hermetic" approach, for his ideas about the universe and poetic theory were largely based on his study of theosophy, astrology and alchemy, magic, and spiritualism.[35] Having lost his childhood faith in Christianity he made "a new religion ... of a fardel of stories and of personages, and of emotions, ... passed on from generation to generation by poets and painters, with some help from philosophers and theologians. I wished for a world where I could discover this tradition perpetually" ("The Trembling of the Veil").

He found this world easily enough by looking within.

> Almost every one who has ever busied himself with such matters has come, in trance or dream, upon some new and strange symbol or event, which he has afterwards found in some work he had never read or heard of. Examples of these are . . . proof that there is a memory of nature that reveals events and symbols of distant centuries.

He came to believe in magic and to hold

> (i) That the borders of our mind are ever shifting, and that many minds can flow into one another, as it were, and create or reveal a single mind, a single energy.
> (ii) That the borders of our memories are as shifting, and that our memories are part of one great memory, the memory of Nature herself.
> (iii) That this great mind and great memory can be evoked by symbols.[36]

The images and incantatory verse of poetry were a kind of magic, evoking "the vision of truth in the depths of the mind". But the poet must seek the right images, symbols of the eternal longings and conflicts which man inherited in the cyclical recurrence of history. Hence certain images and certain stories had particular power for Yeats: Leda and the swan stood for the "begetting of Love and War", for "man's realization that he was something more than animal and something less than divine". From Leda's eggs came Helen and Pollux, Castor and Clytemnestra, who embodied the bitter conflict between the animal and the divine in man's nature. Helen of Troy was equated with Deirdre and with his own love Maud Gonne ("Rose of the World"). Other Yeatsian images which he sought in different manifestations were the frustrated hero (Cuchaillan, Countess Markiewicz), the dancing girl (Salome, Maud Gonne's daughter), recurrent revelations (Dionysus, Jesus, the "rough beast" in "The Second Coming"), the Self and its Anti-self. All these are used in accordance with Yeats's vision of the antithetical nature of the world.

> I must lie down where all the ladders start,
> In the foul rag-and-bone shop of the heart

he cries, and

> Love has pitched his mansion in
> The place of excrement.
>
> ("Crazy Jane", vi)

Yet the heart has joy in divine contemplation as well as in lust. Poetry can make a song of delight out of a vision of destruction:

> I would have all know that when all falls
> In ruin, poetry calls out in joy,
> Being the scattering hand, the bursting pod,
> The victim's joy among the holy flame,
> God's laughter at the shattering of the world.
>
> ("The King's Threshold")

For the poet all the tragedy and glory of the past, the correspondences of microcosm and macrocosm, are valuable as incitements to song, and as materials for his art. So the "instructors" in *A Vision* announce, "We have come to give you metaphors for poetry".

Among literary men interest in Comparative Religion, in myth, ritual, and folk-lore grew during the second half of the nineteenth century, when its exponents included Grant Allen and Andrew Lang. Walter Pater wrote essays on *Demeter and Persephone* and on *Dionysus*, and treated the *Bacchae* of Euripides as

> an example of the figurative or imaginative power of poetry, selecting and combining, at will, from that mixed and forbidding mass [of popular beliefs], weaving the many-coloured threads together, blending the various phases of legend, all the light and shade of the subject, into a shape, substantial and firmly set, through which a mere fluctuating tradition might retain a permanent place in men's imaginations.[39]

This was an early instance of the anthropological approach to literary criticism. It is clear from Pater's other studies that he was keenly sensitive to the imaginative tones of various phases of myth. Moreover, inspired partly by Heine's story *Gods in Exile* but mainly by a serious conviction that paganism is permanent to humanity and manifests itself from time to time even in the heart of Christianity by outbursts of witchcraft, superstition, and moral licence, he wrote in *Denys L'Auxerrois* (1887) an "Imaginary

Portrait", the hero of which was a reincarnation of the god Dionysus in mediaeval Auxerre. This story is more firmly based in scholarly knowledge about the myths than Yeats's *Wanderings of Oisin* (1889) in which the bard returns to earth from an enchanted sleep, and finds Ireland converted to Christianity and himself under the ban of St. Patrick. The wordy conflict between them throws light on Yeats's romantic attitude to the heroes of old and belongs to the age of Shelley and Swinburne rather than to that of modern scientific investigation.

Comparative mythology had first made some progress in the first half of the nineteenth century under enthusiasts such as the brothers Grimm and Max Müller. The latter's work was marred by a tendency to see Sun-myths everywhere and by a reliance on an etymology of names based on a faulty system of comparative linguistics.[37] Other one-track approaches came to regard all religions as based on the worship of heroes, or devils, or the dead. More objective work is associated with the names of E. B. Tylor (*Primitive Culture*, 1871), W. Robertson Smith (*The Religion of The Semites*, 1889, etc.), and Sir James Frazer.

Frazer's *The Golden Bough* (1890, etc.) has had as much influence in literature as in science. It is "an essay on the ritual content of naïve drama; that is, it reconstructs the archetypal ritual from which the structure and generic principles of drama may be logically, not chronologically, derived".[38] Apart from this, *The Golden Bough* and similar works, by bringing together from widely different cultures myths and legends with similar features, amassed a great treasure-hoard of story which fostered the modern love of symbolism and gave support to imaginative writers whose own religion included features such as the dying king, the vegetation god, the concepts of miraculous birth and rebirth after burial, by suggesting the universality of certain patterns of religious belief and ritual observance.

In poetry such ideas were first used extensively in *The Waste Land* (1922). Here, from a religious position near to the Perennial

Philosophy later propounded by Mr. Aldous Huxley (1939), Mr. Eliot criticized twentieth-century materialism and moral apathy, and, to show the universality of men's yearning for spiritual regeneration, drew images and ideas from the myths of Osiris and Adonis, the legends of the Holy Grail and the Fisher King, the tradition behind the Tarot pack of cards, as well as from the teaching of the Buddha, St. Augustine of Hippo, and Christ.

I have already suggested that Mr. Eliot's conglomeration of social, literary, and mythological allusions is somewhat self-consciously and arbitrarily arranged. A knowledge of the myths of several cultures is bound to be rare even among educated people, and the ability to get into the state of mind of the devotees of Osiris or Adonis rarer still. Mr. Eliot has not tried to woo us into the spiritual attitudes of Ancient Egypt, Greece, or India. For the most part his allusions to Frazer, Miss J. L. Weston's *From Ritual to Romance*, and the Buddha's Fire Sermon are intellectual pieces in a mosaic of satiric contrast and self-criticism. Mr. Eliot stands in the twentieth century illuminating the darkness of the present by flashes from modern scholarship about the past. The work of Dame Edith Sitwell, on the other hand, displays a remarkable progress towards a real emotional participation in certain phases of myth.

For many years she seemed a technical virtuoso with a gift of song but not much to say. The wonder of words and rhythms and the flow of bright rococo images were enough. That she was one of the first poets in English to write about pagan negro customs showed her early interest in exotic subjects and rhythms. The theme of *Gold Coast Customs* was murderous licence, a fantastic savagery contrasted with the effete civilization of Lady Bamburgher's parties. Although

> The negress Dorothy still feels
> The great gold planet tease her brain.
> And dreaming deep within her blood
> Lay Africa like the dark in the wood,

the poem is mainly a grotesque ballet of shanty-town slum and tribal barbarity:

> And the Amazon queen
> With a bone-black face
> Wears a mask with an ape-skin beard; she grinds
> Her male child's bones in a mortar, binds
> Him for food, and the people buy. . . .

Dame Edith, however, always delighted in images of sun, corn, and gardens, and this elemental motif in her work was increasingly transfused, in *Green Song* and later volumes,[40] with religious feelings combining Christian and classical mythology in a unique lyrical vitality. Even when she writes about old age ("An Old Woman", "The Poet Laments the Coming of Old Age"), and death ("A Song of the Cold", "Metamorphosis"), her major theme is fullness of life, drawn from sunshine, youth, love, or faith. With remarkable power she suggests the unitary forces in stars and gods and men:

> O sons of men, the firmament's beloved,
> The Golden Ones of heaven have us in care—
> With planetary wisdom, changeless laws,
> Ripening our lives and ruling hearts and rhythms,
> Immortal hungers in the veins and heart
> Born from the primal Cause.

She identifies herself with the ripe season, crying

> "I am fecundity, harvest"
> For on each country road,
> Grown from the needs of men as boughs from trees,
> The reapers walk like the harvesters of heaven—
> Jupiter and his great train, and the corn-goddess,
> And Saturn marching in the Dorian mode.
>   ("Harvest")

A few lines later we read of "the Pentecostal Rushing of Flames, God in the wind that comes to the wheat", and "The universal language of the Bread" becomes a symbol of the risen Christ. In a brief "Song for Two Voices" she epitomizes the union of

Dionysus and the Corn Goddess, and in "Eurydice" brings together allusions to Orpheus, Osiris, and other life-death figures. At the mouth of the Tomb she stands

> With one who out came glittering like the wind
> To meet me—Orpheus with the golden mouth,
> You—like Adonis born from the young myrrh-tree, you, the vine-branch
> Broken by the wind of Love. . . . I turned to greet you—
> And when I touched your mouth, it was the Sun.

Just because Dame Edith is less metaphysical than Mr. Eliot, her handling of comparative mythology is more successful than his.

Modern psychology has brought such anthropological interests into line with the treatment of the Unconscious by insisting that many of our dreams and waking images might be racial memories having the same patterns and contents as the figures and incidents in myth and folk-lore. "That which once ruled in the waking state" (wrote Freud) "when the psychical life was still young and impotent, appears to be banished to the dream life, in somewhat the same way as the bow and arrow, those discarded weapons of adult humanity, have been relegated to the nursery."

Jung has developed the idea:

> There is nothing for it but to recognise the irrational as a necessary, because ever-present, psychological function, and to take its contents not as concrete realities—that would be a regression!—but as psychic realities, real because they work. The collective unconscious, being the repository of man's experience, and at the same time the prior condition of this experience, is an image of the world which has taken æons to form. In this image certain features, the archetypes or dominants, have crystallised in the course of time. They are the ruling powers, the *gods*, images of the dominant laws and principles, and of typical regularly recurring events in the soul's cycle of experience.[41]

Thus the "magician" or "demon" type in fiction or drama has his origins in "one of the most ancient stages in the conception of the god. Art provides a higher form of symbolism by which the ancestral fears may be expressed and allayed." Religious myth and ritual may "allow the primitive man adequate means of expression through a vastly developed symbolism".

Jung's influence reached England at a time when interest was growing in Blake's mythology and Yeats's introduction into poetry of theosophical and magical ideas. The psychology of archetypes supported a revival of the conception of the poet as a mythmaker found in some German Romantic philosophers and already practised by Shelley and Keats. Its literary influence has been most remarkable in criticism and in the interpretation of poets like Spenser, Milton, and Coleridge, who draw deeply on themes from romance, epic, and mythology.[42] But archetypal imagery appears in the work of T. S. Eliot, George Barker, Kathleen Raine, and Roy Fuller. A sonnet by Fuller from *Brutus' Orchard* (1957) gives a clear statement of the Jungian position (and incidentally a reply to W. J. Turner's verse-attack on psychoanalysis). It represents the central theory that certain incidents in folk-lore, epic, and romance draw their surprising force from the fears and lusts that we share with our ancestors and with men in all ages throughout the world. He mentions among others the myths of Daphne and Pasiphae:

> "Mythological Sonnet"
> We read of children taken by the heel,
> And tossed over battlements; a sharp hot stake
> Sizzling in a giant's eye; and near a lake
> Two tender virgins lying naked, while
> Unknown to them four indescribable
> Monsters approach. That world, we much would like
> To think, is simply an artistic fake,
> Nothing to do with that in which we dwell.
>
> But could mere images make even now
> Ears drum with lust, the chest run secret shame?
> The myths are here: it was our father's name
> The maiden shrieked in horror as she turned
> To wrinkled bark; our dearest flesh that burned,
> Straddling her legs inside the wooden cow.

It would be wrong to conclude from this that archetypal images are invariably horrific and involved with the darker impulses of human nature. They can be of all kinds and all degrees of intensity and include natural images such as the lily, the rose, the dawn, the stream, as well as those taken from the situations and actions of world-wide legend. The use of these latter may vary greatly. Thus, the poetry of the late Dorothy Wellesley was much concerned with the remote past. Her *Genesis* (1926) surveys the development of civilization and religion from the dawn of man to the coming of Christ:

> North, west, and south and east
> Age upon age eternally the same,
> Scare of the bushman, torment of the priest,
> The simple life-lust troubled by a flame.
> The earth is strewn with shrines.

She notes the permanent tendency of the human mind to create myths, and in the series "Beneath Earth and Sea" she revisits Ancient Egypt and Syria. But far from fusing images of past and present, she believes that we have lost the "gay heroic law", "some secret of the mind and sense" known to the ancients in their mythologies.[43]

On the other hand, Sir Herbert Read's Mediterranean pieces (in *Moon's Farm, and Poems Mostly Elegiac*, 1955) bring classical legends into relationship with poetry and modern attitudes. Remembering Sappho in Sicily, he sees her poems as

> lyric analogues of the rocky kingdom
>   where Minos once
>   fed virgins to a spectral maw.

After visiting Mycenæ he tells his companion

> I saw you then
> Iphigenia or some legendary girl
> Crouched over a fire of withered thyme
> In Agamemnon's tomb. The flames
> Were brief: and left a darkness

> Deeper than the night: into which we walked
> Strangers to our separate doom.

In the elegy "The Gold Disc", celebrating

> The bubbling lymph that makes of man
> An animal susceptible to love,

he explains that by love he means, not lust,

> But some remoter essence, drained from this,
> That foregoes the natural aim, to weave
> Legends of devotion or of mutual bliss—
> The never defin'd, the always unrealiz'd pattern of our delight.

For Read as for Fuller, "the myths are here".

The work of George Barker has developed from Surrealist incoherence towards a more controlled use of images which combine the personal with the archetypal.[44] Now and again he alludes to a specific legend, as in "Heroes and Worms", where "The dragons of the breast" drag down the "Seraphim of the mind", and he becomes a St. George turned against himself:

> I, cowboy with a spear,
> Transfix my own heart
> To kill the worm down there
> Tearing St. George apart—
> But O that worm turns
> Into my heart of hearts.

In "Goodman Jacksin and the Angel" when the Angel bids Jacksin know himself and show the vipers nuzzling in his guts, the latter imagines Man's ignorant confusion as a Cretan labyrinth:

> O Minotaur! A maze! A maze!
> We only know what we have done
> And through what hecatombs have been
> When, there before us, we come upon
> Bleeding our crying footprints run
> Across, ahead. . . .

In the main Barker's imagery becomes archetypal, not by calling on one specific allusion, but by the weight of the context and by accumulating generic associations.

> The monster in a storm
> Is always with us

he asserts, and

> What debars the supreme
> Virtue who shakes her symbols in my dreams
> Save (behemoth walking and talking in all storms)
> I, whom the thundering heart, the talk of lightning
> Forms and deforms.
>
> ("Zennor Idyll I")

Striving after a "Dionysian poetry", "an apotheosis of the word", Mr. Barker often achieves only a welter of clashing symbols, which indicate a deep interior conflict in a mind not "individuated". But his poetic ideal is well expressed in "Letter to a Young Poet":

> From these lyrical waterfalls rise
> Words that bring rainbows to the eyes,
> And memories called up from the ground
> Smile to see their blood around.

Miss Kathleen Raine exemplifies a different kind and use of archetypes. She imagines the old gods as forces in herself:

> Strange that the self's continuum should outlast
> The Virgin, Aphrodite, and the Mourning Mother,
> All loves and griefs, successive deities
> That hold their kingdom in the human heart.

She has been "virgin and Aphrodite The mourning Isis and the queen of corn", and now awaits Persephone, "To dance my dust at last into the tomb" ("The Transit of the Gods").

Such moods and imagery are unusual, however, in her work, the temper of which is nearer to that of Mr. Eliot's *Quartets* than to Mr. Barker's, and happier than either, though severe, almost crystalline in thought and expression. Her favourite symbols are the archetypal images of mystical thought from Plato and Plotinus to Vaughan. She writes, "The ever-recurring forms of nature mirror eternal reality; the never-recurring productions of human history reflect only fallen man, and are therefore not suitable to become a symbolic vocabulary for the kind of poetry I have attempted to write" (Introduction).[45]

Her similitudes are waves, stars, light direct or reflected, the wind, mountains; to these she adds others more obviously metaphysical, such as the ring, the sphere. Hers is a poetry of aspiration to perfection, conscious of immanent deity. Bodily life may be only a temporary manifestation of the spirit:

> Perhaps soul only puts out a hand,
> Antenna or pseudo-podium, an extended touch
> To receive the spectrum of colour, and the lower
>   octave of pain,
> Reaches down into the waves of nature
> As a child drops an arm into the sea,
> And death is the withdrawal of attention
> That has discovered all it needs to know.
>   ("Three Poems on Illusion, II")

Miss Raine, like Mr. Eliot, sees all things as existing in God,

> Whose being is the breath of life,
> The terra firma that we tread,
> The divine body that we eat,
> The incarnation that we live.
>   ("Ex Nihilo")

In "The Sphere" she plays on the popular desire for "a happy ending" and declares,

> There is no end, no ending—steps of a dance, petals of flowers,
> Phrases of music, rays of the sun, the hours
> Succeed each other, and the perfect sphere
> Turns in our hearts the past and future, near and far,
> Our single soul, atom, and universe.

We are back again at the microcosmic view of the world, itself so ancient as to be an archetypal idea and a fount of images to which the Western mind turns easily when it thinks of the soul as emergent from, returning to, or existing in, a Divine Mind.

Here we may fitly close our foray into regions of literature not yet properly mapped. We have travelled far. Beginning in the heaven-enfolded circles of the Ptolemaic universe, we explored the dependence of the human mind on the four elements and the immortal soul. We observed the conflict of reason with the senses and passions in the Renaissance and the age of Descartes. We saw something of thought's mechanism and the associative elements by which the passions were thought to be evoked and made creative. We watched the concepts of soul and immortality endangered by materialistic science, and the efforts of nineteenth-century poets to preserve their intuitions of spiritual energies transcending and outlasting the physical life. We saw too how, when all seemed subjective, poets could make the most of momentary impressions or impose their own imaginative patterns on the flux of experience and find aesthetic and moral discipline in the struggle with language. Finally, we have seen how, rebelling against the booming, buzzing confusion of sensations, the chaos of inner conflict, they have explored the nature of time and either imagined it transcended in timeless moments of spiritual revelation, or have regarded the warring impulses as enforced by unconscious desires and racial memories, expressible in evocative symbols.

It may seem that in moving thus from the correspondences and potential harmony of the microcosm to the interior depths below the individual dream, we have travelled down an ever-narrowing spiral. But this is not an exact figure; for in each age the aim of poetic thought, as of philosophy, has been "Nosce teipsum", and whether the poet postulated first the existence of eternal spirit and secondly his own, or vice versa, the nature of the whole universe has usually been implied in the concept of the individual mind.

Looking back over the relationships between poetry and ideas about the mind since Chaucer, we observe that each phase of the past has led on to its successor, though not by simple development, and certainly not by a Hegelian dialectic of thesis, antithesis, and resolution. There have been revulsions and expansions, specialization, digressions, even an occasional new beginning. In literature the movement has been fugal in character, for certain themes relevant to our study have recurred in each age, but always in slightly different forms; and now one, now another, has been the dominant interest. Thus the conflict between reason, sense, and passion is an ever-returning theme; but ideas about its nature varied, and so did its literary projection in Shakespeare, Milton, Bridges, and Auden, while the portrayal of human beings shifted between the allegorical (Moralities), the individual (Shakespeare and Browning), and the typical (Jonson, Pope, Auden). Similarly, different aspects of the mind's relationship to what is outside it have come to the fore according to whether God, Man, or Nature has been held to be the proper study of mankind. The poets' views about the imagination have also varied greatly, as mechanical and intuitive conceptions have rivalled each other, and as doctrines of sensory impressions, associations, organic emotion, and unconscious promptings have succeeded one another.

The history of literature cannot be explained by the history of philosophy or psychology. Many other factors are involved as art reflects the forms of things in the mind's distorting mirror. But the way in which art reflects and re-creates is governed to a large extent by what, in the light of tradition, custom, and current ideas, the artist believes his mind to be, its powers and proper interests, and its relation to his medium of expression. His science may be rudimentary or wrong, his particular faith an illusion. What matters, in art as in morality, is not the objective truth of his assumptions about himself, but the pervading intensity of their imaginative influence and the spaciousness and precision of his resultant apprehension of man's place in the scale of being.

NOTES

References are to editions published in London unless otherwise indicated.

I. THE POETRY OF THE SOUL'S INSTRUMENTS

1. Cf. E. Dowden, *Essays Modern and Elizabethan* (1910); E. M. W. Tillyard, *The Elizabethan World Picture* (1943, 1948); Hardin Craig, *The Enchanted Glass* (New York, 1936, 1950); J. B. Bamborough, *Little World of Man* (1952); A. D. Lovejoy, *The Great Chain of Being* (Cambridge, Mass., 1936); F. R. Johnson, *Astronomical Thought in Renaissance England* (Baltimore, 1937); D. C. Allen, *The Star-Crossed Renaissance* (Durham, N.C., 1941).

2. These include: T. Vicary, *The Anatomie of the Bodie of Man*, 1548 (E.E.T.S., 1888); Levirus Lemnius, *The Touchstone of Complexions*, tr. Thomas Newton 1565, 1576; Thomas Rogers, *A Philosophicall Discourse, Entituled, the Anatomie of the Mind* 1576; [S.] Batman uppon Bartholome, *His Booke De Proprietatibus Rerum*, 1582; Pierre de la Primaudaye, *The French Academie . . . Book I*, tr. T.B. 1586, tr. T.B.C. 1618; T. Bright, *A Treatise of Melancholie*, 1586 (New York, 1940); Juan de D. H. N. Huarte, *The Examination of Man's Wits*, tr. R.C. 1594; Sir John Davies, *Nosce Teipsum*, 1599 (*Works*, ed. A. B. Grosart, 1869–76, Vol. I; *Poems*, ed. Clare Howard, New York, 1941); John Davies of Hereford (*Complete Works*, ed. A. B. Grosart, Edinburgh, 1878); Thomas Wright, *The Passions of the Minde*, 1601; Pierre Charron, *Of Wisedome Three Bookes*, tr. S. Lennard 1606, 1630, 1640; F. N. Coeffeteau, *A Table of Humane Passions*, tr. E. Grimeston 1621; Robert Burton, *The Anatomie of Melancholy*, 1621 (ed. A. R. Shilleto, 3 vols., 1926–7); Edward Reynolds, *A Treatise of the Faculties of the Soule of Man*, 1640.

3. Cf. W. C. Curry, *Chaucer and the Medieval Sciences* (New York, 1926).

4. Cf. *Songs and Carols from a Manuscript of the Fifteenth Century*, ed. T. Wright, Percy Society, XXIII, 1847, No. iv.

5. Examples are given in *Secular Lyrics of the XIVth and XVth Centuries*, ed. R. H. Robbins (1952).

6. W. R. Mackenzie, *English Moralities: From the Point of View of Allegory* (1921).

7. G. R. Owst, *Literature and Pulpit in Medieval England* (1933), p. 80.

NOTES, PAGES 13-32

8. Editions: *Castle of Perseverance*; *Wisdom which is Christ*; *Mankind*—in *Macro Plays*, ed. F. J. Furnivall and A. W. Pollard (E.E.T.S., 1904), *Tudor Facsimile Texts*, 1907. *Lusty Juventus*, Dodsley-Hazlitt, II; ed. J. S. Farmer, 1905; *T.F.T.* 1907. *Interlude of Youth*, Dodsley-Hazlitt, I; Bang, XII, 1905; *T.F.T.* 1908-9. *Hickscorner*, Dodsley-Hazlitt, I; Manly, I; ed. J. S. Farmer, 1905; *T.F.T.* 1908. *Interlude of the Four Elements*, ed. J. O. Halliwell, *Percy Society*, LXXIV, 1848; Dodsley-Hazlitt, I; ed. J. S. Farmer, 1905; *T.F.T.* 1908. *Wit and Science*, ed. J. O. Halliwell, *Shak. Soc.* 1848; Manly, I; ed. J. S. Farmer, 1907; *T.F.T.* 1908; *Mal. Soc. Reprint*, 1951. *The Marriage of Wit and Science*, Dodsley-Hazlitt, II; *T.F.T.* 1909. *The Marriage of Wit and Wisdom*, ed. J. O. Halliwell, *Shak. Soc.* 1846; *T.F.T.* 1909.

9. Cf. E. Spenser, *Works*, ed. Greenlaw, Osgood, and Padelford (Variorum ed., 8 vols., Baltimore, 1932-49); *Fowre Hymnes*, ed. L. Winstanley (1907); H. S. V. Jones, *A Spenser Handbook* (New York, 1930); J. Spens, *Spenser's Faerie Queene* (1934); C. S. Lewis, *The Allegory of Love* (Oxford, 1951 ed.).

10. [S.] *Batman uppon Bartholome* (1582), cited in J. W. Reeves, *Body and Mind in Western Thought* (1958), pp. 104-5.

11. P. Fletcher, *The Purple Island* (Cambridge, 1633); in *Poetical Works of Giles Fletcher and Phineas Fletcher*, ed. F. S. Boas (2 vols., Cambridge, 1908-9). William Strode, *The Floating Island*, ed. B. Dobell, *Poetical Works of W.S.* (1907); Henry More, *Philosophical Poems* (1647); see *Philosophical Poems of H. More*, ed. G. Bullough (Manchester, 1931).

12. For selections from Bright, Woolton, and Ashley, see the excellent anthology, *The Frame of Order; an outline of Elizabethan belief taken from treatises of the late sixteenth century*, ed. James Winny (1957).

13. Philippe de Mornay, *A Woorke concerning the trewnesse of the Christian religion* . . . , 1587. Part in *Works of Sir Philip Sidney*, ed. A. Feuillerat, Vol. III (Cambridge, 1923). P. de la Primaudaye, *The French Academie*, tr. T.B. 1586; Richard Hooker, *Works*, ed. John Keble, 3 vols. (Oxford, 1865) (Vol. I, ch. V-XII).

14. Sir John Davies, *Nosce Teipsum*, 1599 (*Works*, ed. A. B. Grosart, 3 vols., 1869-76; *Works*, ed. H. Morley, 1889). John Davies of Hereford, *Mirum in Modum*, 1602; *Microcosmos*, 1603; *Summa Totalis*, 1607 (*Complete Works*, ed. A. B. Grosart, Edinburgh, 1878). Fulke Greville, *Certaine learned and elegant workes*, 1633 (*Works*, ed. A. B. Grosart, 4 vols., 1870; *Poems and Dramas*, ed. G. Bullough, Edinburgh, 1939).

15. John Wilmot, Earl of Rochester, *A Satyr against Mankind* (anon.), 1675 (*Poems*, ed. V. de S. Pinto, 1953).

16. Citations here are from N. Ault, *Elizabethan Lyrics* (1925).

17. See L. C. John, *The Elizabethan Sonnet Sequences: Studies in Conventional*

Conceits (New York, 1938); M. B. Ogle, "The Classical Origin and Tradition of Literary Conceits", *American Journal of Philosophy*, XXXIV, 1913, 125–53; D. Bush, *Mythology and the Renaissance Tradition in English Poetry* (Minneapolis, 1932).

18. P. Sidney, *Works*, ed. A. Feuillerat (1922), II, 236, 302.
19. *Ibid.*, pp. 293–4.
20. *Ibid.*, pp. 312–14.
21. *Ibid.*, p. 212.
22. *Ibid.*, p. 237.
23. R. Graves, *Poems (1914–26)* (1927), p. 150.
24. For Donne's use of the word "Ecstasy" and for various interpretations of the poem see M. Y. Hughes, "Some of Donne's 'Ecstasies' ", *PMLA*, LXXV (1960), 509–18.
25. Louis L. Martz, *The Poetry of Meditation* (New Haven, Conn., 1954), pp. 121–2. Martz treats the subject mainly through Roman Catholic writings. Many translations from foreign masters were published at Douai or St. Omer, for example, St. François de Sales (1614), Tomás de Villacastin (1618), G. Loarte (1584), Robert Bellarmine (1616), Antonio de Molina (1617), Jean Pierre de Camus (1632), Luis de Granada (1612). Some of these were certainly studied by Anglicans and Puritans both before and after the Civil War.
26. These may come from the "Scala Meditoria" in the *Rosetum* of Joannes Mauburnus Zwolle, 1494. See the facsimile in Martz, p. 63, which includes many more stages.

II. THE DEVELOPMENT OF SHAKESPEARE'S ATTITUDE TO THE MIND

1. Hardin Craig, *The Enchanted Glass* (New York, 1936), p. 195.
2. G. Bullough ed., *Narrative and Dramatic Sources of Shakespeare*, I (1957), 108.
3. P. Charron, *Of Wisdom*, tr. S. Lennard (1630 ed.), p. 169.
4. Cf. references in L. B. Wright, *Middle-Class Culture in Elizabethan England* (Chapel Hill, 1935), ch. VII.
5. Pierre de la Primaudaye, *The French Academie, newly translated by T.B.* (1586), p. 474.
6. *Ibid.*, p. 292.
7. G. Bullough, ed., *Narrative and Dramatic Sources*, I, 212–53.
8. L. B. Campbell, *Shakespeare's Tragic Heroes: Slaves of Passion* (Cambridge, Mass., 1930), p. 105.
9. Cf. facsimile in Students' Facsimile Edition (1912); *Shakespeare's Library*, ed. W. C. Hazlitt (1875), Pt. II, Vol. I. For Falstaff, see J. D. Wilson, *The*

NOTES, PAGES 72–101   259

Fortunes of Falstaff (Cambridge, 1943); H. B. Charlton, *Shakespearian Comedy* (1938), pp. 161–207.

  10. Cf. L. Babb, *The Elizabethan Malady* (East Lansing, 1951), ch. IV.

  11. E. Dowden, *Shakspere: A Critical Study of his Mind and his Art* (1875); C. J. Sisson, *The Mythical Sorrows of Shakespeare*, British Academy Lecture, 1934; R. W. Chambers, *The Jacobean Shakespeare and "Measure for Measure"*, British Academy Lecture, 1937.

  12. Both quoted in Campbell, *Shakespeare's Tragic Heroes*, pp. 95, 102.

  13. T. Bright, *A Treatise of Melancholy* (1586); see L. B. Campbell, *Shakespeare's Tragic Heroes*, p. 76.

  14. Cf. E. M. Wilson, "Family Honour in the Plays of Shakespeare's Predecessors and Contemporaries", *Essays and Studies of the English Association* (1953).

III. REASON, THE PASSIONS, AND ASSOCIATIONS

  1. T. S. Eliot, *Selected Essays* (1932), pp. 267–77.

  2. M. H. Carré, *Phases of Thought in England* (Oxford, 1949), p. 246.

  3. J. Glanvill, *The Vanity of Dogmatising* (1661), p. 211; cited by Carré, *op. cit.*, p. 250.

  4. Cited by Carré, *op. cit.*, p. 251.

  5. *Essay towards the Theory of an Ideal and Intelligible World*, 2 parts (1701, 1704); it expounds Malebranche's doctrines.

  6. Cf. the valuable notes in *The Literary Works of Matthew Prior*, ed. H. B. Wright and M. K. Spears (1959); also W. P. Barrett, "Matthew Prior's *Alma*", *MLR*, XXVII (1932); E. K. Spears, "The Meaning of Prior's *Alma*", *ELH*, XIII (1946).

  7. Cf. E. K. Spears, *op. cit.*, pp. 271–8.

  8. Edward Young, *Conjectures on Original Composition*, ed. E. J. Morley (Manchester, 1918), pp. 22–33.

  9. " 'The business of a poet', said Imlac, 'is to examine not the individual but the species; to remark general properties and large appearances. He does not number the streaks of the tulip, or describe the different shades in the verdure of the forest' " (S. Johnson, *Rasselas*, ch. x).

  10. Cf. K. MacLean, *John Locke and English Literature of the Eighteenth Century* (Yale University Press, 1936); T. Fowler, *Locke* (1880); D. G. James, *The Life of Reason (Hobbes, Locke, Bolingbroke)* (1949).

  11. René Descartes, *Oeuvres*, ed. C. Adam and P. Tannery (Paris, 1897), I. 5–13 (Latin Defence of Balzac's *Letters*). Cf. B. Willey, *The Seventeenth Century Background* (1934), ch. V.

12. Cf. G. Tillotson, "Augustan Poetic Diction", I and II, *Augustan Studies*, (1961).

13. E. Krantz, *Essai sur l'Esthétique de Descartes: rapports de la doctrine cartésienne avec la littérature classique française au 17e siècle* (Paris, 1898).

14. J. E. Spingarn, *Critical Essays of the Seventeenth Century* (Oxford, 1908), II, 59. Vol. II also contains the essays by Mulgrave and Roscommon cited later; Vol. III, Granville's *Essay upon Unnatural Flights in Poetry*.

15. "Pope on Wit: The Essay on Criticism", by E. N. Hooker, in *The Seventeenth Century: Studies in the History of English Thought and Literature from Bacon to Pope*, by R. F. Jones et al. (Stanford, Calif., 1951).

16. John Dennis, *The Impartial Critick*, Dial. 3; in Spingarn, *Critical Essays of the Seventeenth Century*, III, 184.

17. A. Pope, *An Essay on Man*, ed. Maynard Mack (1950).

18. S. Johnson, *Lives of the Poets*, I (Oxford, 1926 ed.), p. 133. See also R. Trickett, "The Augustan Pantheon", *Essays and Studies*, N.S. Vol. VI, ed. G. Bullough (1953).

19. David Hume, *Treatise of Human Nature*, ed. T. H. Green and T. H. Grose (2 vols., 1874), I. 311-33, 439-46, etc.

20. Citations from *Essays, Literary, Moral, and Political*, by David Hume (1870 ed.), pp. 316-37. Cf. B. Willey, *The Eighteenth Century Background* (1940), ch. VII.

21. Citations from 6th edition, 1834.

22. M. Akenside, *The Pleasures of Imagination* (1744), Bk. I, "The Argument".

23. Abbie Findlay Potts explores (and maybe exaggerates) Wordsworth's debt to Akenside, in *Wordsworth's Prelude: A Study of its Literary Form* (Ithaca, 1953), pp. 244-78.

IV. ASSOCIATIONS, INTUITION, AND IMMORTAL LONGINGS

1. J. S. Mill, *A System of Logic Ratiocinative and Inductive* (1843), 1919 ed., p. 558.

2. David Hartley, *Observations on Man* (1749), cited from 6th ed. 1834, ch. IV, sect. I, pp. 263-4. Cf. B. Willey, *op. cit.*, ch. VIII.

3. Quoted in A. Alison, *Essays on the Nature and Principles of Taste* (1790), 1817 ed., I, 61-2.

4. Dugald Stewart, *Elements of the Philosophy of the Human Mind* (1792-1827), cited from 1837 ed., p. 220.

5. *The Letters of John Keats*, ed. M. B. Forman (3rd ed., 1947). Letters 55-64.

6. See the illuminating comments on this poem in D. G. James, *The Romantic Comedy* (1948), pp. 118-21.

7. In *John Keats: A Reassessment*, ed. K. Muir (Liverpool, 1959), pp. 68–9.
8. Cf. E. B. F. D'Auvergne, *The Dear Emma* (1936), pp. 88, 89, 101; O. A. Sherrard, *A Life of Emma, Lady Hamilton* (1927); M. Bowen, *Patriotic Lady* (1935).
9. Hartley, *op. cit.*, ch. IV, sect. 4, p. 295.
10. Cf. W. J. Bate, *Negative Capability: The Intuitive Approach in Keats* (Cambridge, Mass., 1939), pp. 29–33; "Keats and Hazlitt", by K. Muir, in *John Keats: A Reassessment*, pp. 139–58.
11. Hartley, *op. cit.*, ch. IV, sect. 5, p. 307.
12. A. Beattie, *William Wordsworth* (University of Wisconsin Press, 1927).
13. Cf. R. H. Thouless, *General and Social Psychology* (1937 ed.), pp. 103, 255, 279; C. Spearman, *The Nature of Intelligence and the Principles of Cognition* (1923).
14. D. Stewart, *Elements of the Philosophy of the Human Mind* (1837 ed.), p. 17; further page references are given in the text.
15. C. E. Pulos, *The Deep Truth* (University of Nebraska Press, 1954), discusses Shelley's debt to the sceptics.
16. *Shelley's Prose, or The Trumpet of a Prophecy*, ed. D. L. Clark (Albuquerque, 1954), p. 174.
17. L. Winstanley, "Shelley's Platonism", *Essays and Studies* (1913); and Pulos, *op. cit.*, ch. V.
18. R. S. Crane, *The Language of Criticism and the Structure of Poetry* (Toronto, 1953), p. 161.
19. J. S. Mill, *A System of Logic* (1843), 1919 ed., Bk. VI, ch. IV, pp. 555–8.
20. T. H. Huxley, *Method and Results* (1893), pp. 242–4.
21. E. Hering, "On Memory as a Universal Function of Organized Matter", tr. by S. Butler in *Unconscious Memory* (1910 ed.), p. 67. Cf. L. W. Reeves, *Body and Mind in Western Thought* (1958), pp. 376–84.
22. T. H. Huxley, "On the Physical Basis of Life" (1868) in *Method and Results* (1893), p. 160.
23. John Tyndall, *Address delivered before the British Association assembled at Belfast, with additions* (1874). Reprinted in *Fragments of Science*, Vol. II (1879).
24. Cf. *Life of Clerk Maxwell* (1882), by Campbell and Garnett, pp. 639–41.
25. References in this paragraph are from M. H. Carré, *Phases of Thought in England* (1949), pp. 320–5.
26. R. Knox, *Enthusiasm: A Chapter in the History of Religion* (Oxford, 1950), pp. 422 ff.
27. William Law, *A Demonstration of the Gross and Fundamental Errors of a Late Book*, 1757 (*Works*, 1892, Vol. V, pp. 1–131).
28. Cf. H. Adams, *Blake and Yeats: The Contrary Vision* (Ithaca, 1955), pp. 23–7, 308.

29. H. L. Mansel, *Limits of Religious Thought* (1848); J. B. Mozley, *On Miracles* (1865), Carré, *Phases of Thought in England*, pp. 340-2.
30. Newman, *An Essay in Aid of A Grammar of Assent* (1870), 3rd ed., p. 232.
31. *Ibid.*, p. 382.
32. Herbert Spencer, *Principles of Psychology*, 1872 ed., II, xvii.
33. Cf. J. M. Bramwell, *Hypnotism, its History, Practice and Theory* (1903); E. G. Boring, *A History of Experimental Psychology* (New York, 1929), ch. 7.
34. Cf. W. C. De Vane, *A Browning Handbook* (New York, 1955), p. 225.
35. William Whewell, *Astronomy and general Physics considered with reference to Natural Theology* (The Bridgewater Treatises, III (1833), Introduction; Bk. I, II).
36. E. D. H. Johnson, *The Alien Vision of Victorian Poetry*, Princeton Studies in English, no. 34 (Princeton, New Jersey, 1952).
37. Gerard Manley Hopkins, *Sermons and Devotional Writings*, ed. C. Devlin (1959), p. 122.
38. Quoted by E. Thompson in *Robert Bridges, 1844-1930* (1944), p. 120.
39. O. Elton, *Robert Bridges and the "Testament of Beauty"* (1932).
40. M. L. V. Hughes, *Everyman's "Testament of Beauty"* (1932), pp. 156-7.
41. J. Martineau, *Types of Ethical Theory* (1892), II, 365-7.

V. THE INDIVIDUAL AND THE RACIAL IMAGE

1. Cf. E. G. Boring, *A History of Experimental Psychology* (New York, 1929), chs. 17-23; R. S. Peters ed., *Brett's History of Psychology* (1953), Part IV.
2. Charles Berman, *The Glands Regulating Personality* (New York, 1928).
3. E.g. *Antic Hay* (1923), ch. 22; *Point Counterpoint* (1928), ch. 3.
4. D. Hume, *A Treatise of Human Nature* (1739-40), ed. T. H. Green and T. H. Grose (1874), Bk. I, Pt. IV, sect. 6, Vol. I, p. 534.
5. Étienne Bonnot, Abbé de Condillac, *Traité des sensations* (1754) in *Œuvres* (Paris, 1947), I, 313, etc.
6. W. Pater, *The Renaissance: Studies in Art and Poetry* (1873), cited from 1910 ed., pp. 233 ff.
7. For the ideas of French Impressionist and later painters, see A. Lhote, *De la palette à l'escritoire* (Paris, 1946).
8. F. Galton, *Inquiries into Human Faculty and its Development* (1883); other quotations from M. Nordau, *Decadence* (1895), ch. 3.
9. G. J. Romanes, *Animal Intelligence* (1881); *Mental Evolution in Animals* (1883); *Mental Evolution in Man* (1888).
10. C. Ll. Morgan, *Introduction to Comparative Psychology* (1894); *Animal Behaviour* (1900).

11. Sir John Lubbock, *Ants, Bees and Wasps* (1882); J. H. Fabre, *Souvenirs entomologiques*, 9 vols. (Paris, 1879-1904); A. Bethe, "Dürfen wir den Ameisen und Bienen psychische Qualitäten zuschreiben," *Arch. f. d. ges. Physiol.*, LXX (1898), LXXIX (1900), 39-52; J. Loeb, *Comparative Physiology of the Brain and Comparative Psychology* (New York, 1900); M. F. Washburn, *Animal Mind* (New York, 1908); E. L. Thorndike, *Animal Intelligence* (New York, 1898).

12. J. M. Whistler, *The Gentle Art of Making Enemies* (1890), pp. 135-59.

13. W. James, *Pragmatism* (1907), p. 257.

14. Cited in B. Russell, *History of Western Philosophy* (1946), p. 851.

15. On the aesthetic ideas in modern art, see H. Read, *Art Now* (1933).

16. J. A. Symonds, *Essays Speculative and Suggestive* (1890), 3rd ed. 1907, p. 227.

17. Useful information about Mr. Eliot's early life and work is given in Grover Smith, *T. S. Eliot's Poetry and Plays* (Chicago, 1956).

18. Cf. W. F. Lofthouse, *F. H. Bradley* (1949).

19. T. S. Eliot, *Selected Essays* (1932), p. 400.

20. Boring, op. cit., ch. 22, especially pp. 578-9.

21. *The Letters of Ezra Pound, 1907-41*, ed. D. D. Paige (1951). For Pound's technique cf. H. H. Watts. *E. Pound and the Cantos* (1958).

22. Grover Smith, *T. S. Eliot's Poetry and Plays*, p. 251. Cf. K. Smidt, *Poetry and Belief in the Work of T. S. Eliot* (Oslo, 1949).

23. Cf. M. E. Cleugh, *Time* (1937) and its Bibliography. The best study of literary conceptions of time is G. Poulet's *Studies in Human Time* (Baltimore, 1956), which has a section on American writers, including Eliot.

24. H. Bergson, *Creative Evolution* (1910), Eng. trans. 1911.

25. J. S. Mill, *A System of Logic* (1904 ed.), p. 40.

26. H. L. Mansel, *Metaphysics* (1860), pp. 354-5.

27. Cf. the Bibliography in *Freud and the Twentieth Century*, ed. B. Nelson (1958); Pfister, *The Psychoanalytic Method* (1915); J. A. Hadfield, *Dreams and Nightmares* (1954).

28. H. Read, *Collected Essays in Literary Criticism* (1938, 1950), p. 126 n.

29. Cf. his critical writings, *Poetic Unreason* (1925); *The Common Asphodel* (1949); *The Crowning Privilege* (1955).

30. Cf. David Gascoyne, *Surrealism* (1935).

31. Cf. E. H. J. Gombrich, "Psychoanalysis and Art", *Freud and the Twentieth Century* (1958), pp. 184, 200.

32. Cf. W. Bromberg, *The Mind of Man: A History of Psychotherapy and Psychoanalysis* (New York, 1959), ch. 9.

33. A. Adler, *The Neurotic Constitution* (New York, 1917); *Problems of Neurosis* (1929); L. Way, *Alfred Adler: An Introduction to his Psychology* (1956).

34. A. Adler, *Problems of Neurosis* (1929), p. 130.

35. Cf. R. Ellman, *Yeats, the Man and the Masks* (1949) and *The Identity of Yeats* (1954); H. Adams, *Blake and Yeats: The Contrary Vision*, Cornell Studies in English, XL (Ithaca, 1955).

36. W. B. Yeats, "Ideas of Good and Evil", *Essays* (1924), p. 13.

37. Cf. J. Grimm, *Deutsche Mythologie* (Berlin, 1875–8, trans. J. S. Stallybrass, 1882–8); F. Max Müller, *Lectures on the Science of Language* (1871) and *Selected Essays* (1881); Andrew Lang, *Myth, Ritual and Religion* (1887). For a sketch of modern reinterpretations of the Greek myths see G. Highet, *The Classical Tradition* (Oxford, 1949), ch. 23. Cf. also D. Bush, *Mythology and the Romantic Tradition in English Poetry* (Cambridge, Mass., 1937).

38. N. Frye, *Anatomy of Criticism: Four Essays* (Princeton, 1957).

39. W. Pater, *Greek Studies* (1895), pp. 53–4.

40. Citations here are from *Song of the Cold* (1945).

41. C. G. Jung, *The Collected Works*, ed. H. Read, M. Fordham, G. Adler (1953–), VII, p. 93. Cf. *The Integration of the Personality*, tr. S. Del. (1946); *The Interpretation of Nature and the Psyche* (1949). Also J. Jacobi, *The Psychology of C. G. Jung* (1942); P. W. Martin, *Experiment in Depth* (1955).

42. Cf. Maud Bodkin, *Archetypal Patterns in Poetry* (1934) and *Studies of Type-Images in Poetry, Religion and Philosophy* (1951); Northrop Frye, *Anatomy of Criticism: Four Essays* (Princeton, 1957).

43. Cf. *Early Light: The Collected Poems of Dorothy Wellesley* (1955).

44. George Barker, *Collected Poems, 1930–55* (1957).

45. Kathleen Raine, *Collected Poems* (1956). Cf. H. Foltinek, "The Primitive Element in the Poetry of Kathleen Raine", *English Studies*, XLII, February, 1961.

INDEX

Addison, J., 92, 100, 130
Adler, A., 234, 235–6
'Aesthetes', 189–92
Ages of Man, 4
Agrippa, C., 24
Akenside, M., 125, 130–3, 135
Alanus de Insulis, 18
Alexander, S., 223
Alison, A., 213
All's Well that Ends Well, 8, 74
Alma, 93–5
Alma, House of, 18–21
Amiel, H-F., 182
Animal spirits, 4
Anti-Jacobin, The, 204
Apperception, 211–12, 236
Aquinas, St. Thomas, 2, 3, 75, 94
Arcadia, 32, 34
Archetypes, 242–53
Ariosto, L., 16, 18
Aristotle, 2, 4, 17, 18, 21, 43, 94–5, 126, 183, 237
Armstrong, J., 107–8
Arnold, M., 169, 192, 241
Arthur (*The Faerie Queene*), 17, 18, 20
Ascham, R., 9
Ashley, R., 22
Association theory, 126–52, 157
As You Like It, 72–3
Auden, W. H., 234–42, 255
Augustine, St., 2, 17, 42, 55
Averroes, 178

Bacon, F., 9, 10, 91, 163
Bain, A., 160
Baldwin, M., 237

Barker, G., 249, 251–2
Bartolomeus Anglicanus, 21
Batman, S., 21
Baudelaire, C., 197
Baxter, R., 42
Beardsley, A., 197
Beattie, A., 144
Beaumont, F. and Fletcher, J., 49
Benevolence, 125
Bentley, R., 162
Bergson, H., 223–7
Berkeley, Bp. G., 152, 154
Berman, C., 189
Bernard, C., 188
Bernard, St., 18, 42
Bethe, A., 203
Betterton, T., 71
Blake, W., 162–3, 249
Blood, 4
Boccaccio, G., 5
Bodin, J., 22
Boehme, J., 162
Boileau, N., 101
Boring, E. G., 202, 203
Bouhours, D., 104
Boyle, R., 43, 91
Bradley, F. H., 214–15
Braid, J., 172
Bramston, J., 106
Braque, G., 210, 213
Breton, A., 233
Breuer, J., 227–8
Bridges, R., 141, 183–7, 255
Bright, T., 17, 22, 80
Brooke, R., 200–2, 206–7
Browning, R., 90, 164–75, 177, 178, 183

Burton, R., 72
Butler, Bp. J., 161, 168, 171
Butler, S., 160
Byron, Lord, 136, 138-9, 204

Cambridge Platonists, 41, 92, 94, 96, 162
Campbell, L. B., 71, 79, 80, 84
Cardinal virtues, 10, 29
Carlyle, T., 169
Casanova motif, 36
Castiglione, B., 9
Castle of Love, 18
Castle of Perseverance, 11 12
Chambers, R., 175, 186
Chapman, G., 49, 74
Charcot, J. M., 227
Charleton, W., 91
Chaucer, G., 5-8, 143, 254
Choler, 4
Chrétien de Troyes, 6, 35
Clarke, S., 121, 162
Claude Lorraine, 140
Clough, A. H., 179-82, 215
Coleridge, H., 151
Coleridge, S. T. C., 125, 133, 143, 147, 148, 150, 152, 204, 227
Collins, W., 90, 123
Comedy of Errors, 56-7, 59, 60, 71
Common sense, 3, 23, 34
Comparative mythology, 244-8
Condillac, Abbé de, 190-1
Condorcet, M. J., 149
Conflict of Conscience, 12
Conquest of Granada, 113-14
Constable, T., 31
Contemplation, 34-5
Coward, W., 93, 94
Cowley, A., 45-6
Cowper, W., 136
Craig, H., 49
Crane, R. S., 157
Crashaw, R., 43
Cubism, 210, 212
Cudworth, R., 162

Cunningham, J., 123
Cuvier, L. C., 175
Cymbeline, 87

Daniel, S., 32
Dante, 8, 34, 90
Darwin, C., 173, 186, 195, 203
Davenant, Sir W., 102
Davies, Sir J., 23, 24, 40, 45, 92
Davies, J., 23, 40, 45
Davies, W. H., 198-9
'Decadence', 195-8
Degas, H-G. E., 194
de la Mare, W., 229-31
Dennis, J., 105, 113
Descartes, R., 21, 47, 91, 92, 94, 98, 99, 101, 111, 116, 144, 160, 174, 202, 254
Despine, P. C., 195
Dewey, J., 211-12
Digby, Sir K., 20-1
Dodsley, R., 119-20
Donne, J., 7, 35-41, 90, 97, 137
Dowson, E. C., 198
Drayton, M., 31
Dreams, 55-9, 122, 176, 229, 230
Drury, E., 39
Dryden, J., 100, 105, 106, 112-14, 118-19, 122-3, 196
Du Bartas, G. de S., 19
Du Maurier, G., 172
Dunne, J. W., 223
Dürer, A., 182
Duty of a Player, 71
Dyer, J., 106, 135

Ehrenfels, C. von, 215
Einstein, A., 223
Eliot, Sir T., 9
Eliot, T. S., 48, 90, 212-27, 239, 245-6, 249, 252, 253
Elliotson, J., 171
Ellis, H., 196
Elton, O., 183
Empiricus, Sextus, 24

INDEX

Enthusiasm, 144
Epicurus, 91, 94
Ernst, M., 233
Etty, W., 121
Evolution theory, 134, 167, 173, 178, 183–7, 223–6, 248
Eyes and heart, 31–2

Fabre, J. H., 203
Faerie Queene, The, 16–21, 23, 92
Fall of Man, 10, 24, 26, 41
Famous Victories, 72
Fancy, 3, 19, 23, 45, 102, 105, 128, 129, 130, 131, 133, 144–8, 150–1
'Fauves', 210
Ferrar, N., 42
Fichte, J. G., 169
Ficino, M., 17
Fitzgerald, E., 182
Flaubert, G., 226
Fletcher, G., 12
Fletcher, P., 21
Folk-psychology, 6
Ford, J., 49
Four Elements, 13
Frazer, Sir J., 245–6
Free will, 26–9
Freud, S., 1, 228, 233, 241, 248
Froude, J. A., 179
Fuller, R., 249
Fuller, T., 42

Galen, 2, 8
Galileo, 91
Gall, F. J., 195
Galton, F., 196
Gascoyne, D., 233
Gassendi, P., 91, 95, 161
Gauguin, P., 210
Gautier, T., 192
Gay, J., 101
Georgian poets, 131, 198–207
Gestalt psychology, 215–17, 238
Glanvill, J., 91, 122

Gogh, V. van, 210, 212
Golding, A., 23
Goldsmith, O., 118, 137
Gonne, M., 243
Gower, J., 17
Grace, 17, 30
Granville, G., 104
Graves, R., 35, 229–32
Gray, T., 90, 121
Green, M., 107, 108–10
Greene, R., 49
Greville, F., 23–5, 40
Griffin, B., 32
Grimm brothers, 245
Grosseteste, Robert, 18
Guérinsen, O., 196
Gunn, J. A., 223

Hall, J., 42
Hallam, A., 176–7
Hamilton, E. Lady, 142
Hamilton, Sir W. (ambassador), 142
Hamilton, Sir W. (philosopher), 134
Hamlet, 22, 44–5, 68–9, 80–3, 85, 86
Hardy, T., 182, 184
Hartley, D., 128–30, 130–3, 134, 136, 139, 143–4, 146, 163
Hazlitt, W., 139, 143
Heard, G., 235
Heine, H., 244
Helmholtz, H. von, 188
Henley, W. E., 193, 197
Henry IV, Pt. 1, 68, 69–71
Henry IV, Pt. 2, 74
Henry VI, Pt. 1, 50, 55
Henry VI, Pt. 2, 50, 54, 55, 79
Henry VI, Pt. 3, 50, 51–3, 55, 79
Heraclitus, 201
Herbert, G., 42, 43
Hering, E., 160
Hermetic images, 242–3
Hick Scorner, 13
Hobbes, T., 21, 25, 46, 92, 102, 114, 122, 126, 235

INDEX

Hodgson, R., 205
Hogarth, W., 117, 139
Home, D. D., 171
Hooker, E. N., 105
Hooker, R., 23
Hopkins, G. M., 185
Horace, 98, 106, 110, 117
Hume, D., 127–8, 130, 134, 152–3, 163, 189–91
Humours, 1, 4, 49, 70, 112
Huon of Bordeaux, 18
Hurd, Bp. R., 137
Hutcheson, F., 125
Huxley, A., 170, 189, 246
Huxley, T. H., 160, 189
Huysmans, J. K., 197

Ibsen, H., 198
'Illative sense', 163–4
Imagination, 3, 23, 24, 129–30, 146–8, 157, 159, 165
Impressionists (painters), 192, 194, 198, 210; (poets), 193–202
Inchbald, Mrs., 117
Interlude of Youth, 12, 13, 72
Intuition, 30, 150–1, 154, 157, 167–71, 178, 185–6

James, H., 2
James, W., 211, 213, 214
Janet, P., 227
Jennings, E., 227
John of the Cross, St., 42
Johnson, E. D. H., 176
Johnson, S., 90, 110–11, 120, 130
Jonson, B., 49, 68, 112, 255
Judgement, 3, 46, 100, 102–5, 126–7
Juliana of Norwich, 222
Julius Caesar, 74, 82
Jung, C. G., 234, 248–9
Juvenal, 117

Keats, J., 139–43, 157–8, 165, 181, 249
King, W., 93, 106, 122
King Lear, 84–6, 88

Knox, R., 162
Koffka, K., 215
Köhler, W., 215
Krafft-Ebbing, R. von, 195

Lamarck, J. B., 173
Lambeth Homilies, 12
Lane, H., 235
Langland, W., 17
Laplace, P. S., 175
Lautréamont, I. D., 233
Law, W., 162
Lawrence, D. H., 202, 208–10, 212
Layard, J., 234
Lear, E., 241
Legrain, 196
Le Roy, 22
Locke, J., 47, 92, 93, 99–100, 104–5, 126–7, 128, 132, 163
Loeb, J., 203
Lombroso, C., 195, 196, 198
Longer thou livest, The, 12
Love's Labour's Lost, 62–4, 68
Lubbock, Sir J., 203
Lucas, P., 195
Lucretius, 94, 161, 183
Lusty Juventus, 12, 13
Lyly, J., 49
Lytton, E. B., 172

Macbeth, 84, 86
McEvoy, A., 192
Mack, M., 114
Mackenzie, W. R., 11
Macrobius, 55
McTaggart, J. M. E., 223
Magendie, F., 188
Magnan, V., 196
Magnificence, 12
Manchester, E. of, 43
Manet, E., 192, 194
Mankind, 11
Mansel, H. L., 163, 227
Markiewicz, Countess, 243

INDEX

Marlowe, C., 13, 35, 49, 55
Marriage of Wit and Science, 12, 15, 16
Marriage of Wit and Wisdom, 12, 15
Marston, J., 117
Martial, 36, 110
Martineau, J., 186
Martz, L., 42
Marvell, A., 44, 90
Marxism, 234, 235, 237
Masefield, J., 199–200, 205–6
Maudsley, H., 160, 195, 196
Maxwell, C., 162
Measure for Measure, 74, 87
Melancholy, 4, 124
Memory, 3, 17, 18–19, 20, 22, 24, 80, 129, 131–2, 157
Mental chemistry, 135
Merchant of Venice, 65–8, 83
Mesmer, F. A., 171
Microcosmic theory, 2–4, 11, 90, 105, 167, 173, 217, 253
Middleton, T., 6, 49
Midsummer Night's Dream, 58–9, 71, 88, 123
Mill, James, 134–5
Mill, J. S., 134–5, 159, 188, 190–1, 227
Milton, J., 13, 25–30, 122, 123, 255
Montaigne, M., 95, 115
Montemayor, J. de, 61
Morality Plays, 11–16, 92
More, H., 22, 92, 122
Morel, B. A., 195
Morgan, C. Ll., 203
Mornay, P. de, 23
Mozley, J. B., 163
Much Ado about Nothing, 73
Muir, K., 141
Mulgrave, E. of, 102–3, 118, 122
Müller, F. M., 245
Murger, H., 196
Murray, J., 138

Natural spirits, 4
Nature, 11

Neoplatonism, 151
Newman, J. H., 97, 163, 168
Newton, I., 115, 135, 162, 163
Nichols, R., 202
Nicholson, J., 195
Nietzsche, F. W., 211, 235
Nisbet, J. F., 196
Nordau, M., 198
Norris, J., 92

Oldham, J., 118
O'Neill, E., 48
Othello, 73, 83, 86
Ovid, 6, 8, 35, 36, 39, 106
Owst, G. R., 12

Parnell, T., 120
Pascal, B., 240, 241
Passions, 3, 24, 26, 28, 30, 34, 49, 53, 71, 79, 98, 111, 112–21, 165, 255
Pater, W., 41, 189–92, 202, 214, 216, 220, 244–5
Pavlov, I., 203
Peele, G., 49
Periphrasis, 102
Perseverance, 11
Petrarch, 30
Petronius, 122
Philips, J., 106
Phlegm, 4
Picasso, P., 20, 210, 213
Plato, 17, 154–7, 165, 183, 185, 186, 252
Poe, E. A., 214, 232
Pope, A., 1, 97, 101, 105, 114–17, 137, 138, 157, 255
Post-Impressionism, 210–14
Pound, E., 212–13, 216
Praz, M., 195
Pre-existence, 44
Priestley, J. B., 48
Primaudaye, P. de la, 23, 60–1
Prior, M., 93–5, 101
Prudentius, 12
Pythagorean, 21

Racial memories, 248–53
Racine, J., 216
Raine, K., 227, 249, 252–3
Ray, J., 162
Read, Sir H., 228, 250–1
Reason, 3, 15, 16, 21, 23–8, 33, 34, 37, 96, 115–16
Redford, J., 15–16
Reichenbach, K. von, 172
Reid, T., 125, 134, 146, 147
Reynolds, J. H., 139
Rice, J., 139
Richard III, 50, 53–4, 55, 79
Rochester, E. of, 24–5
Rogers, S., 135–6
Roman de la Rose, 6
Romanes, G. J., 203
Romeo and Juliet, 79–80
Roscommon, E. of, 103–4
Rossetti, D. G., 198
Rousseau, J-J., 98, 124
Royal Society, 91, 100, 122
Ruling Passion, 98, 114–17
Ruskin, J., 210
'Rutherford, Mark', 179

Sackville, T., 17
Schiller, J. C. F., 195–6
Senecan, 50, 53, 55
Senses, 14, 18, 20, 23–5, 30, 33, 128–31, 138, 140, 144, 152, 157, 174, 255
Sensibility, 1, 121–5, 137, 145
Sensitive principle, 3, 21, 37
Seven Deadly Sins, 10, 17, 20, 120
Shadwell, T., 112
Shaftesbury, E. of, 114, 121, 125
Shakespeare, W., 1, 2, 5, 8, 31, 48–89, 139, 143, 210, 216, 229, 231, 232, 255; plays are indexed separately under titles
Shannon, C., 192
Shaw, G. B., 48, 168
Shelley, P. B., 152–7, 166, 167, 183, 204, 249

Sickert, W., 192
Sidney, Sir P., 10, 23, 32–4, 35, 117
Sitwell, Dame E., 212, 246–8
Smith, A., 149
Soul, triple, 21, 37
Southey, R., 125
Spencer, H., 161, 169, 223
Spenser, E., 5, 16–21, 23, 32–3, 35, 92, 121
Sprat, T., 100, 122
Steer, W., 192, 194
Sterne, L., 128, 204
Stewart, D., 134, 137–8, 146–9
Stoicism, 49
Strode, W., 22
Supernatural, 56–7, 88, 122–3
Surrealism, 232–3
Surrey, E. of, 6, 62
Symbolistes, 192, 198, 212
Symonds, J. A., 215
Symons, A., 193–7, 202

Taming of the Shrew, 7, 57–8, 60–1, 62
Tempest, The, 87–9
Tennyson, A., Lord, 90, 166, 175–9
Teresa, St., 42, 43
Theologia Germanica, 42, 53
Thomas, D., 233–4
Thomson, J., 102, 135, 136, 137
Thomson, J. ('B.V.'), 182
Thorndike, E. L., 203
Tiedemann, F., 175
Tischbein, J. H. W., 142
Titian, 141
Titus and Gisippus, 61
Titus Andronicus, 56, 83
Toulouse-Lautrec, H. de, 194
Tourneur, C., 49
Traherne, T., 44, 45
Transitions, 137, 213–14
Troilus and Cressida, 73, 74–8, 84
Turner, W. J., 228, 249
Two Gentlemen of Verona, 61–2, 71

INDEX 271

Tylor, E. B., 245
Tyndall, J., 161

Unconscious, 186, 209, 227–53
Understanding, 3, 14, 23, 24
Upton, J., 21

Valdes, J. de, 42
Vaughan, H., 43, 252
Vegetative principle, 3, 21, 37
Velasquez, D. de S. y, 211
Verlaine, P., 196, 241
Vincent of Beauvais, 55
Vital spirits, 4
Voltaire, F. M. A. de, 241

Walpole, H., 142
Warner, R., 202
Warton, J., 121–2
Warton, T. (elder), 123–4
Warton, T. (younger), 124
Washburn, M. F., 207
Watson, J. B., 203
Watson, T., 31
Webster, J., 49
Wellesley, D., 250
Wells, H. G., 168
Wertheimer, M., 215
Wesley, J., 162

Weston, J. L., 246
Whateley, R., 136–7
Whewell, W., 175
Whichcote, B., 41
Whistler, J. McN., 192, 210–11
Whiter, W., 138
Whitman, W., 22, 181
Wilde, O., 192, 198
Will, 3, 13–15, 16, 26, 182, 211, 215, 218, 220
Williams, T., 48
Wilson, T., 9, 10
Winter's Tale, A, 87
Wisdom Who is Christ, 12, 14–15
Wit, 15, 16, 45, 101, 104–5
Wit and Science, 15–16
Woodhouse, R., 139
Woolf, V., 212
Woolton, J., 22
Worde, W. de, 42
Wordsworth, W., 125, 131, 135, 139, 143, 145–52, 157, 158–9, 160, 178, 185, 192, 195, 197, 204, 239, 242
Wright, T., 79
Wyatt, Sir T., 6, 30, 62

Yeats, W. B., 21, 198, 222, 242–4, 245, 249
Young, E., 95–8, 117–18

www.ingramcontent.com/pod-product-compliance
Lightning Source LLC
Chambersburg PA
CBHW020359080526
44584CB00014B/1086